POSTCARD HISTORY SERIES

Coney Island

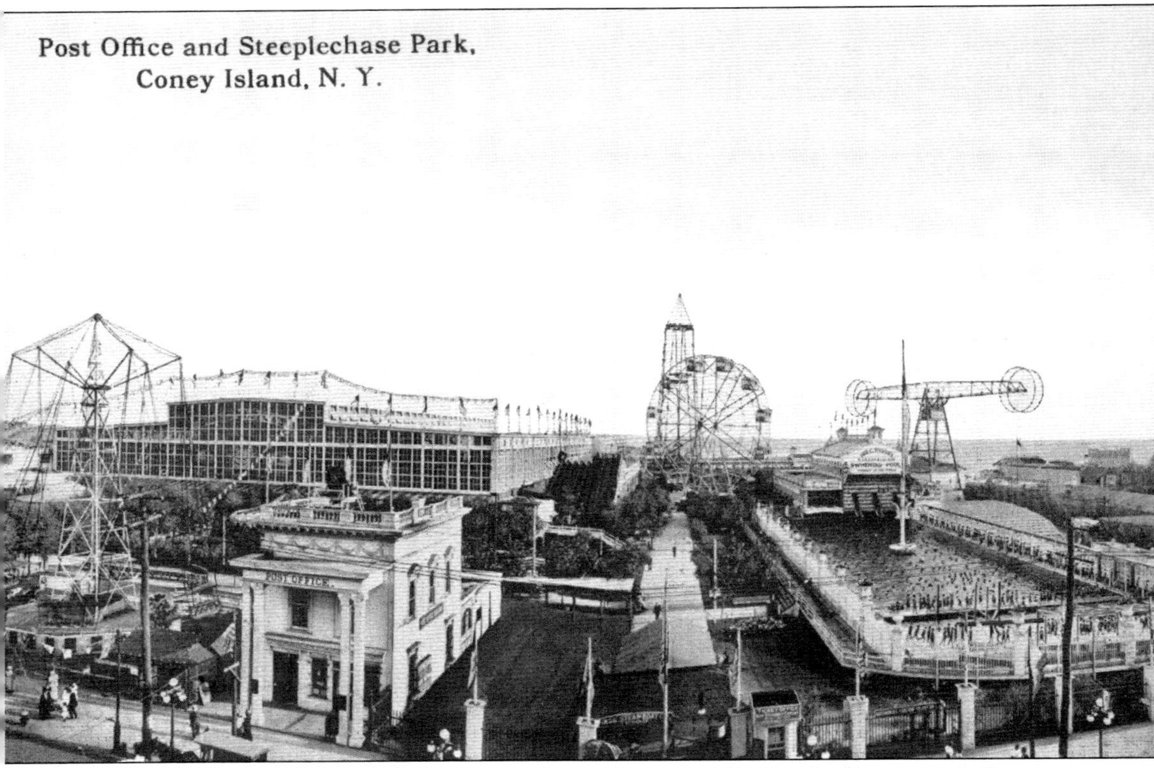

This aerial view of Steeplechase Park shows the post office in the foreground. On an average summer weekend in 1907, visitors to Coney Island mailed 250,000 postcards to family and friends. In 1907, it cost 1¢ to mail a postcard. (Courtesy of the author.)

On the Front Cover: Dreamland was open from 1904 to 1911. The lagoon that separated Dreamland's east and west promenades was situated seaward of the Beacon Tower. The 130-foot-wide lake extended 300 feet to the base of the Shoot-the-Chutes. A wide pedestrian bridge arched over the water where the descending boats hit the lagoon. (Courtesy of the author.)

On the Back Cover: Steeplechase Park, Coney Island's longest-lasting amusement park, was open from 1897 to 1964. It was created by George C. Tilyou and was advertised as the "Funny Place." Today, the Steeplechase Park site is occupied by MCU Park, home of the Brooklyn Cyclones, a New York Mets–affiliated minor-league baseball team. The Parachute Jump is the only structure that remains from Steeplechase Park. (Courtesy of the author.)

POSTCARD HISTORY SERIES

Coney Island

Laura J. Hoffman

ARCADIA
PUBLISHING

ISBN 978-1-4671-2131-6

Published by Arcadia Publishing
Charleston, South Carolina

Printed in the United States of America

Library of Congress Control Number: 2013946828

For all general information contact Arcadia Publishing at:
Telephone 843-853-2070
Fax 843-853-0044
E-mail sales@arcadiapublishing.com
For customer service and orders:
Toll-Free 1-888-313-2665

Visit us on the Internet at www.arcadiapublishing.com

Many people are involved in Coney Island's preservation efforts, and this book is dedicated to them. The ride is not over yet.

Contents

Acknowledgments

This book would not have been possible without the support of my family and friends.

I would like to thank the folks at the Coney Island History Project and Coney Island USA for all their hard work and dedication.

All of the images in this book are from the author's collection.

I wish to thank my editors at Arcadia Publishing, especially Rémy Thurston, for the continuous support and belief in this project.

Last but not least, I would like to thank Mike Galloway for leaving the house when I needed to get work done.

INTRODUCTION

Through the years, Coney Island has been many things to many people. It was known as the People's Playground, the Nickel Empire, and Sodom by the Sea. It has represented the epitome of free expression and the American spirit of entrepreneurship. It has become home to hundreds of thousands of immigrants from every corner of the world. It is fascinating, strange, and sometimes highly offensive; by today's standards, it would definitely be deemed politically incorrect. Despite all that, some amazing achievements have emerged from Coney Island.

For instance, in the early 1900s, babies born prematurely often died because there were no incubators in hospitals. The medical establishment did not begin to widely accept the technology in the United States until the late 1930s. Dr. Martin A. Couney, a German, came to Coney Island and opened sideshow exhibits that charged admission (25¢) to crowds who wanted to view the babies in incubators. Dr. Couney would then use the proceeds to pay for incubators and nurses to care for the babies. The parents of the premature babies were never charged for this care. Reports vary, but Dr. Couney is credited with saving the lives of at least 5,000 babies. According to Dr. Couney's obituary printed in the *New York Times* on March 2, 1950, "For years he had shows at both Dreamland and Luna Park, and the night Dreamland was destroyed by fire the babies were saved by a quick transfer to the Luna Park incubators, some of the lodgers doubling up."

In addition to baby incubators, many other inventions supposedly originated in Coney Island, including the hot dog, the enclosed amusement park, the roller coaster, and the carousel. Although these may not have been truly invented there, they were certainly perfected in Coney Island.

Many famous people have worked in Coney Island. Cary Grant—then known as Archibald Leach—was a stilt walker who was paid to advertise various attractions. Al Capone got his "scarface" while working at the Harvard Inn in Coney Island. Harry Houdini met his future wife, Bess, while performing at Henderson's Music Hall with his brother Theo. Eddie Cantor and Jimmy Durante worked as singing waiters at Carey Walsh's fine establishment.

Postcards were the social media of the early 1900s, and there are few better places to spotlight this than Coney Island. On an average summer weekend in 1907, visitors to Coney Island mailed more than a quarter-million postcards to family and friends. On a single day in 1906, the Coney Island post office processed over 200,000 postcards. Many more postcards were never mailed but instead saved in scrapbooks.

Various types of postcards have existed in the United States throughout the years. Private mailing cards, authorized by an act of Congress on May 19, 1898, used the back of the card for the address only. These are easy to identify, as they say "private mailing card" on the side where the address is to be written. The undivided-back postcard replaced the private mailing card.

On December 24, 1901, the US government allowed the words "post card" to be included on the undivided back of privately printed cards where the name and address of the recipient were to be written. On March 1, 1907, the post office authorized the divided back postcard, which included space for a note. White border cards first appeared in 1915, and "linen" cards—which were not actually linen but had a textured front that resembled cloth—began to dominate in the 1930s.

Because this book is a postcard history, the time frame it covers is limited, but there are important Coney Island landmarks that were destroyed before postcards existed. In 1885, James V. Lafferty built the Elephant Hotel (also known as the Elephant Colossus)—a hotel in the shape of an elephant. There is still one in Atlantic City, but this one was twice its size. It stood 122 feet high with legs that were 60 feet in circumference. A cigar store operated out of one the front legs. A spiral staircase in one of the hind legs led visitors upstairs to the 31 guest rooms. For 10 years, the elephant's huge head, which faced the ocean, appeared in the sight line of immigrants arriving in New York even before they could see the Statue of Liberty. Unfortunately, the Elephant Hotel burned down in 1896, so it never had a chance to appear on any postcards.

Four main amusement parks have existed in Coney Island: Steeplechase, Luna, Dreamland, and Astroland; this postcard history covers the first three parks. Astroland, with its outer-space theme, opened in 1962 at Surf Avenue and West Tenth Street. It ceased operations in September 2008, but Dewey Albert, his son Jerry, and, later, Jerry's wife, Carol, kept Astroland going during some difficult times, which helped to keep Coney Island alive as an amusement destination for millions of people. Charles Denson covered Astroland extensively in his Arcadia Publishing book, Images of America: *Coney Island and Astroland*. The new Luna Park opened on the Astroland site in 2010.

The biggest enemy of Coney Island has been fire. Five fires, in particular, caused the most devastation. The 1903 fire in the Bowery destroyed 260 buildings between West Tenth Street and Steeplechase Park. In 1907, a fire at Steeplechase Park erased 35 acres of the iconic amusement area. The 1911 fire at Dreamland destroyed the entire park, along with many surrounding buildings. In 1932, the worst fire in Coney Island's history consumed 100 feet of the Boardwalk and destroyed apartment buildings and bathhouses all the way from the beach to Surf Avenue and from West Twenty-first to West Twenty-fourth Streets. In 1944, a pair of fires at Luna Park wiped out most of the 22-acre park.

Coney Island is a fascinating place to visit, especially during the summer months. Landmarks abound, and history is alive and well at the Coney Island History Project, which runs a newly expanded exhibition center on West Twelfth Street at the entrance to Deno's Wonder Wheel Amusement Park. One of the mechanical horses from the legendary Steeplechase Park ride is on display at the center, along with many other pieces of history. Visitors can take a ride on the legendary Wonder Wheel (built in 1920), stroll on the Boardwalk (built in 1923), and check out the newly renovated Steeplechase Pier—with its spectacular view of Coney Island—and the Parachute Jump, which has been in the same location since 1941. Coney Island's last remaining historic carousel, the B&B Carousell (built in 1919), has been fully restored and is now the centerpiece of the new Steeplechase Plaza located near the pier. Don't miss taking a ride on the original Coney Island Cyclone roller coaster (built in 1927). After working up an appetite, hungry guests can chow down at Nathan's Famous (founded in 1916), Totonno's Pizzeria Napolitano (same location since 1924), and Gargiulo's Restaurant (established in 1907), all of which are within walking distance of the amusements.

One

The Early Days

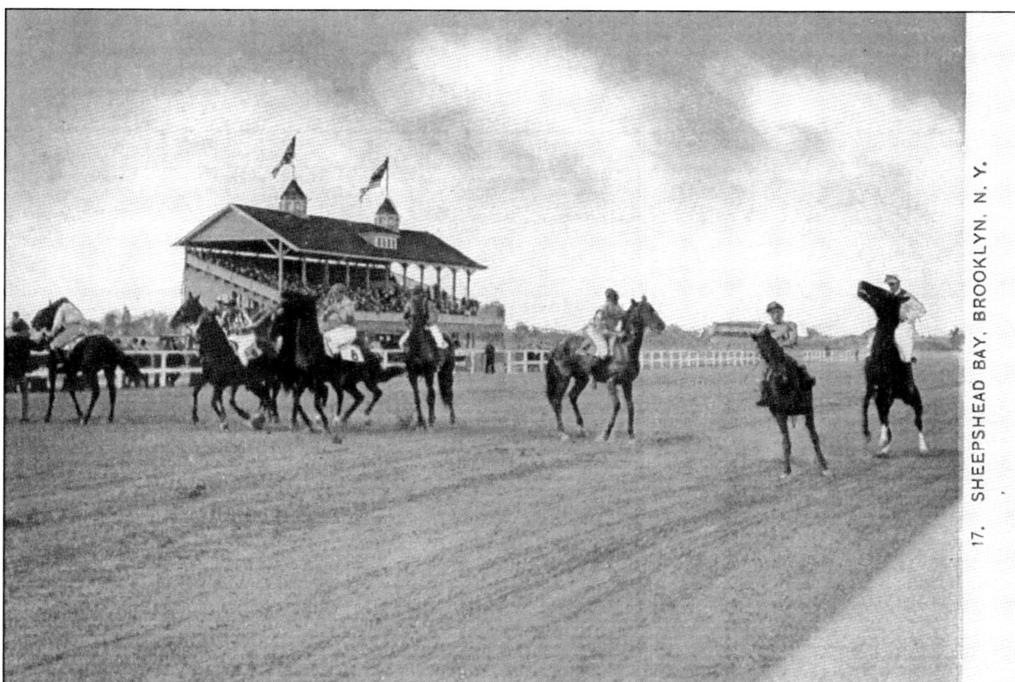

The Coney Island Jockey Club—founded by a consortium of businessmen led by Leonard Jerome, the grandfather of Winston Churchill—opened Sheepshead Bay Race Track, Brooklyn's most magnificent horse-racing track, in 1880. Horse racing was big business in the late 19th century. At the time, there were two other racetracks in the immediate area: Brighton Beach Race Course and Gravesend Race Track. The Sheepshead Bay track closed in 1910.

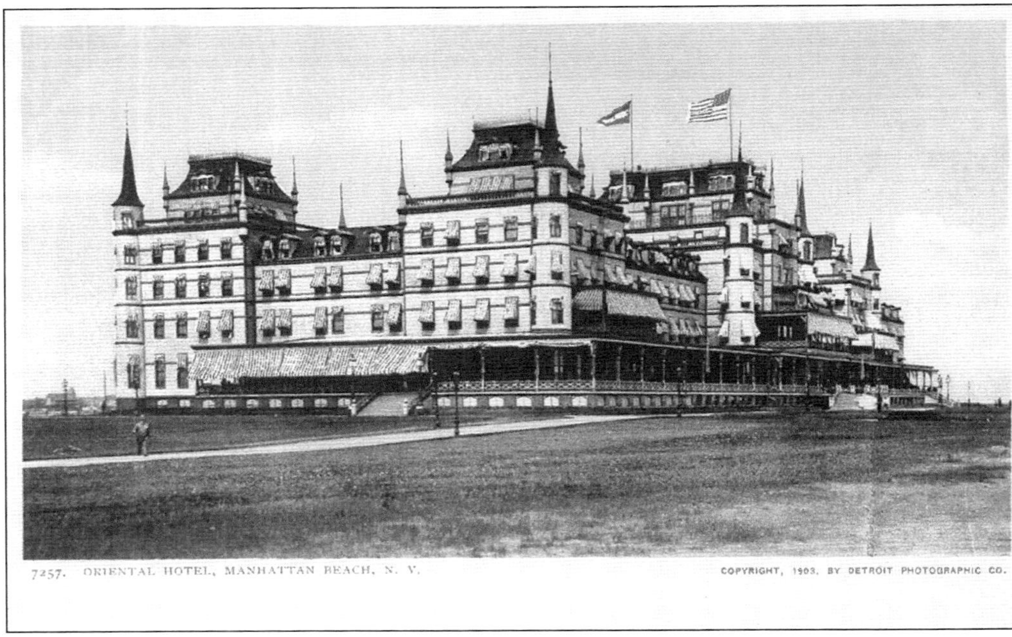

The Oriental Hotel, built at the east end of Coney Island in 1876, served rich guests and their families, who often stayed for the entire summer. Kingsborough Community College is now located near the former site of the Oriental Hotel, which was demolished in 1916.

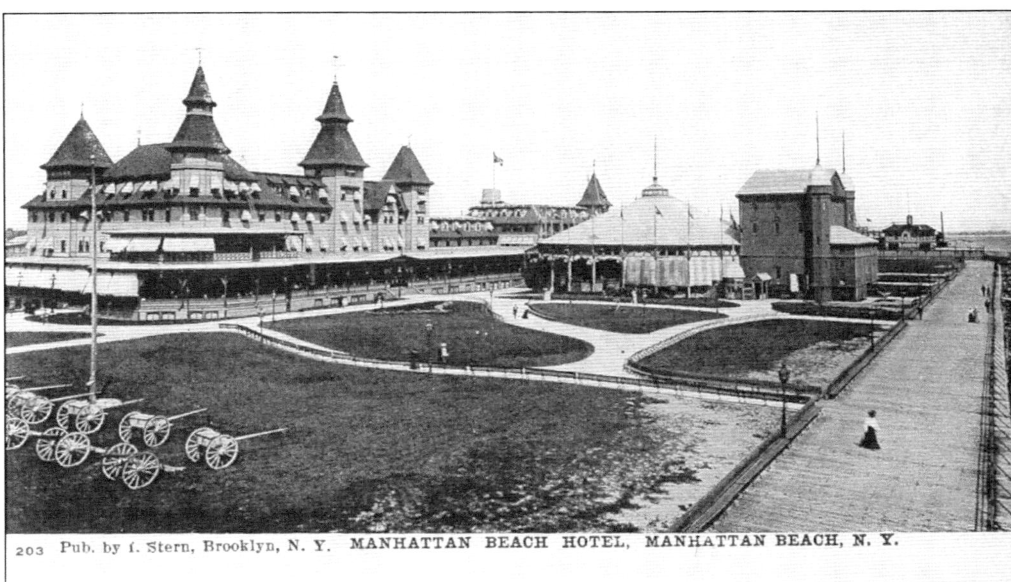

Austin Corbin opened the Manhattan Beach Hotel in 1877 on the far eastern shore of Coney Island. Architect J. Pickering Putnam set the hotel's nearly 700-foot-long front, with its covered verandas and acres of manicured lawns, to face the sea. Considered the most elegant and fashionable hotel in the United States in its time, it featured 258 lavish rooms, restaurants, a ballroom, and shops. The hotel closed in 1911.

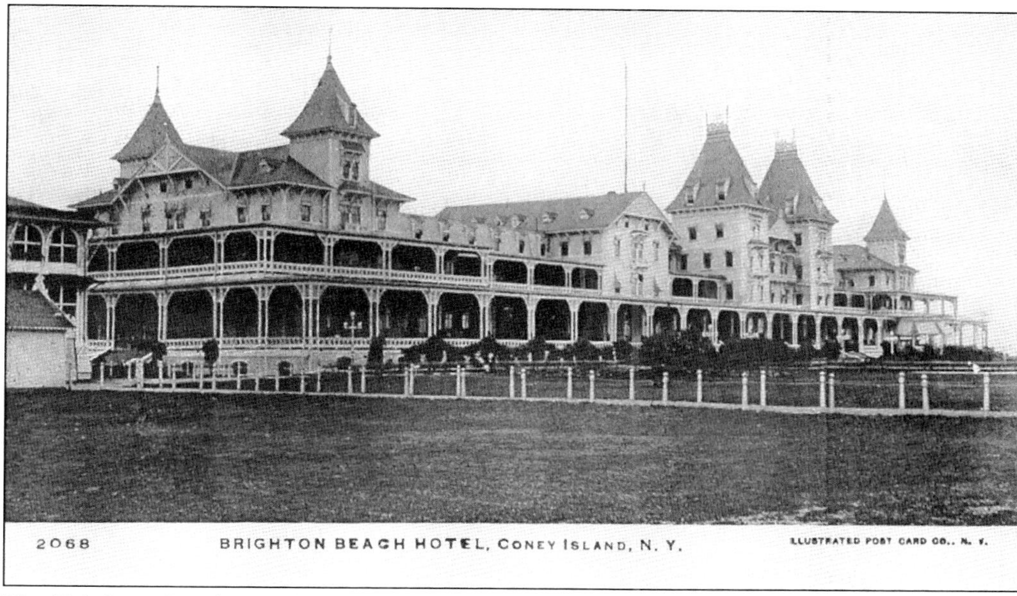

The Brighton Beach Hotel, constructed in time for the 1878 season, catered to the growing upper-middle class. This vast wooden hotel, which contained accommodations for nearly 5,000 guests, also had the resources to feed 20,000 people per day.

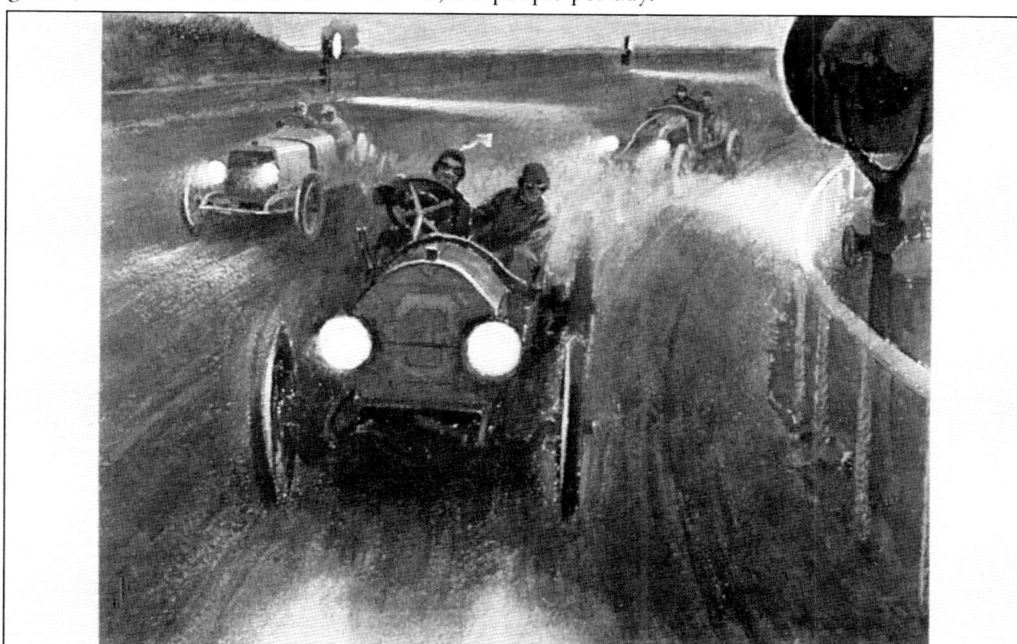

In June 1908, the New York State Senate passed the Hart-Agnew Law, which placed tight restrictions on racetrack betting. After horse racing ended in the Coney Island area, the Brighton Beach Race Course hosted automobile racing events until 1916. Several big races were held there, including the Brighton Beach 24 Hour Race. This postcard features a 1974 painting by Peter Helck that commemorates the 24-hour race held in July 1909 that was won by George Robertson and Al Poole. No trace of the track remains today.

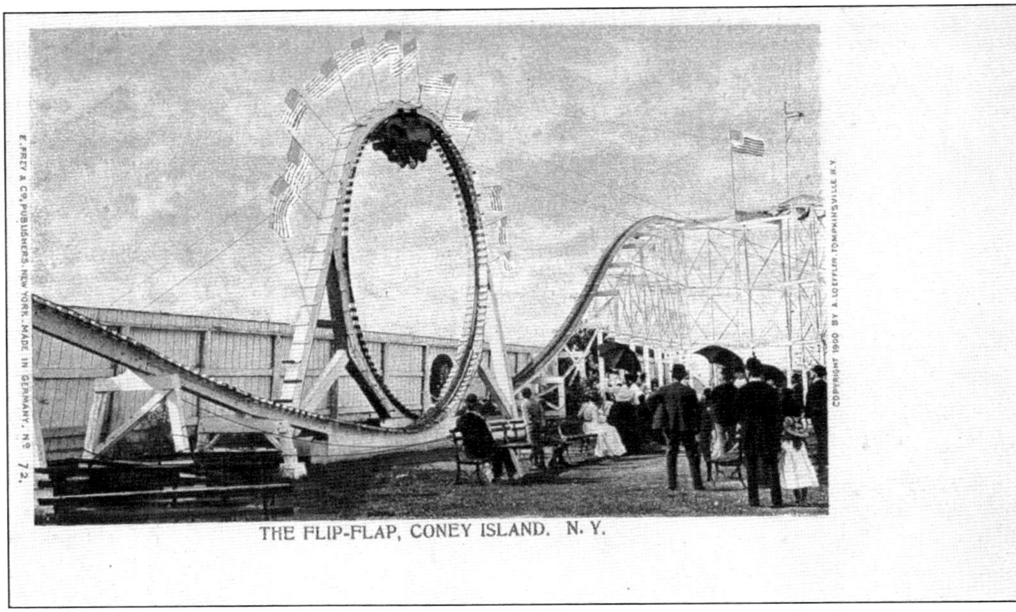

In 1895, adventurer Paul Boyton bought 16 acres of land on Coney Island and opened Sea Lion Park. He fenced the property and charged admission, ushering in the era of the enclosed amusement park. This undivided-back postcard shows the most daring of rides, the Flip-Flap, a looping coaster that caused a number of neck injuries and was dismantled in 1902.

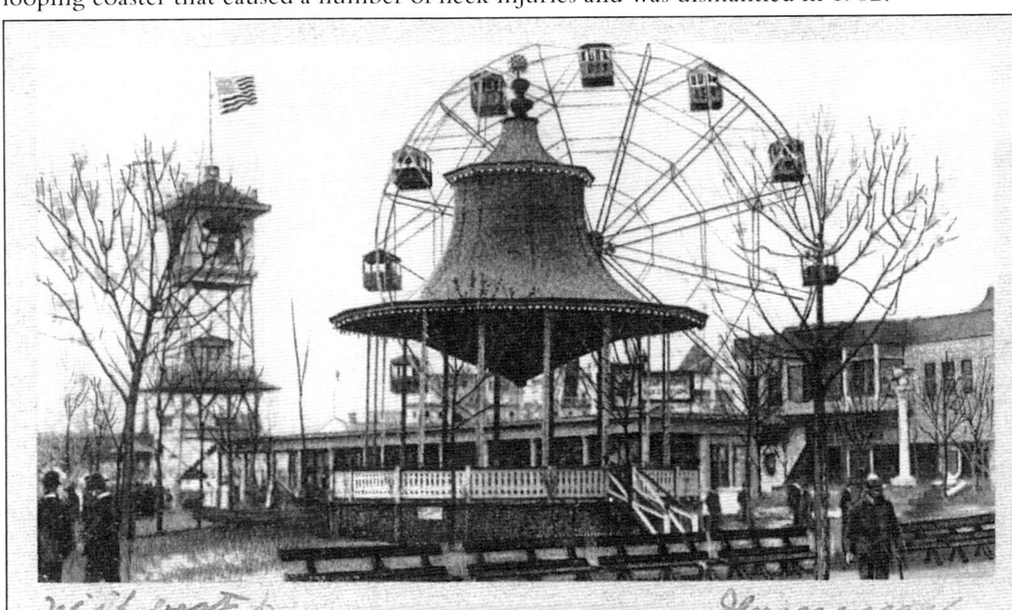

George C. Tilyou grew up in Coney Island. While visiting the World's Columbian Exposition in Chicago in 1893, he saw a magnificent Ferris wheel but was unable to purchase it. Instead, he purchased another, smaller Ferris wheel and returned to Coney Island, where he posted a sign that said: "On This Site Will Be Erected the World's Largest Ferris Wheel." Tilyou was able to sell enough concessions space around the wheel to pay for its delivery in 1894.

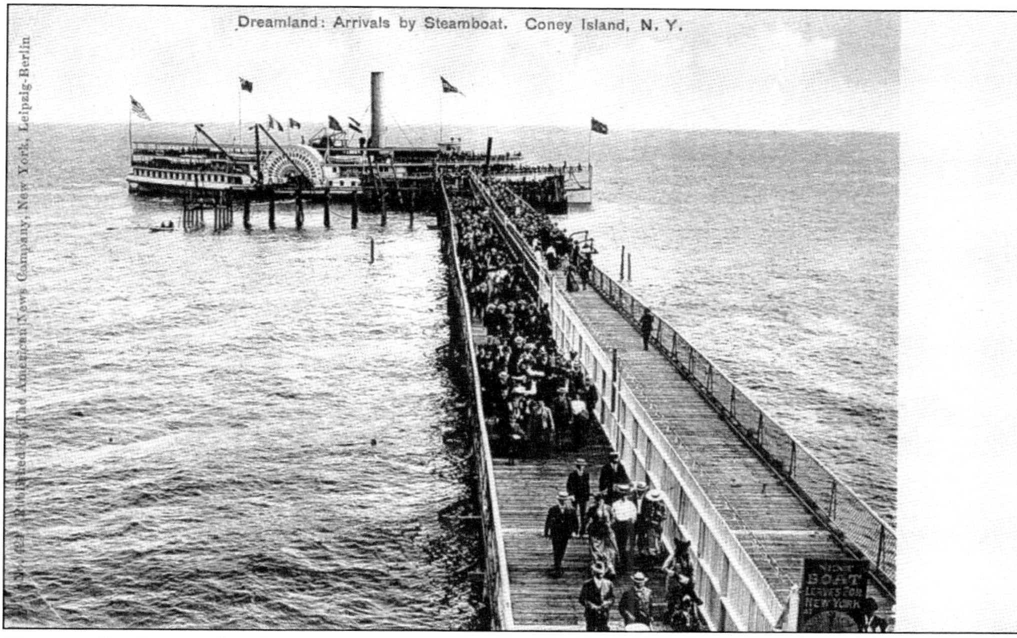

Coney Island started to become a vacation destination after the Civil War. Excursion railroads and the Coney Island & Brooklyn Railroad reached the area in the 1860s, and the Iron Steamboat Company arrived in 1881. The Dreamland pier served as a dock for steamboats until it was destroyed in a devastating fire in 1911.

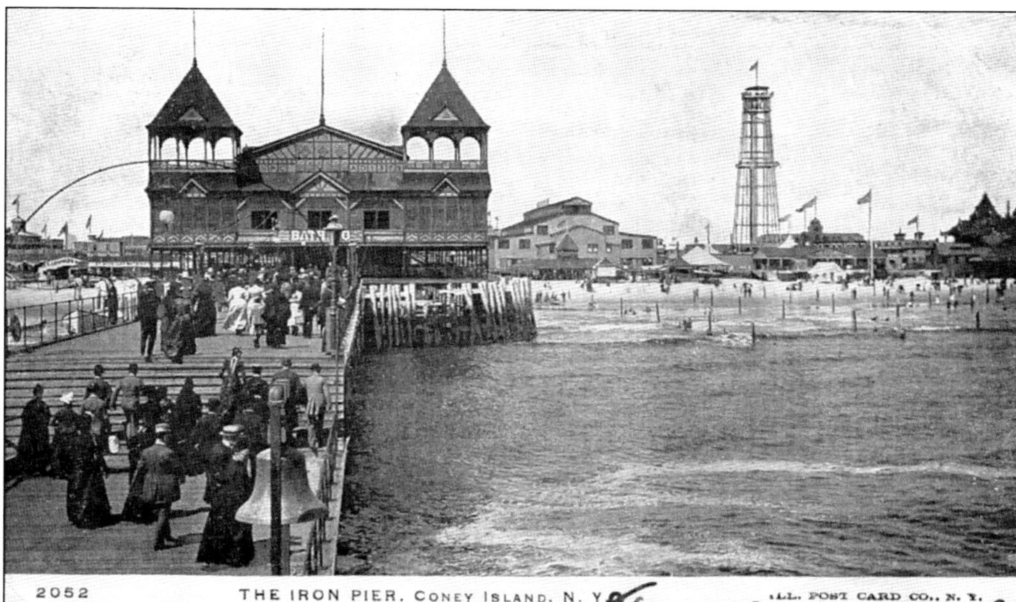

This undivided-back postcard shows crowds arriving at the Iron Pier by steamboat. For many immigrants who came to New York City in the first 10 years of the 20th century, Coney Island represented the freedom to escape the city for the day. Sigmund Freud came to Coney Island via steamboat in September 1909 during his first and only visit to the United States.

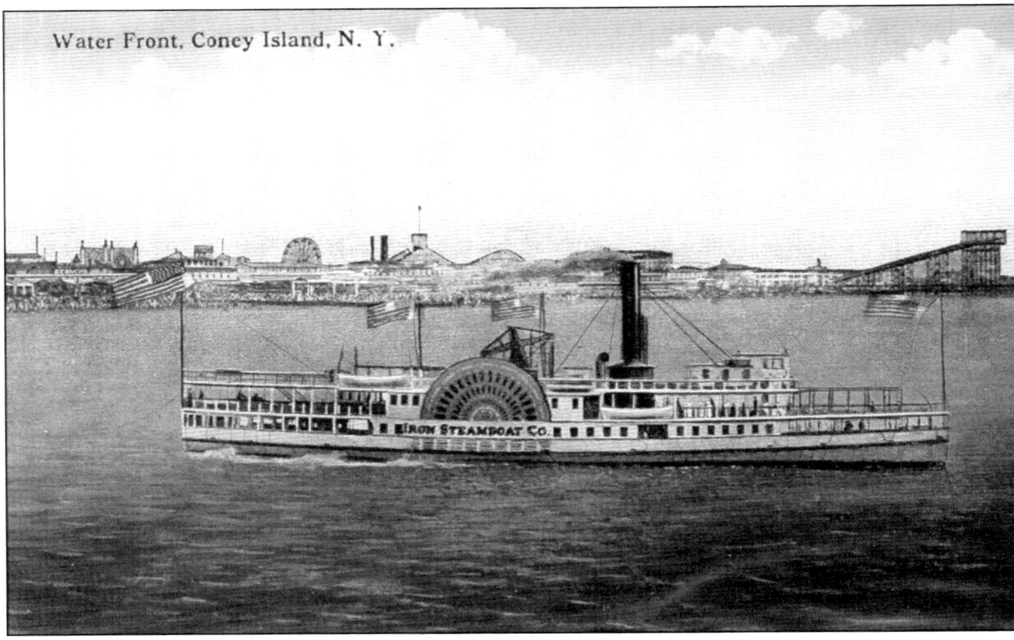

The Iron Steamboat Company provided ferry service between Manhattan and Coney Island. The original fleet consisted of seven iron-hulled steamboats, each named after a constellation: Cygnus, Cepheus, Cetus, Pegasus, Perseus, Sirius, and Taurus. In later years, two older wooden steamboats—the *Columbia* and the *Grand Republic*—were added to the fleet.

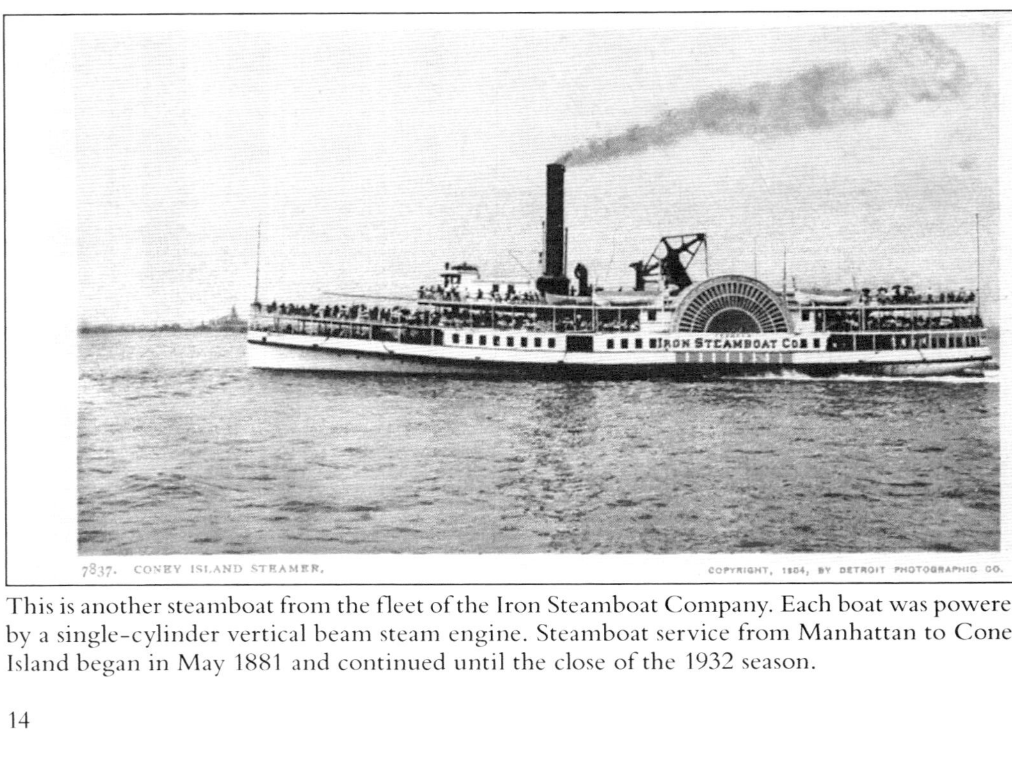

This is another steamboat from the fleet of the Iron Steamboat Company. Each boat was powered by a single-cylinder vertical beam steam engine. Steamboat service from Manhattan to Coney Island began in May 1881 and continued until the close of the 1932 season.

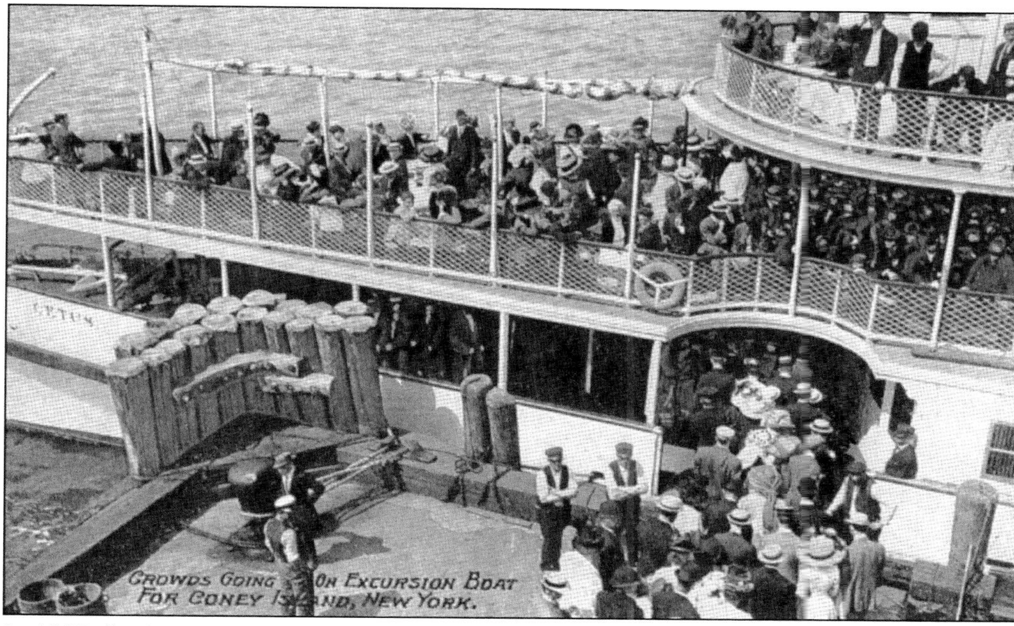

In 1907, for 35¢, visitors could arrive by steamship and spend the day at Dreamland before returning to a Manhattan terminal at the Battery, Twenty-third Street, or Harlem.

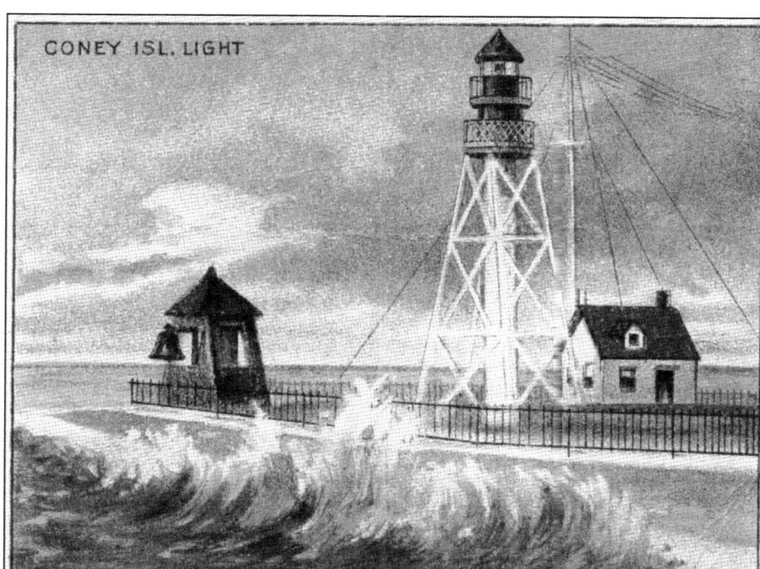

Hassan Cork Tip Cigarettes issued the Lighthouse series of collectible cards in 1912. This one shows the Coney Island Light (or Nortons Point Light), which was built in 1890 at the western end of Coney Island. The area, known as Nortons Point, is now part of the gated community of Sea Gate. The lighthouse is still in operation.

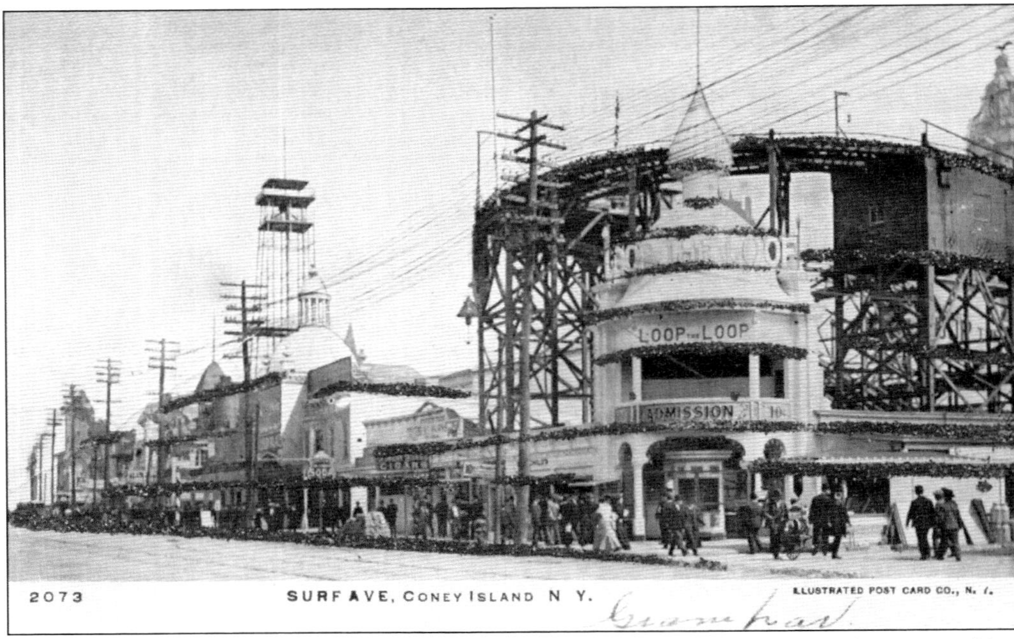

In 1901, Edwin Prescott erected a steel looping coaster—the Loop the Loop—on the corner of Surf Avenue and West Tenth Street. The ride's elliptical loop—a change from the traditional circular loops used on previous looping coasters—helped reduce the strain on passengers' necks.

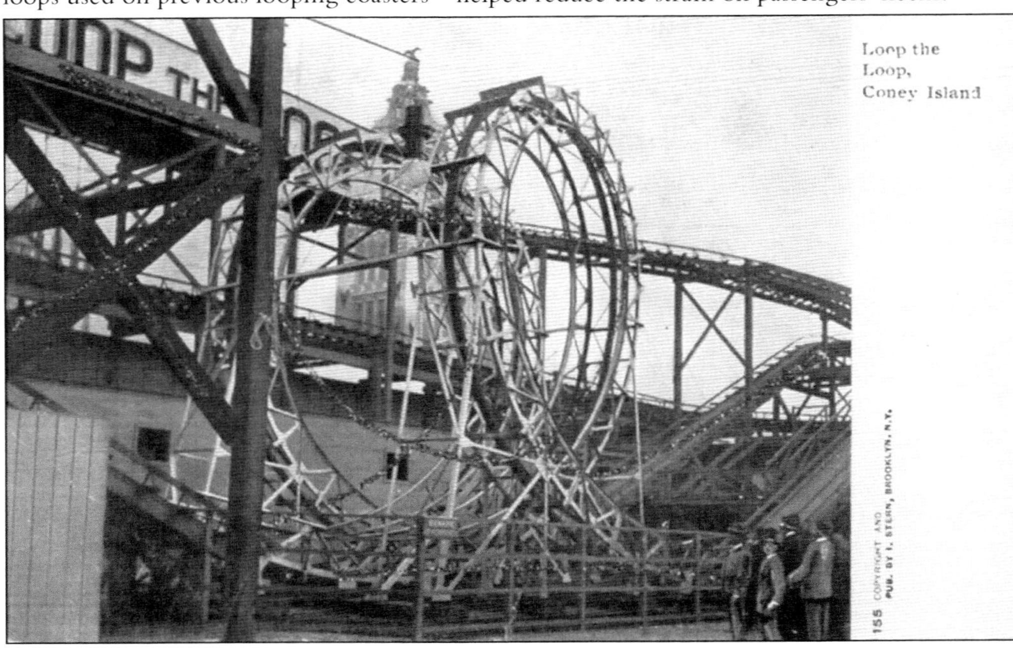

At 10¢ a ride, the Loop the Loop might have been profitable if safety inspectors had not prohibited the operation of more than one car at a time. Releasing one four-passenger car every five minutes proved to be unprofitable, and despite charging admission to watch the ride, it was dismantled after the 1910 season. During the early 1900s, to make postcards stand out, some manufacturers added silver and/or gold glitter (as shown on the postcard pictured here).

Two

STEEPLECHASE PARK

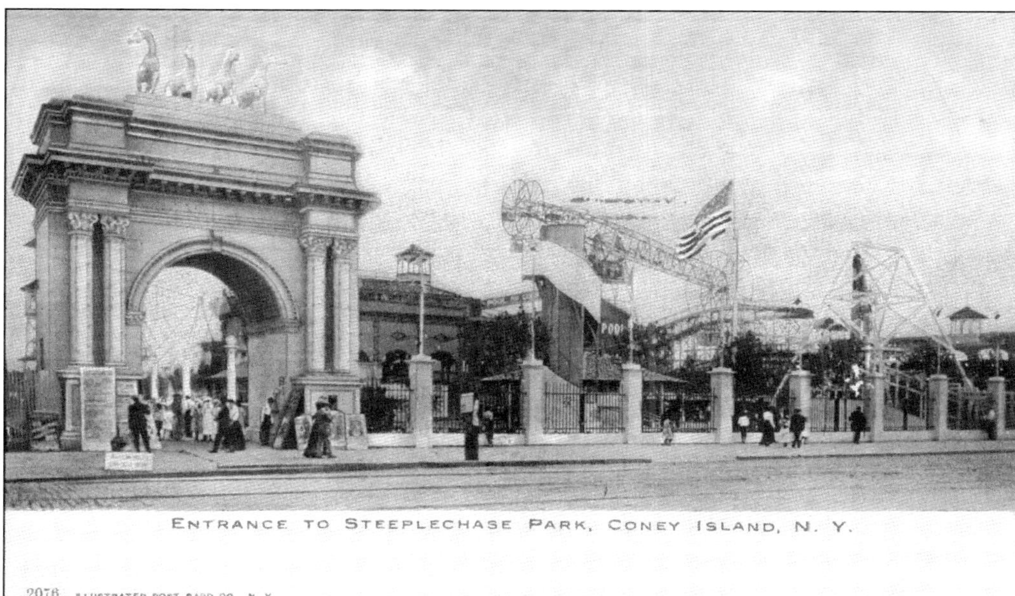

The original Steeplechase Park entrance on Surf Avenue was a grand archway with pillars and four horses on top. George C. Tilyou (1862–1914) grew up in Coney Island and understood the concept of the amusement park. He chose horse racing as the theme of his Steeplechase Park, which opened on 15 acres of oceanfront property in 1897.

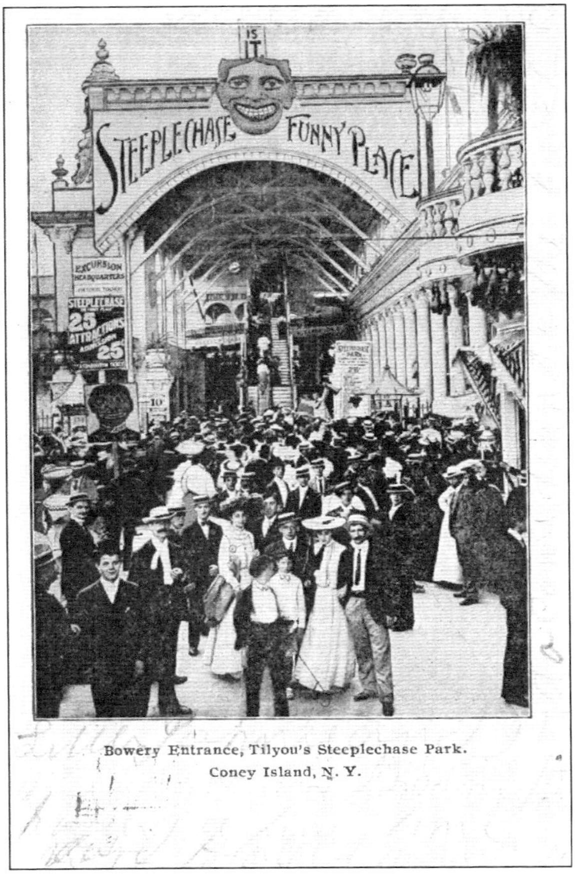

Bowery Entrance, Tilyou's Steeplechase Park.
Coney Island, N. Y.

Steeplechase Park's nickname was the "Funny Place." This private mailing card shows the original Bowery entrance, with its recognizable big, smiling, happy face. George Tilyou created the narrow street known as the Bowery in the 1890s to guide customers to Steeplechase Park. The street was originally named Ocean Walk Avenue and ran five blocks from Jones Walk to West Sixteenth Street.

Steeplechase Park was open for 67 seasons—longer than any other amusement park in Coney Island. Tilyou wanted to create family entertainment, so he made Steeplechase an enclosed park, and visitors paid a fee to enter. Tilyou felt that by charging admission, he could keep the seedier element out and foster a fun and safe environment for young people and families.

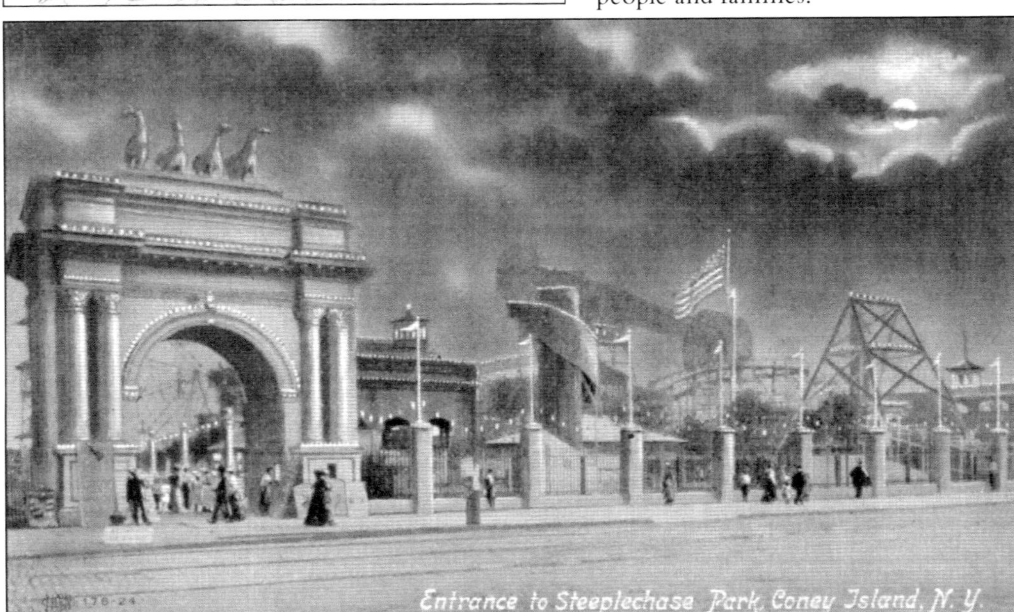

Entrance to Steeplechase Park, Coney Island, N. Y.

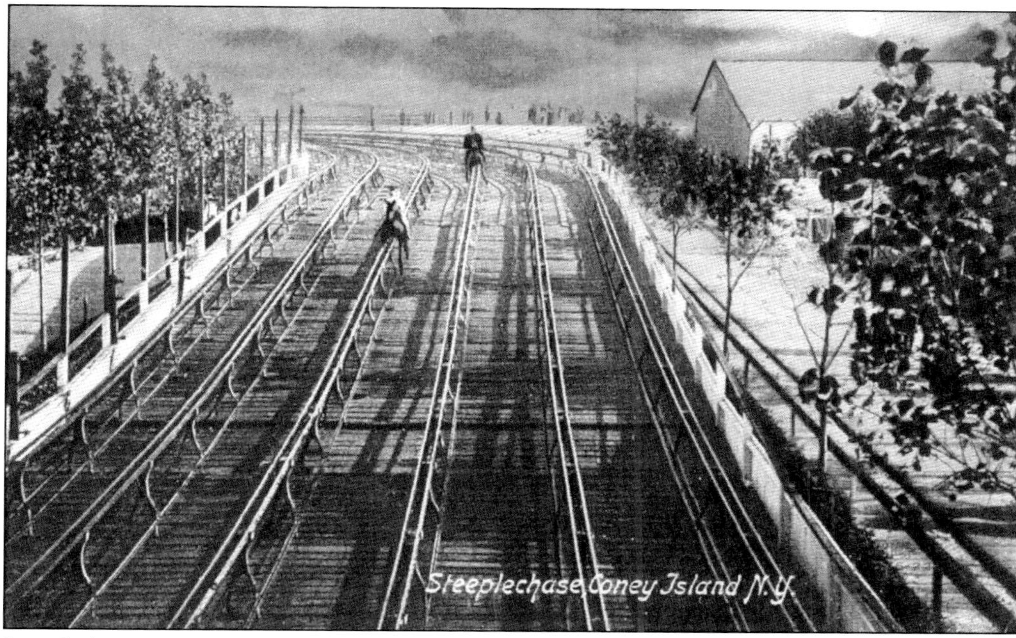

Steeplechase Race Course was the main attraction at Steeplechase Park. It featured a 1,100-foot-long curved metal racetrack with six double-saddled wooden horses on wheels, and it operated on gravity. The second version of the race course had two separate courses running somewhat parallel with each other. One had four horses and ran completely outside the Pavilion of Fun. The other also had four horses but ran mostly inside the structure. After riding the Steeplechase horses, patrons entered the Blowhole Theater, where little people dressed as clowns used electric cattle prods to separate the men from the women while jets of compressed air were blown up the women's skirts. Patrons could then join the audience and watch the same fate befall others.

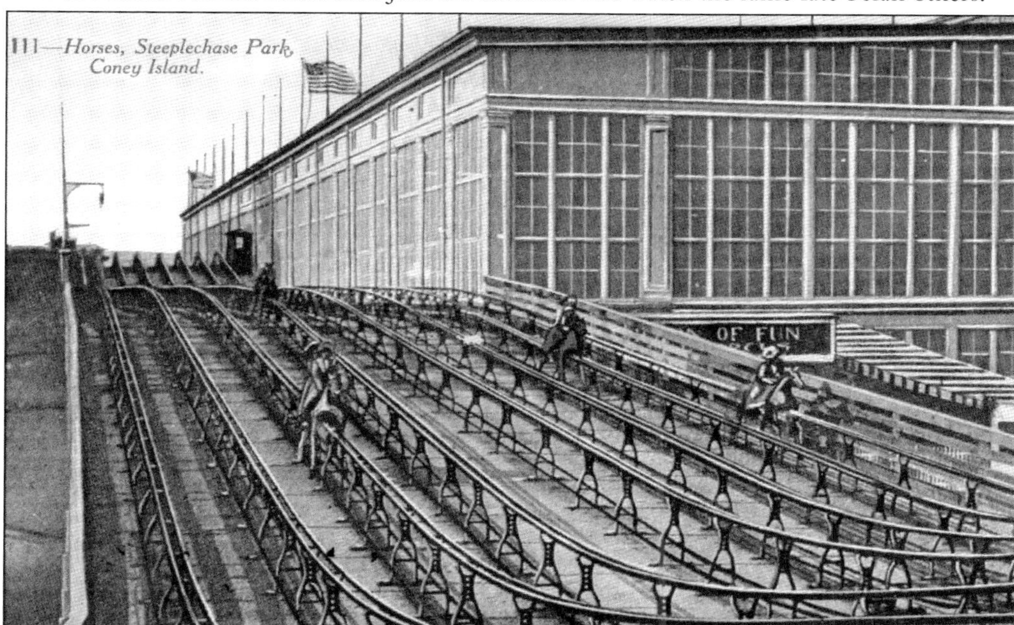

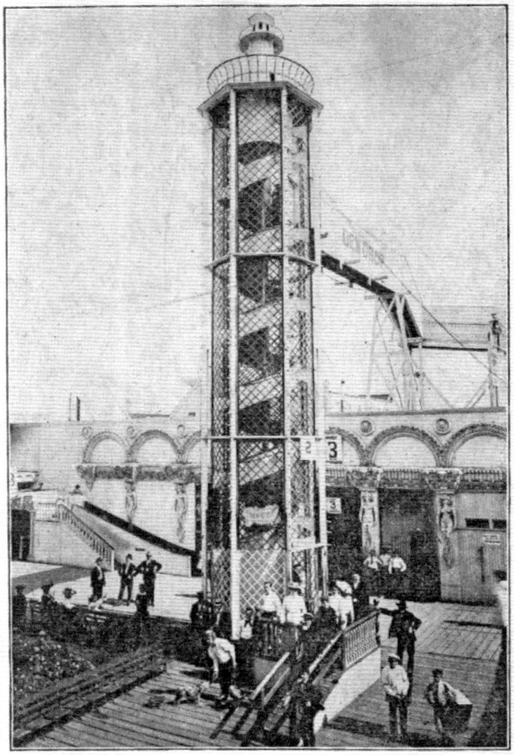

"Dewdrop," Tilyou's Steeplechase Park.
Coney Island, N. Y.

This private mailing card shows the Dewdrop, a spiral tower slide located just inside the Bowery entrance. Another George C. Tilyou invention, the Dewdrop had patrons climb to the top of a 50-foot-tall tower before whirling feet first in a downward spiral and being ejected onto a billowy platform.

Steeplechase Park opened in 1897 on 15 acres. Half the park burned in 1907. Ever the businessman, owner George C. Tilyou erected a fence around the property and posted a sign that said, "I have troubles today that I did not have yesterday. I had troubles yesterday that I have not today. On this site will be erected shortly a bigger, better Steeplechase Park—Admission to the burning ruins—10 cents."

E 1256 Birds Eye View of Steeplechase Park, Coney Island, N. Y.

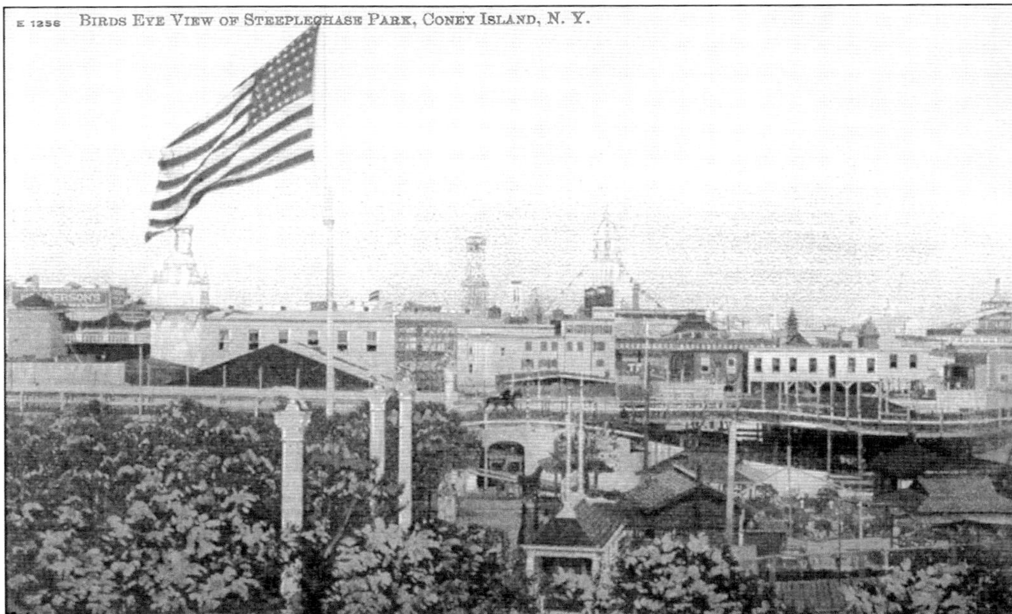

The Gladys' Chime Tower was a focal point for Steeplechase Park. The bells could be heard throughout the park as they chimed every hour on the hour.

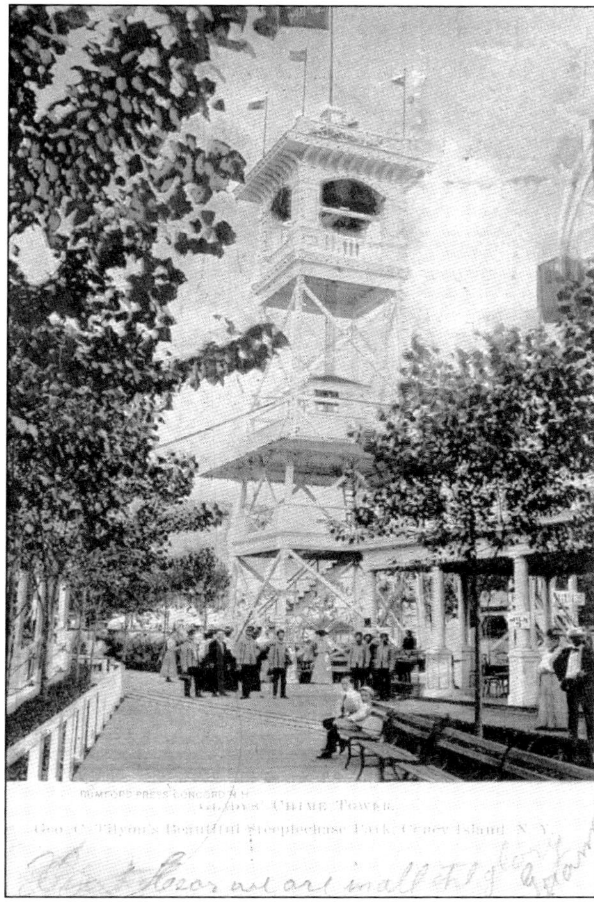

Japanese tea gardens were very popular in Coney Island; each of the big three amusement parks had their own version. The postcard below shows the tea garden at Steeplechase Park as painted by Charles E. Flowers. This postcard is part of Raphael Tuck & Sons' postcard series no. 2072, issued in 1905, which features scenes from Coney Island.

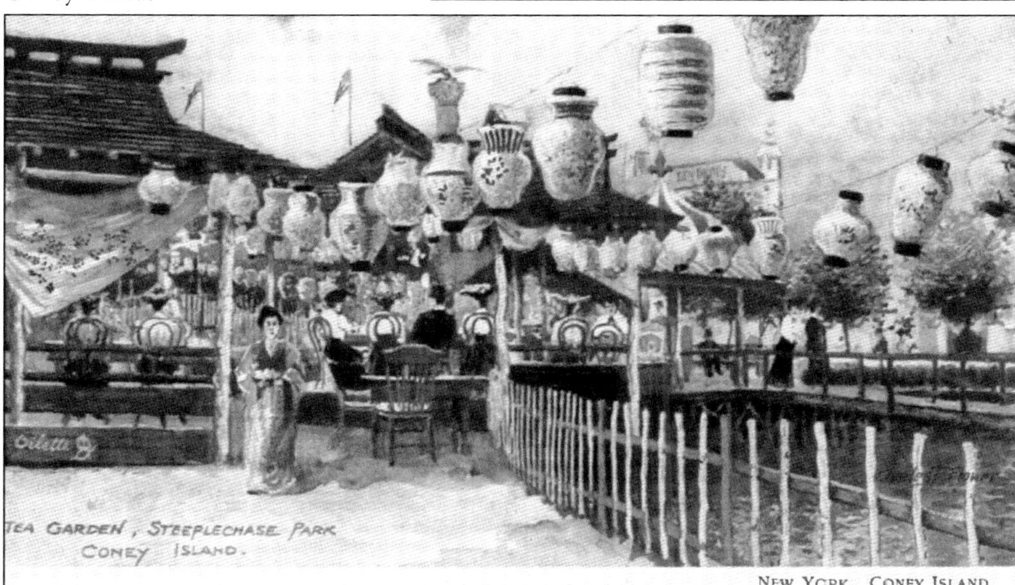

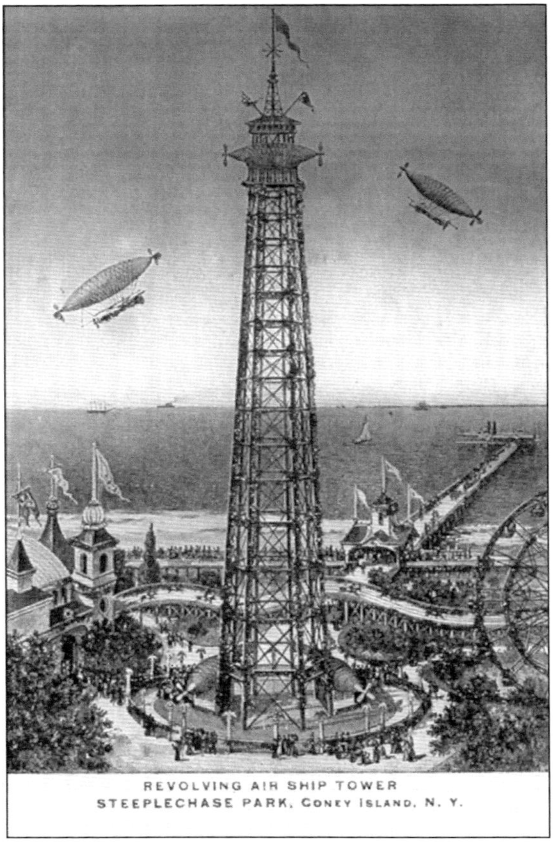

The Revolving Air Ship Tower, shown here with the Steeplechase Track and the Steeplechase Pier in the background, was one of the early rides at Steeplechase Park. The Revolving Air Ship Tower, an aerial corkscrew ride, was converted into a water tower after the 1907 fire destroyed half the park.

This postcard offers a glimpse of Steeplechase Park as it may have been seen from the top of the Revolving Air Ship Tower.

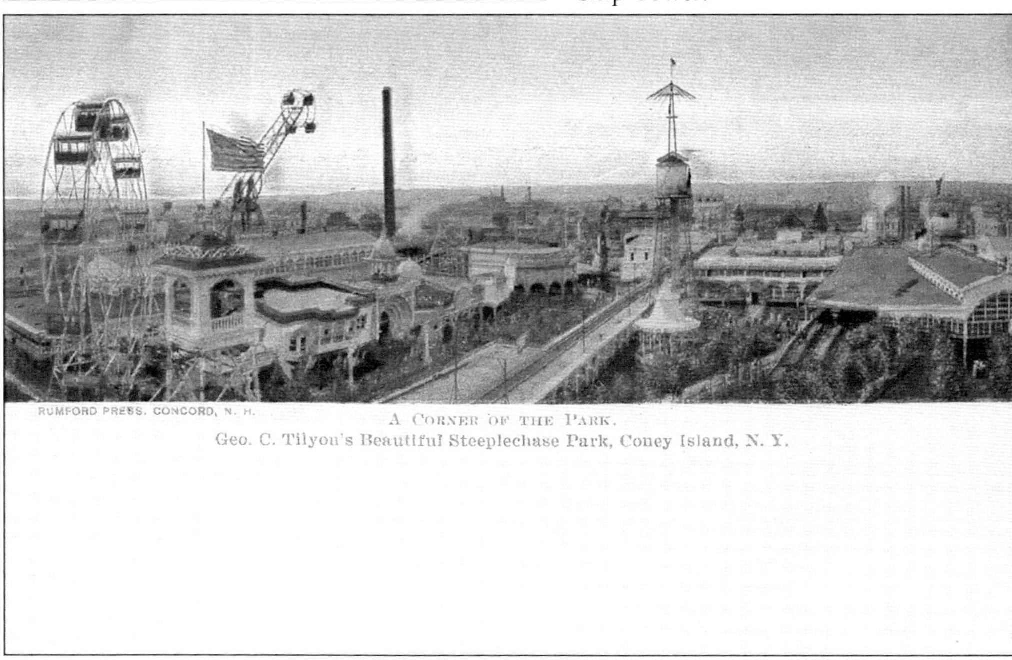

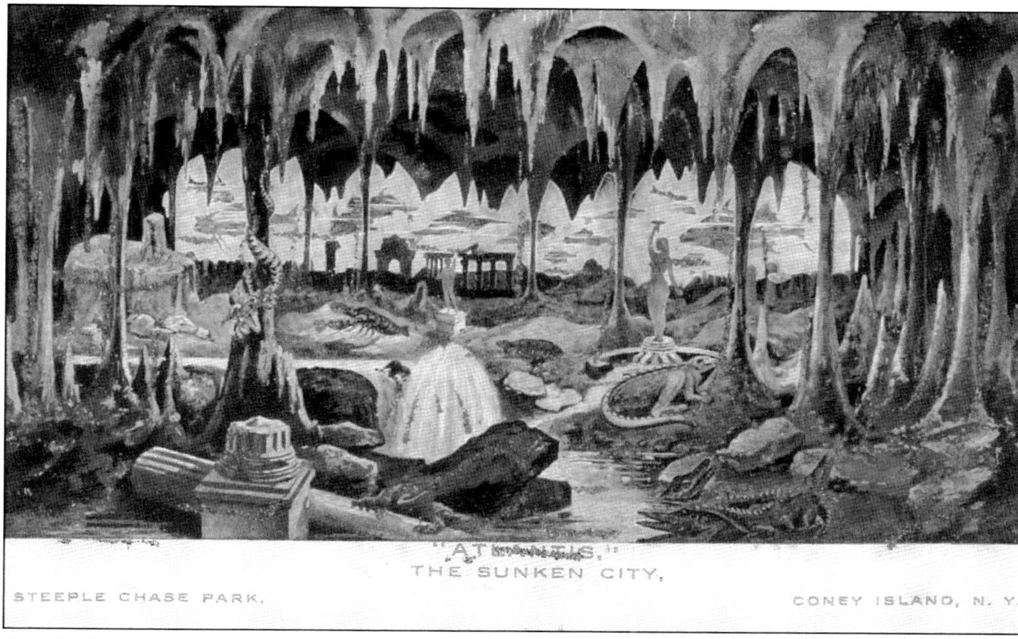

Steeplechase Park owner George C. Tilyou knew that he needed to make constant additions and changes in his park to keep it exciting. In 1905, he added a ride that took patrons through the "Sunken City" of Atlantis.

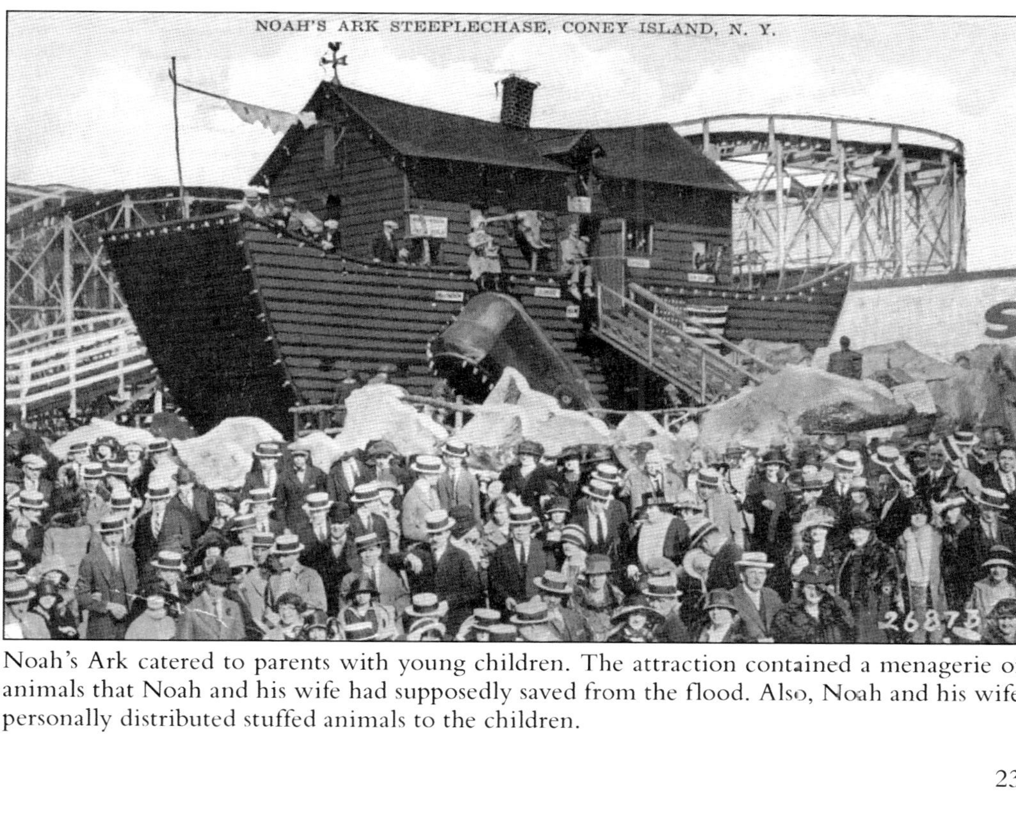

Noah's Ark catered to parents with young children. The attraction contained a menagerie of animals that Noah and his wife had supposedly saved from the flood. Also, Noah and his wife personally distributed stuffed animals to the children.

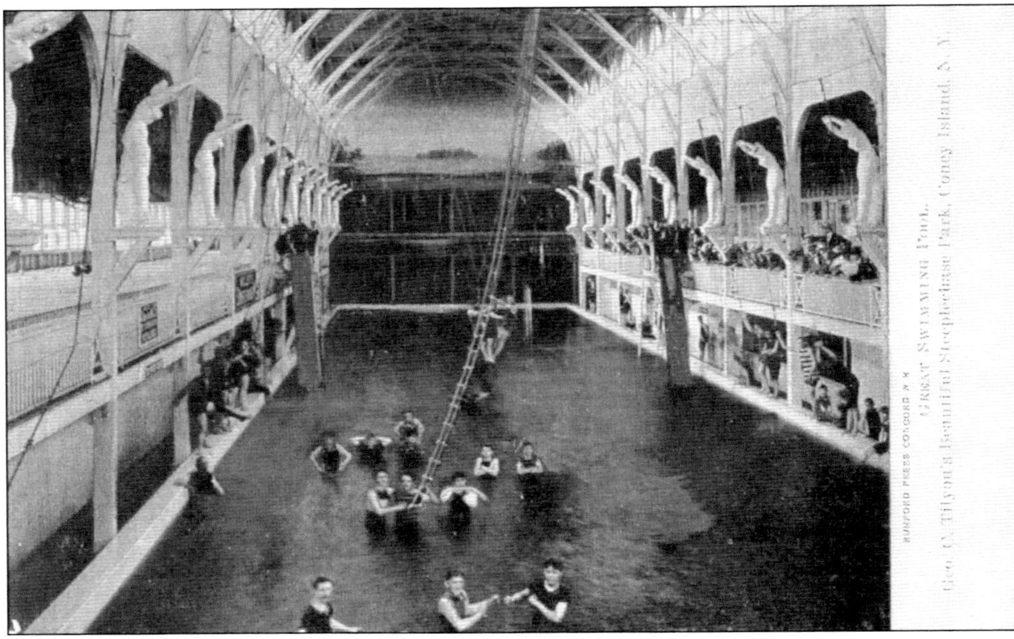

Steeplechase Park owner George C. Tilyou, a born promoter, released this statement to reporters after the 1907 fire that destroyed half of the park: "Steeplechase, although scorched a little, still has 25 attractions for 25 cents. I have completed the Boardwalk from Surf Avenue to the unburned part of the park and soon another will be built from the Bowery entrance. Five acres are OK. The swimming pool will be sacrificed and I'm building a human roulette wheel in its place."

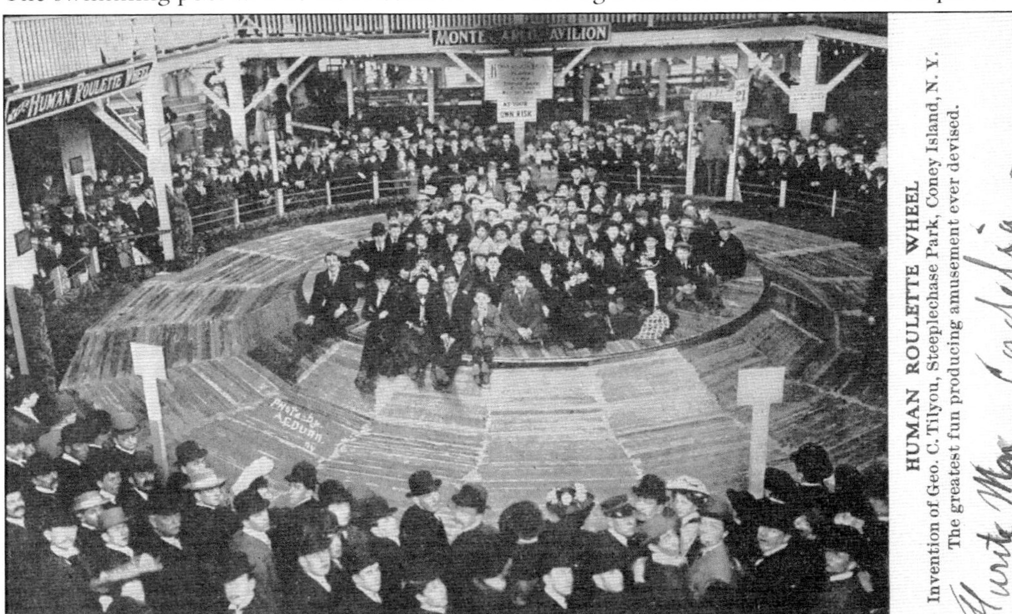

The Human Roulette Wheel, which became one of the favorite attractions at Steeplechase Park, was a large spinning wheel—riders tried to hang on as long as possible, but most were flung off of the spinning platform by centrifugal force.

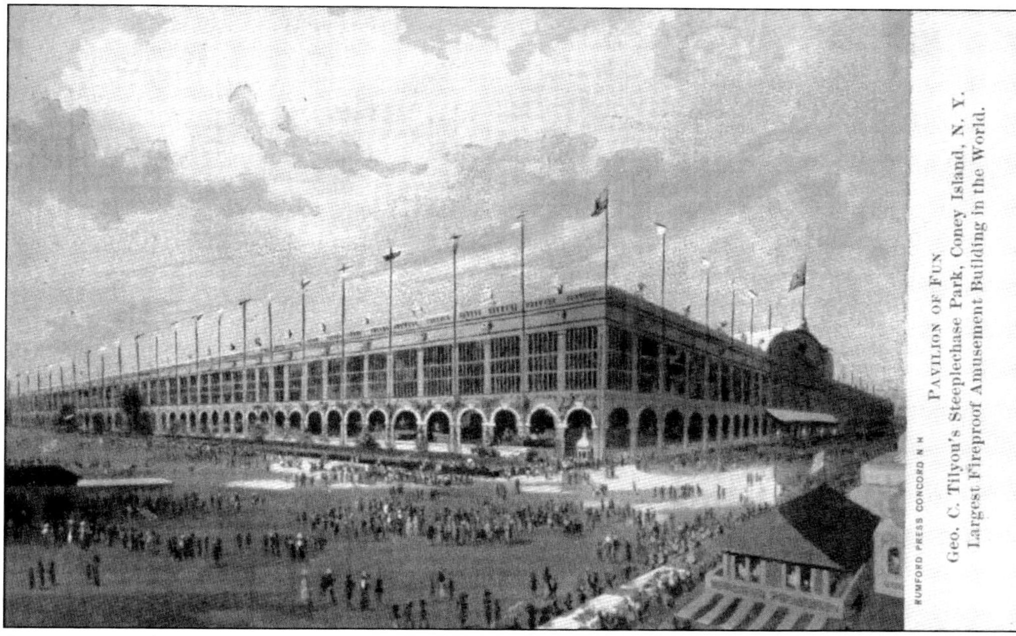

George C. Tilyou realized, after the 1907 fire, that the fun does not have to end when it rains. When he built the Pavilion of Fun, it included amusements like the Insanitarium, Blowhole Theater, Comedy Lane, Battleship Roll, Laughing Gallery, Bounding Billows, Uncle Sam, Down & Out, Bicycle Carousel, Human Pool Table, Hoop-la, Panama Slide, and many others.

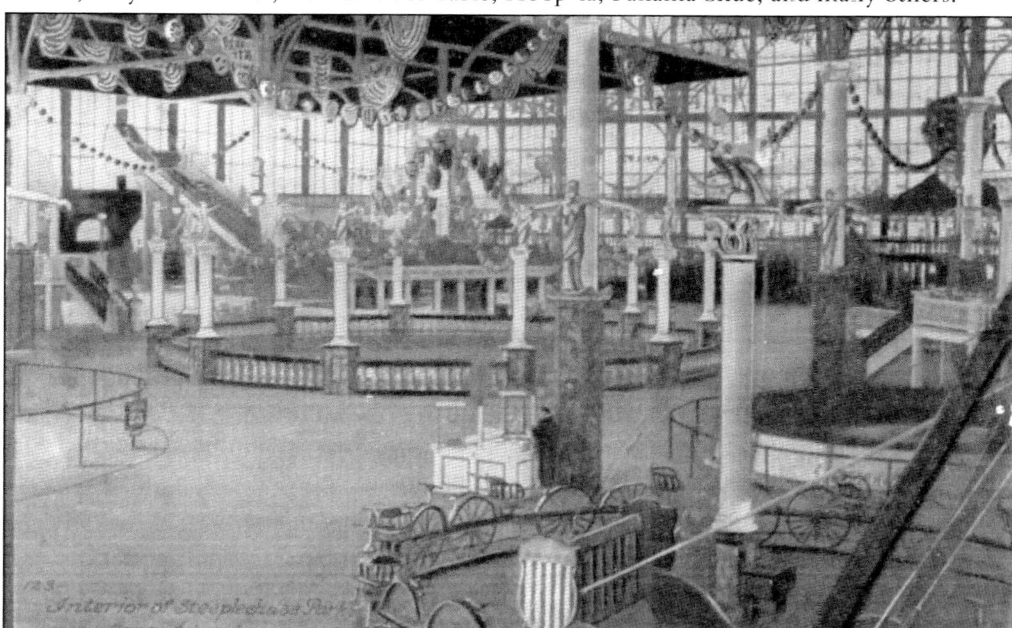

Inside the Pavilion of Fun at Steeplechase Park, guests could be entertained for hours by participating or watching others. According to rumor, the churchgoing Tilyou would pray for rain so that crowds would flock to the Pavilion of Fun. After Steeplechase Park closed in 1964, many of the rides from the Pavilion of Fun were relocated to Astroland.

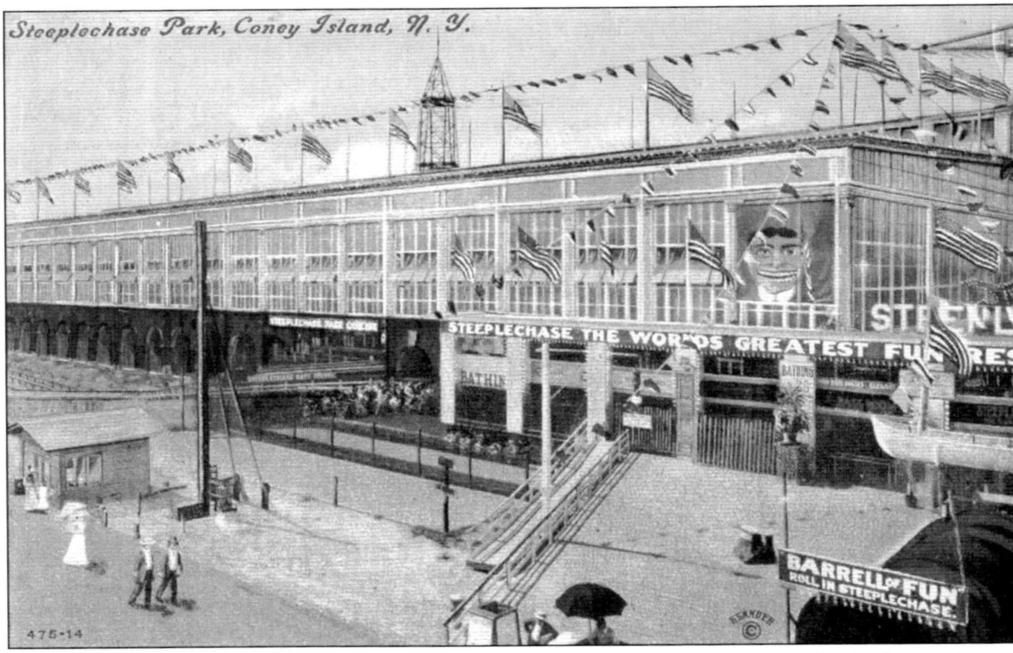

After the fire of 1907, George C. Tilyou had the new Pavilion of Fun built of glass and steel, and it covered five acres. This postcard shows the Barrell of Fun entrance, where patrons tried to maneuver through a large revolving barrel.

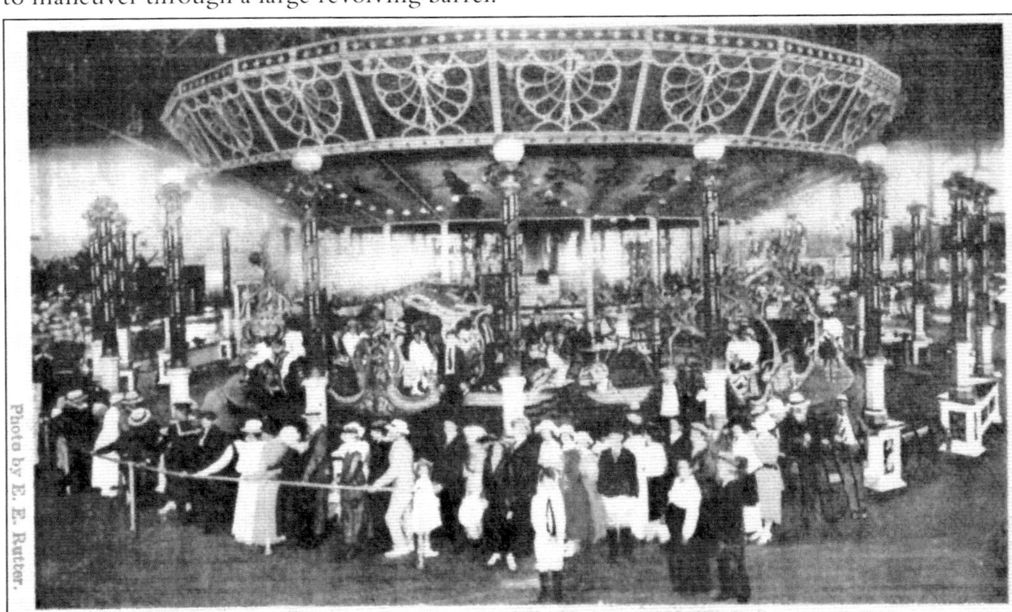

The El Dorado Carousel was located at Surf Avenue and West Fifth Street until it was transferred to Steeplechase's Pavilion of Fun after the ride's paint was blistered in the Dreamland fire of 1911. The carousel featured horses, pigs, and other barnyard animals, had three platforms revolving at different speeds, and was illuminated by 5,000 lights. After Steeplechase Park closed in 1964, the carousel remained in storage until it was sent to Japan in 1970 for the Osaka World's Fair.

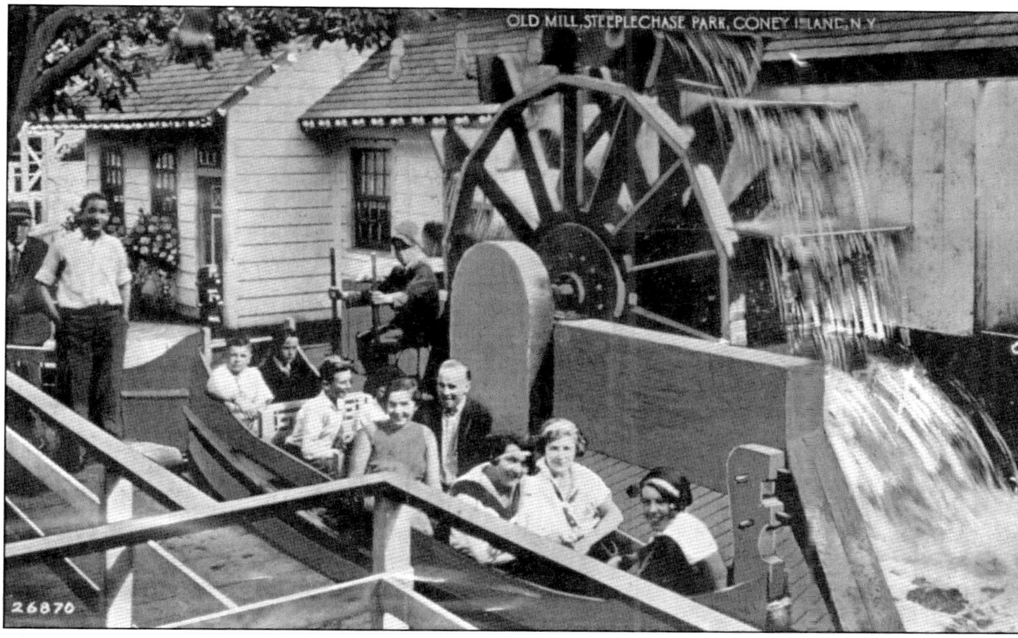

The Old Mill boat rides in Steeplechase Park were very popular, especially with young couples. The Old Mill, invented by George W. Schofield in 1902, was a vast improvement upon earlier rides thanks to its use of a large paddle wheel.

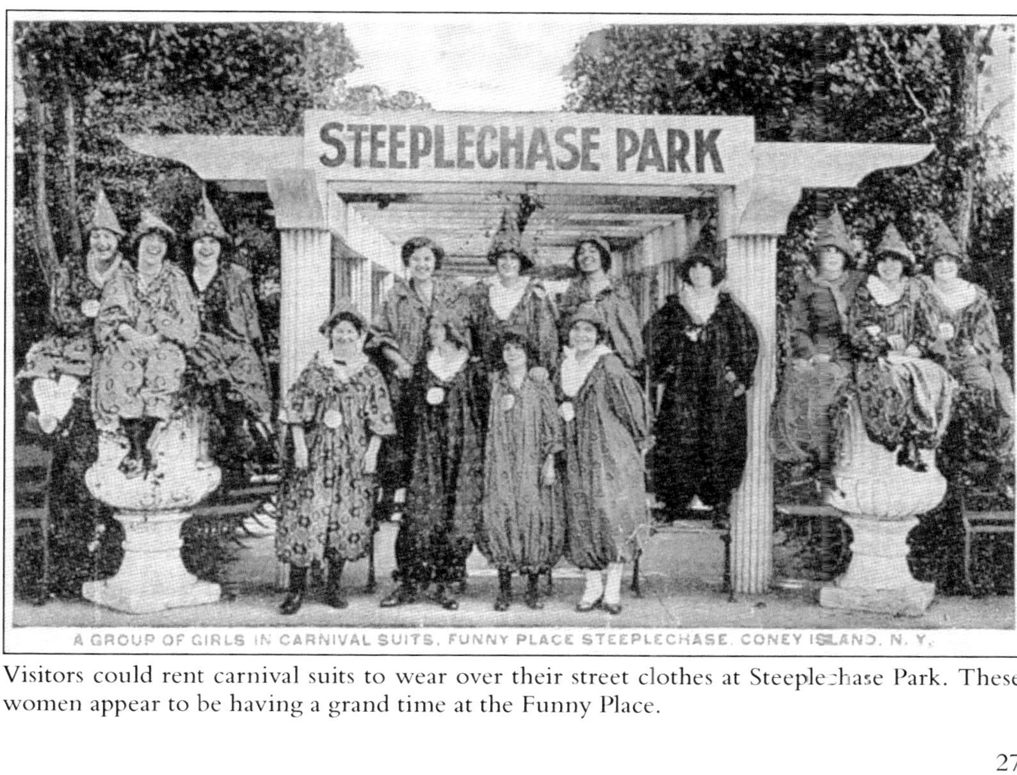

Visitors could rent carnival suits to wear over their street clothes at Steeplechase Park. These women appear to be having a grand time at the Funny Place.

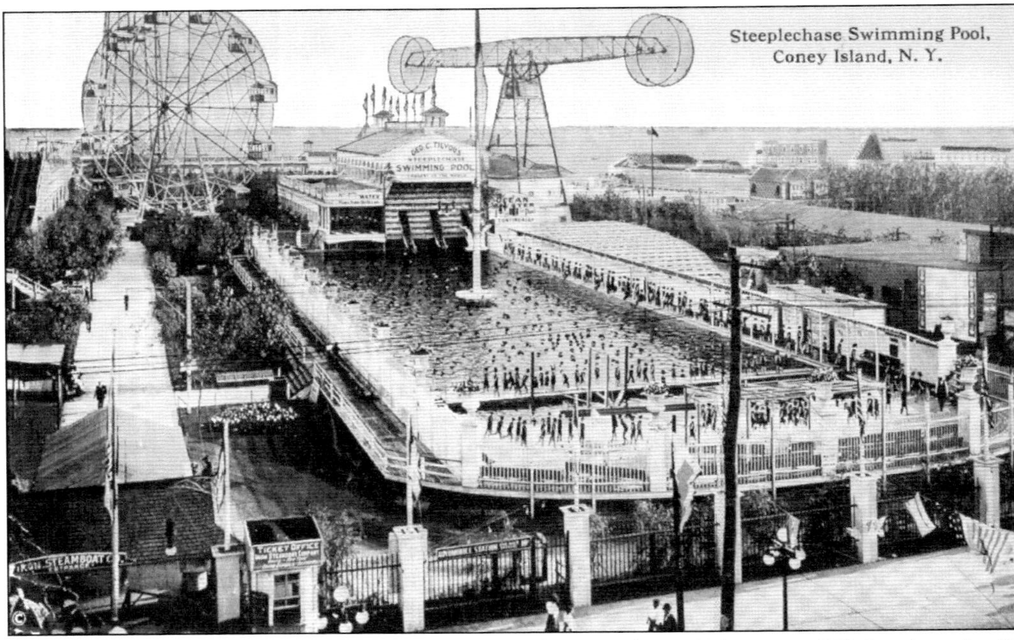

The outdoor swimming pool at Steeplechase Park opened in 1910. It was 270 feet long by 90 feet wide and contained 670,000 gallons of saltwater. Starting in 1945, the pool was reserved for those who paid for a season pass.

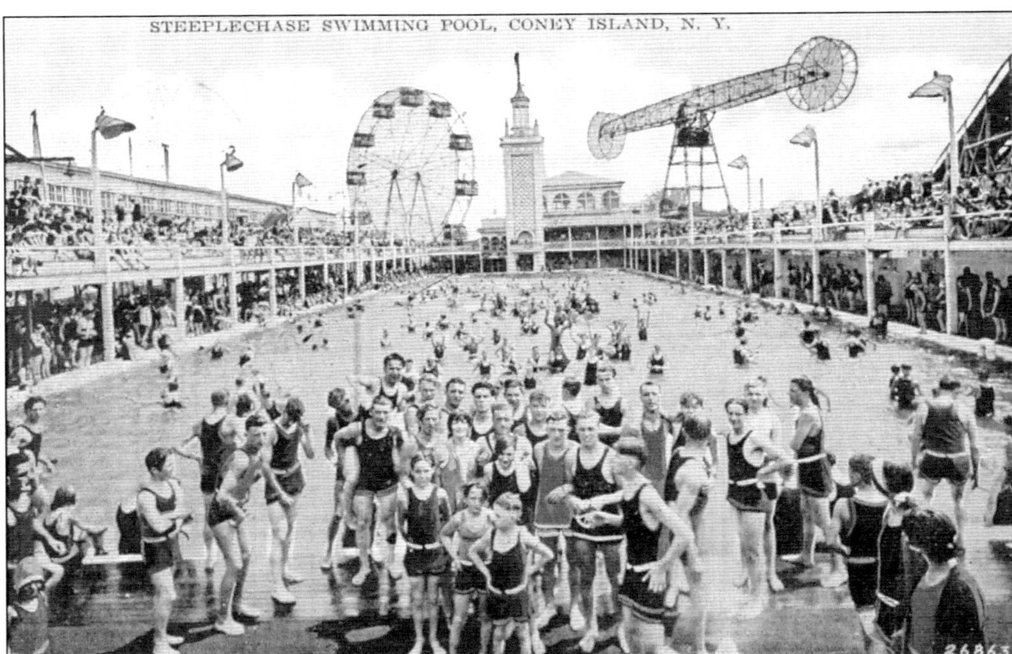

Another view of the Steeplechase swimming pool shows the Ferris wheel and the Giant See-Saw in the background. The Giant See-Saw featured two small Ferris wheels on each end of a giant lever. This ride would lift passengers nearly 170 feet into the sky.

At night, the view from the Ferris wheel was spectacular. Fortunately, the Ferris wheel was salvaged from the old park after the 1907 fire. The lowest-hanging cars of the giant wheel were burned, but the steel structure was undamaged, so it was able to be refurbished.

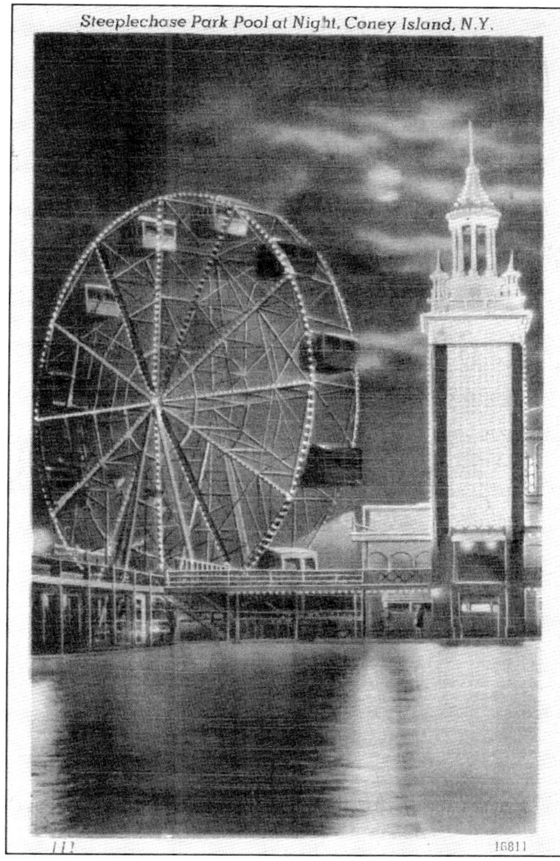

As early as 1925, bathing-beauty contests became popular at Coney Island. Steeplechase Park held the "Modern Venus" bathing-beauty contest each year, and the winner would go on to represent Coney Island in the national bathing-beauty contest in Atlantic City. Not to be outdone, Luna Park held its own "Red-headed" bathing-beauty contest. In the 1930s, Steeplechase began holding a "Most Beautiful Grandmother" bathing-beauty contest. A variation of this tradition continues today at the Miss Coney Island Burlesque Beauty Pageant, which is held each September and sponsored by Coney Island USA.

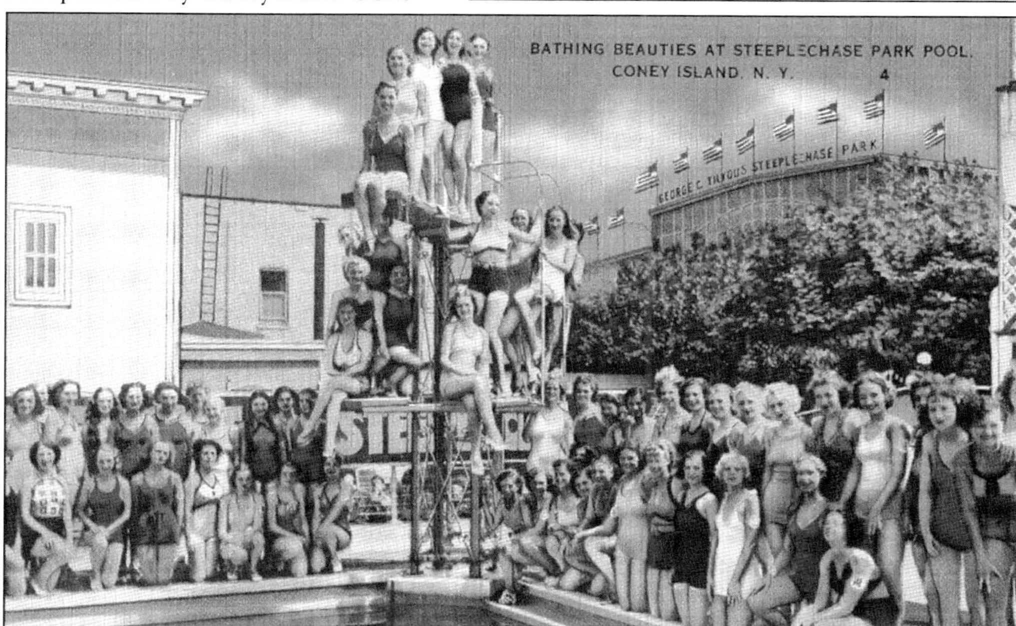

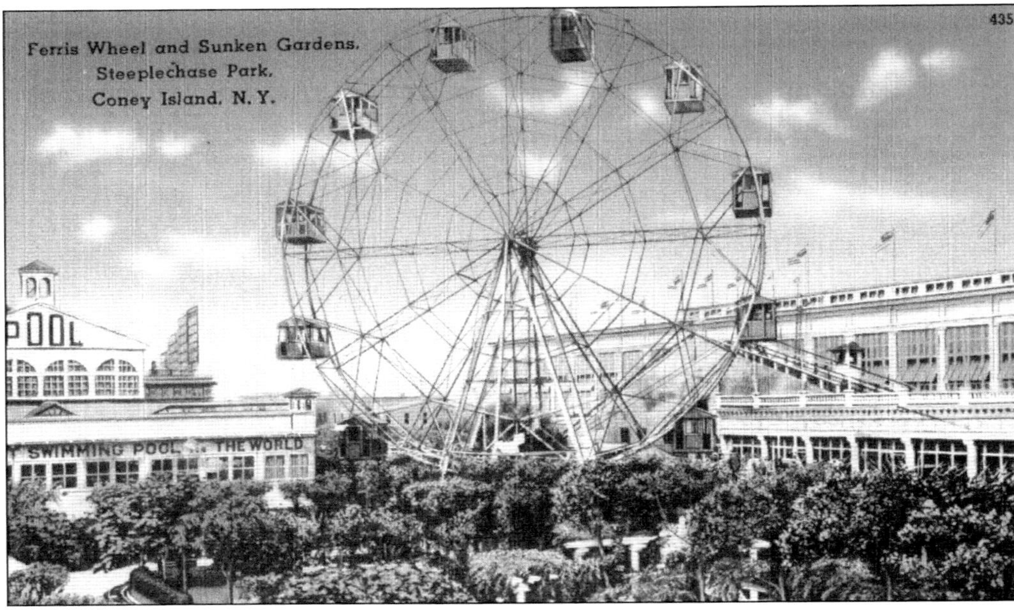

Steeplechase Park owner George C. Tilyou's Ferris wheel, originally located at the Bowery and West Eighth Street, was transferred to the Sunken Gardens in 1905. It had 12 cars that each held up to 18 passengers. It functioned from 1894 to 1964.

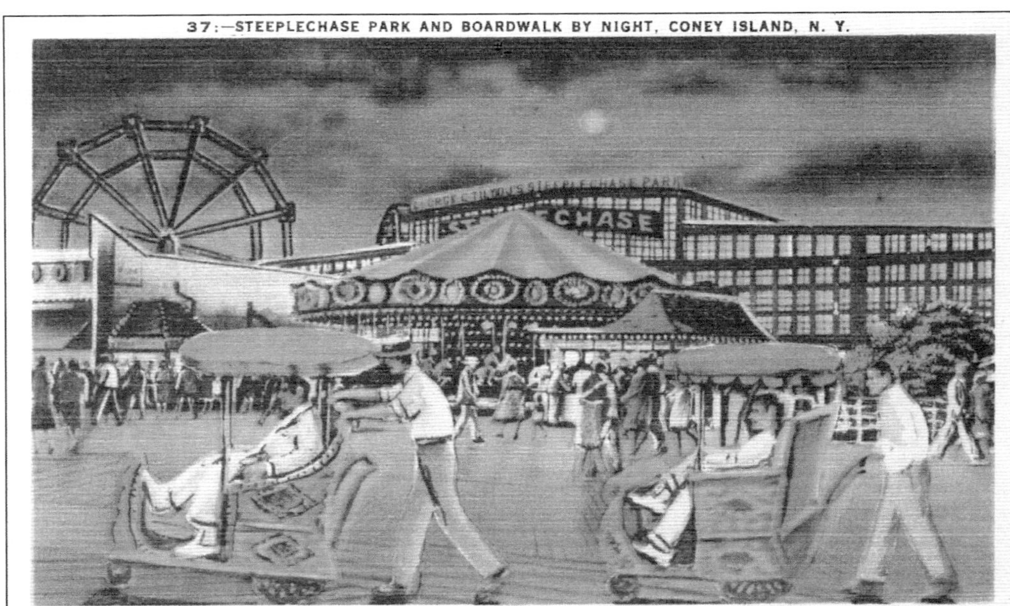

In this depiction of Steeplechase Park from the boardwalk at night, the Rolling Chairs are traveling down the boardwalk. When George Tilyou died in 1914, he left the care of the park to his children, who continued to operate it for the next 50 years.

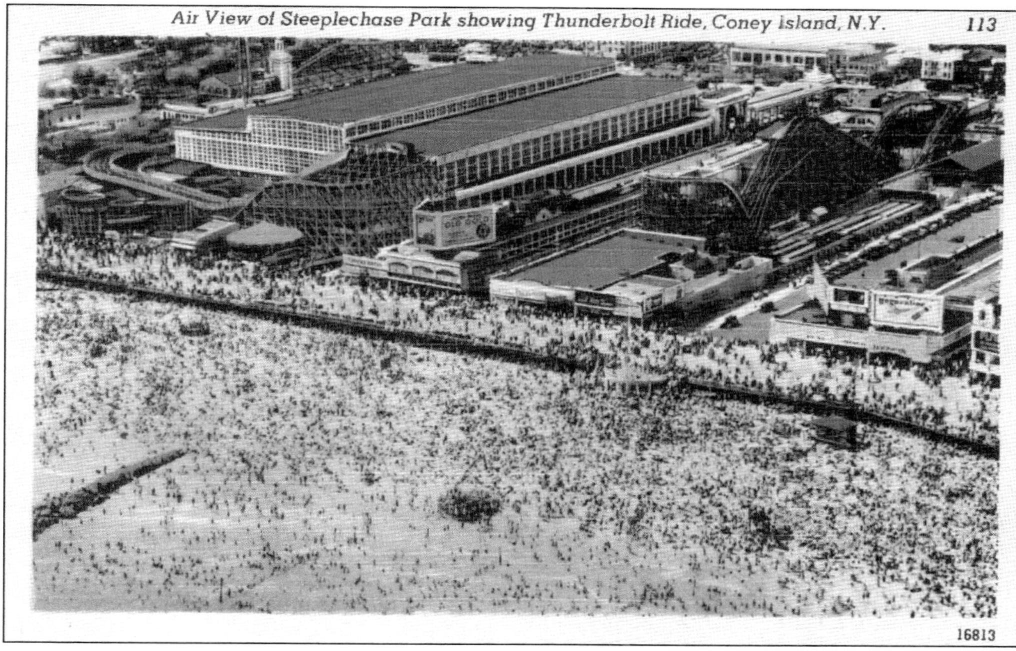

This aerial view of Steeplechase Park shows the expanded Pavilion of Fun and the Thunderbolt, a wooden roller coaster that operated from 1925 until 1982. In June 2013, the New York City Economic Development Corporation announced that the Thunderbolt would be rebuilt as a new steel coaster with speeds that will reach 65 mph over 2,000 feet of track. The 125-foot-tall coaster will be near the new Steeplechase Plaza and the historic B&B Carousell. The original Thunderbolt, built over the Kensington Hotel, was featured in the 1977 Woody Allen film *Annie Hall*.

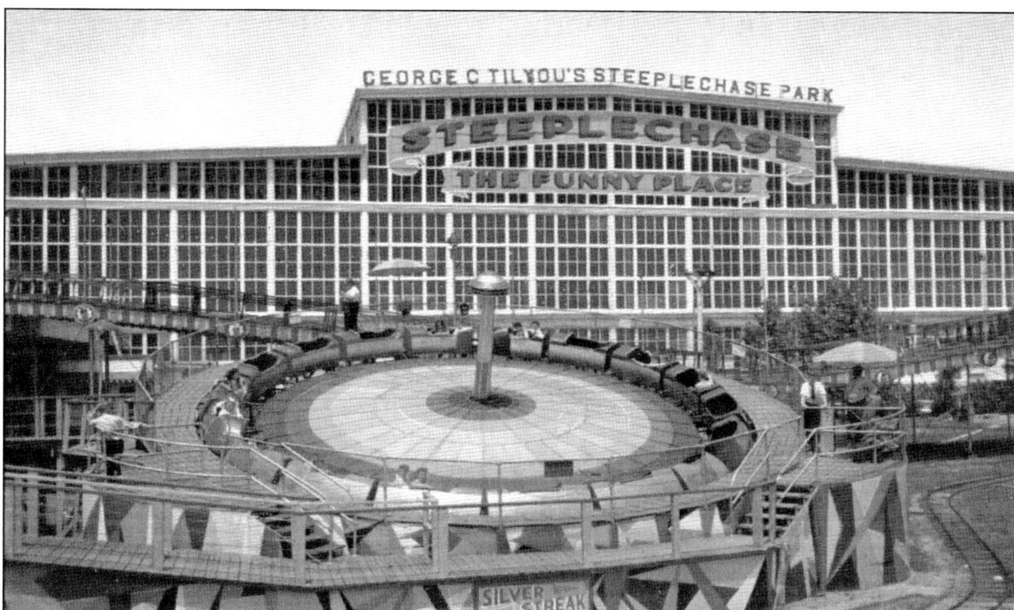

This chrome postcard shows the Pavilion of Fun with the Silver Streak ride in front.

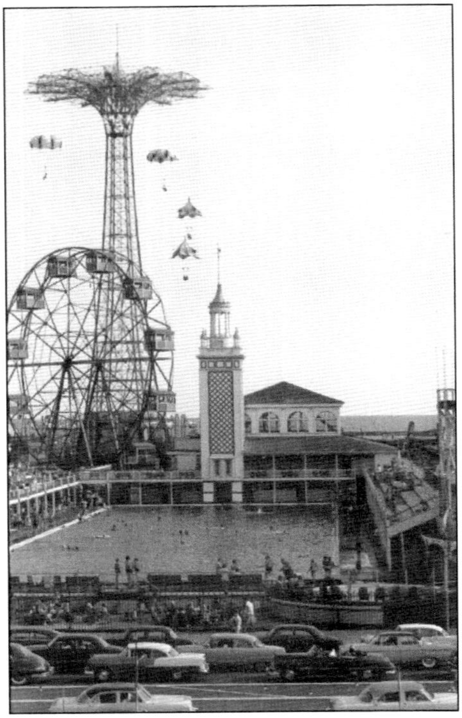

Ret. Lt. Comdr. James Hale Strong (1890–1961) built the machine that would become the Parachute Drop (now called the Parachute Jump) as a training device for paratroopers. He then redesigned the device for civilian use for the 1939 New York World's Fair. It was moved to its current site, which was then part of Steeplechase Park, in 1941. The ride is 250 feet tall and had 12 arms that supported two-seater parachutes that drop from the top of the ride to the ground.

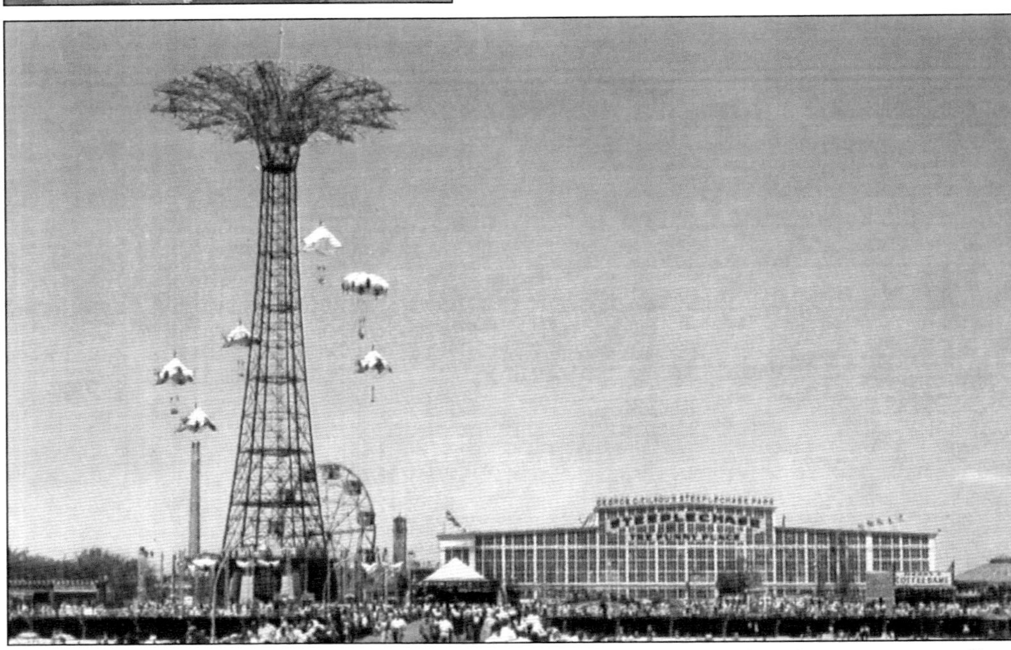

The Parachute Jump ride ceased operations when Steeplechase Park closed in 1964. It was listed in the National Register of Historic Places in 1980, and the City of New York recognized it as a city landmark in 1988. Today, the Parachute Jump looms over the right-field corner of MCU Park, home of the Brooklyn Cyclones baseball team (a New York Mets affiliate). At night, neon lights make the "Eiffel Tower of Brooklyn" visible throughout New York City.

Three

Luna Park

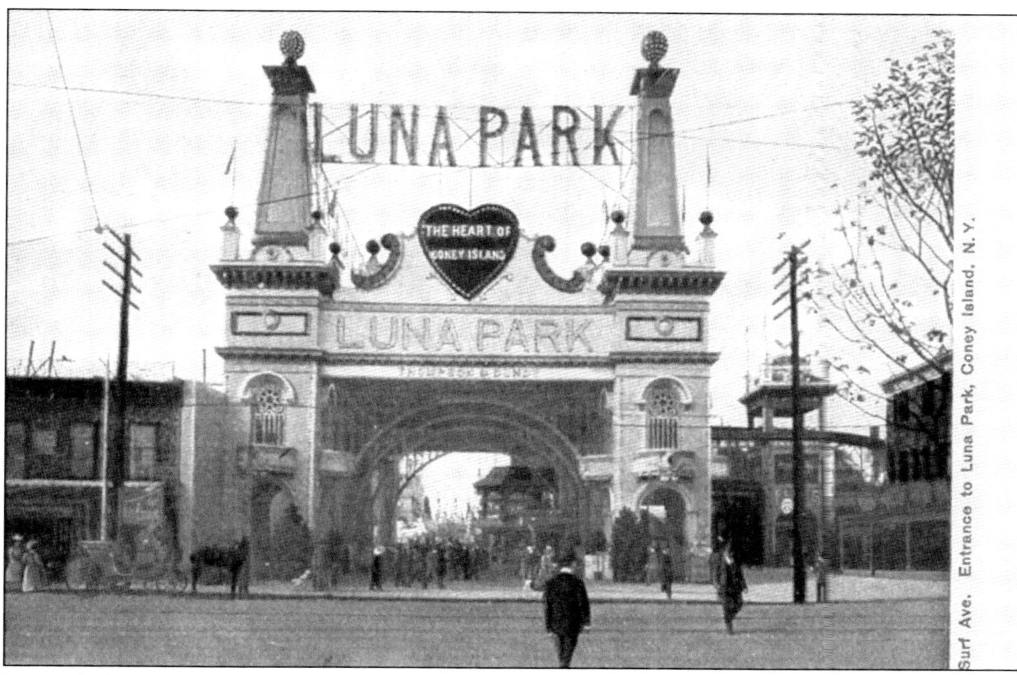

In 1901, George C. Tilyou attended the Pan-American Exposition in Buffalo to scout for new attractions. The one that caught his eye—A Trip to the Moon—was owned and operated by Fred Thompson and Elmer "Skip" Dundy. Tilyou brought the partners and the ride to Steeplechase Park. After witnessing the success of Steeplechase, Thompson and Dundy, after one season, ventured out and opened their own amusement park in May 1903.

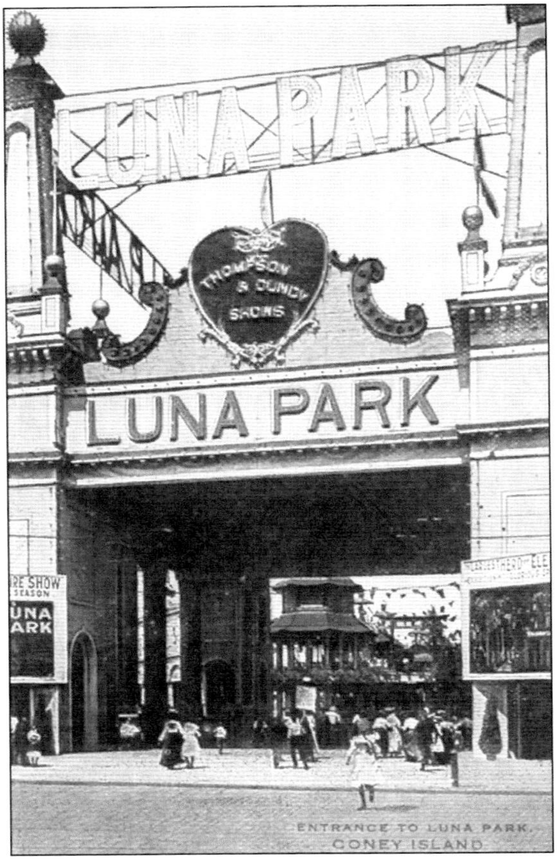

Sea Lion Park closed after a financially disastrous 1902 season. Fred Thompson and Skip Dundy leased the property from Paul Boyton and kept the Shoot-the-Chutes ride. They moved their Trip to the Moon ride to the park and added new attractions after acquiring the adjacent property where the Elephant Hotel once stood. This undivided-back postcard shows the original entrance to Luna Park off Surf Avenue. After Thompson and Dundy added hundreds of thousands of incandescent lights, Luna Park opened on May 16, 1903.

Thompson and Dundy were forever changing the park's attractions. Their philosophy was that if an attraction failed to pay for itself in a single season, it would be scrapped. One of the first casualties of the 1905 season was the 20,000 Leagues Under the Sea show, which was replaced by a small indoor scenic railway called the Dragon's Gorge. Its mammoth archway, illuminated by 10,000 lights at night, was flanked by two enormous dragons.

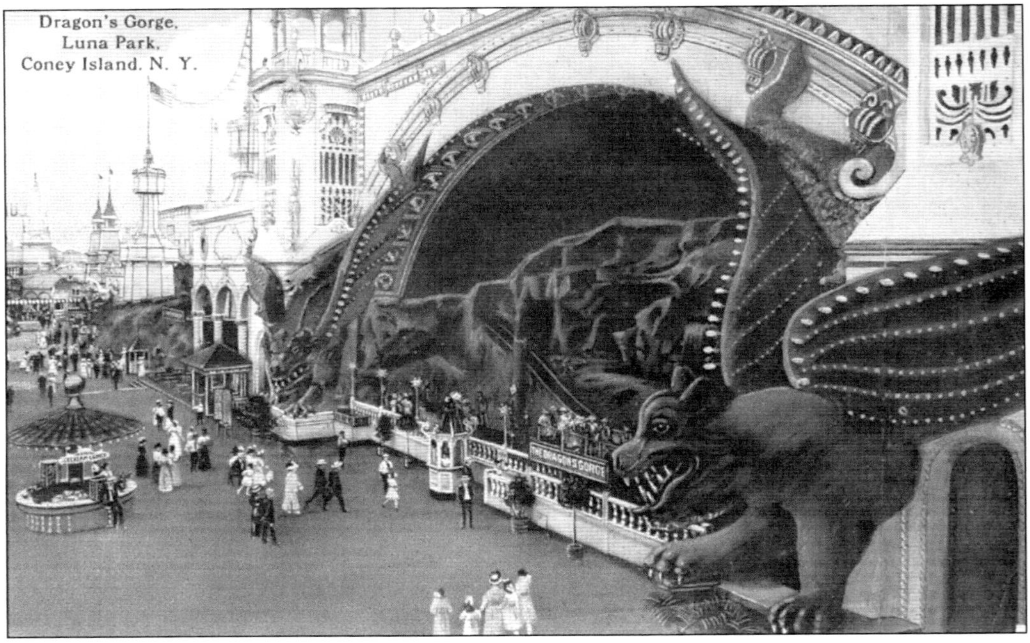

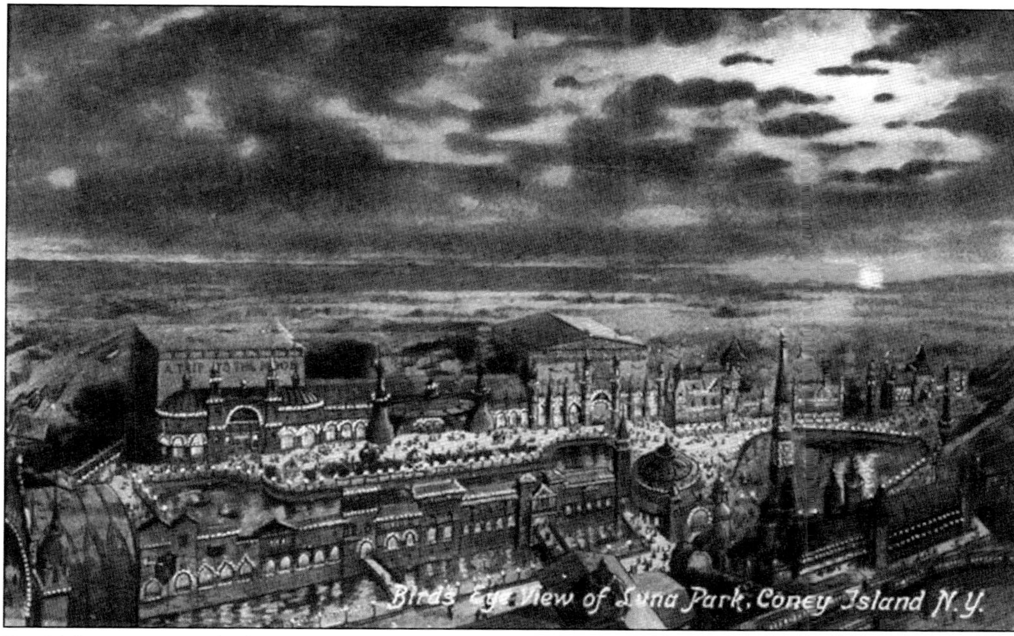

Fred Thompson and Skip Dundy created the A Trip to the Moon ride and presented it at the Pan-American Exposition held in Buffalo in 1901. The two men then came to Coney Island and duplicated the attraction for Steeplechase Park. In 1903, it became the centerpiece of their newly opened Luna Park. This bird's-eye view of Luna Park at night during a full moon includes the A Trip to the Moon building in the background.

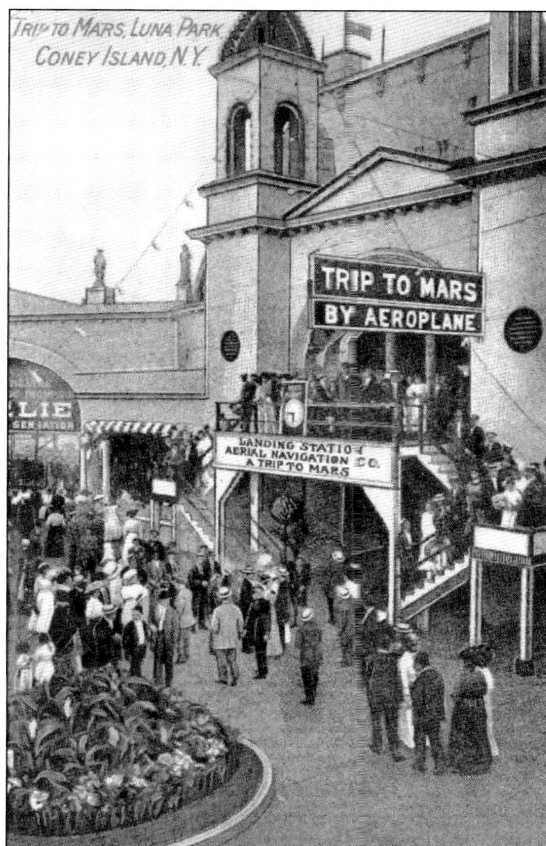

In 1912, A Trip to the Moon was transformed into A Trip to Mars by Aeroplane. In this ride, 30 passengers took a simulated airplane ride up through the clouds toward the stars. The trip's narration told passengers which stars they were visiting on their Martian odyssey.

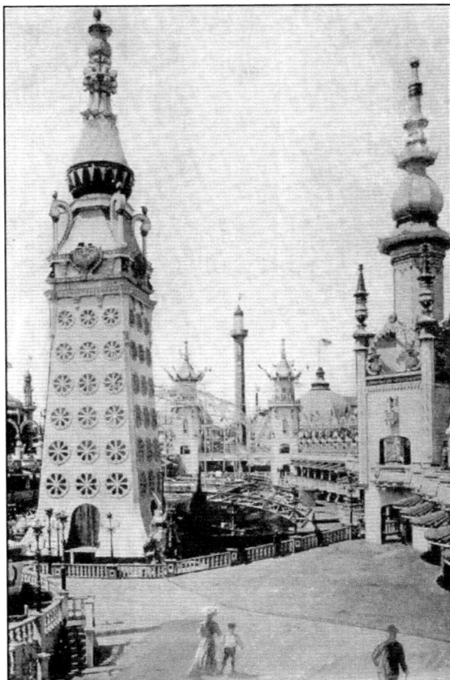

SOUVENIR POST CARD CO., NEW YORK

4718—*Tower and General View, Luna Park, Coney Island.*

The Tower was the centerpiece of Luna Park, where curves and colors were everywhere. Luna Park was designed to amaze rather than amuse.

This back of this postcard depicting Luna Park proclaims that "Luna Park is the largest private amusement enterprise at Coney Island, containing hundreds of electrical amusement devices and other concessions that are daily enjoyed by the visiting crowds. At night it is the most brilliant spot in Coney Island, being illuminated by thousands of electric lights."

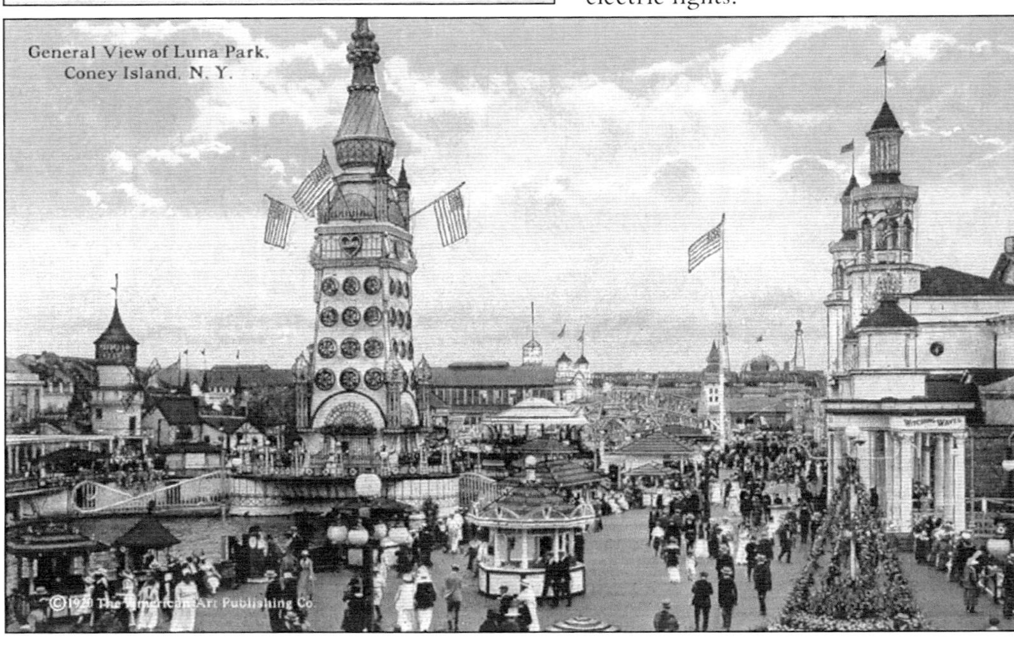

At night, the structures at Luna Park glowed with the power of 250,000 electric lights. Four million paying customers visited Luna Park in 1904, making it the most popular of the three Coney Island parks. Many people expressly came at night to view the amazing lights. Luna Park's constant change of attractions continued to bring repeat business to the park.

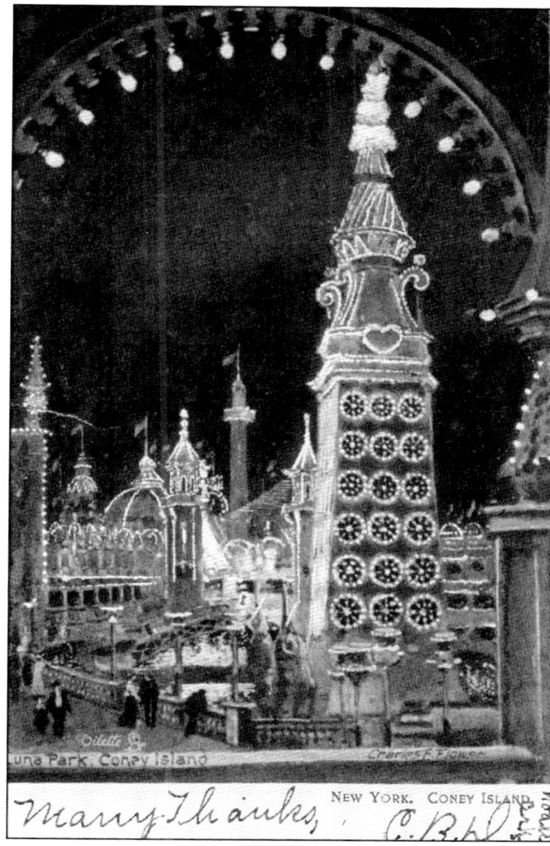

Owners Fred Thompson and Skip Dundy built a court of fountains near the lagoon and the 200-foot tall electric tower. Luna Park was such an immediate success that Thompson and Dundy were able to pay back their bank loans for the park less than a year after it opened.

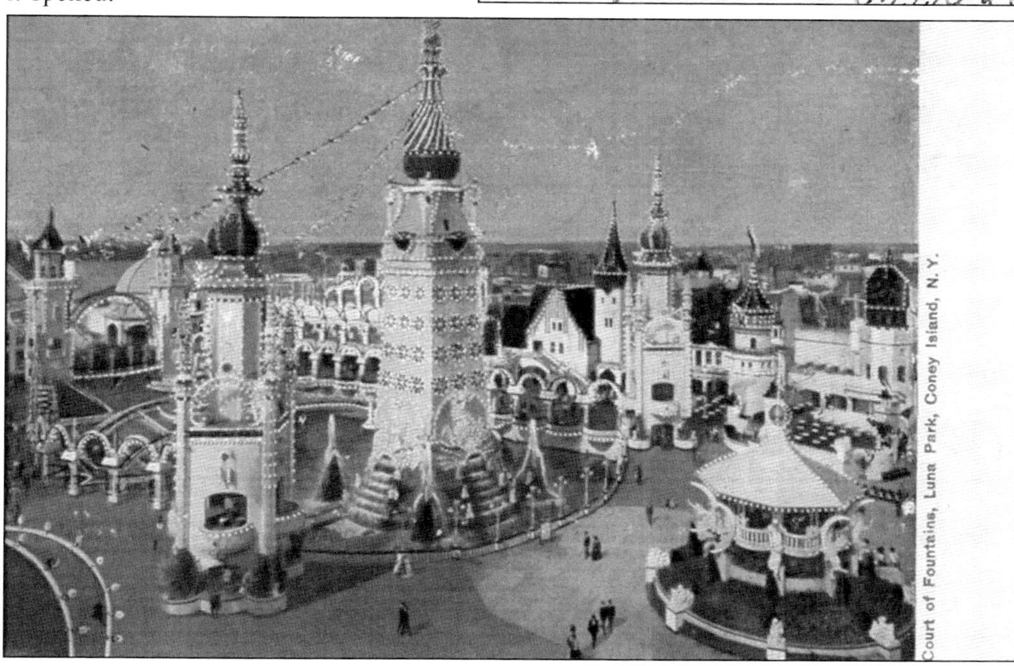

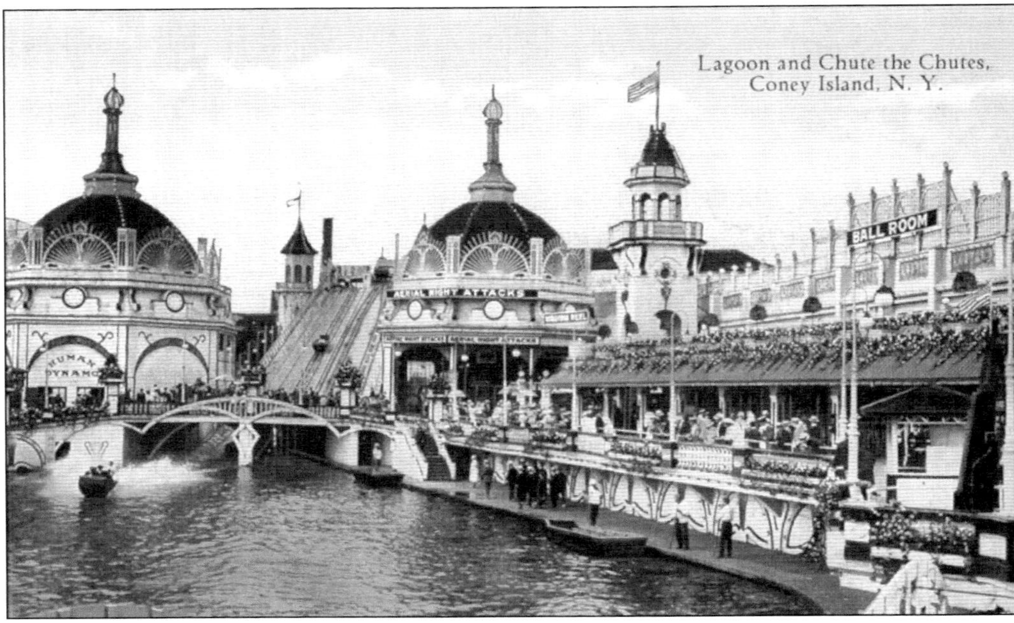

The Shoot-the-Chutes was the only ride that Luna Park owners Fred Thompson and Skip Dundy salvaged from Sea Lion Park. The ride consisted of flat-bottomed boats that slid down a steep slide into the lagoon. The boat was then guided to a landing by a boatman, who sat in the back. After the passengers disembarked, the boat was pulled up the ramp by a cable to be ready for the next group of riders.

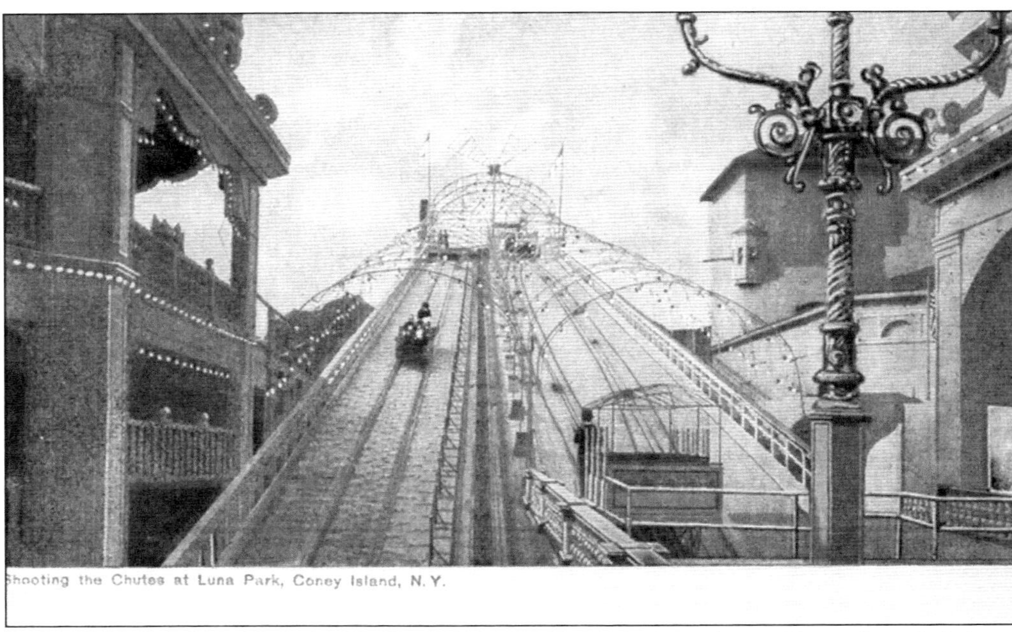

A pedestrian bridge crossed over the lagoon, and friends and family could watch as their loved ones came down the chute and splashed into the lagoon. When the boat hit the water, it bounced and became airborne for a short distance—to the screaming delight of its passengers.

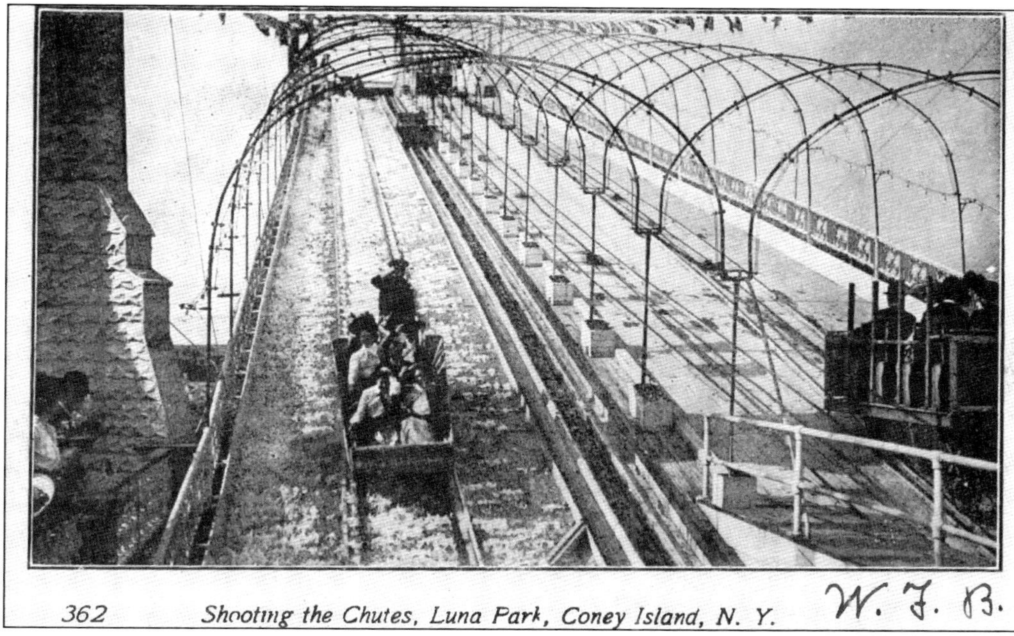

These postcards offer two views of the Shoot-the-Chutes ride at Luna Park. The park always had plenty of new attractions, and to please his partner Skip Dundy, who loved the circus, owner Fred Thompson included multiple animal acts. Thompson was able to keep crowds moving by carefully spacing his most outstanding attractions at particular sites in the park.

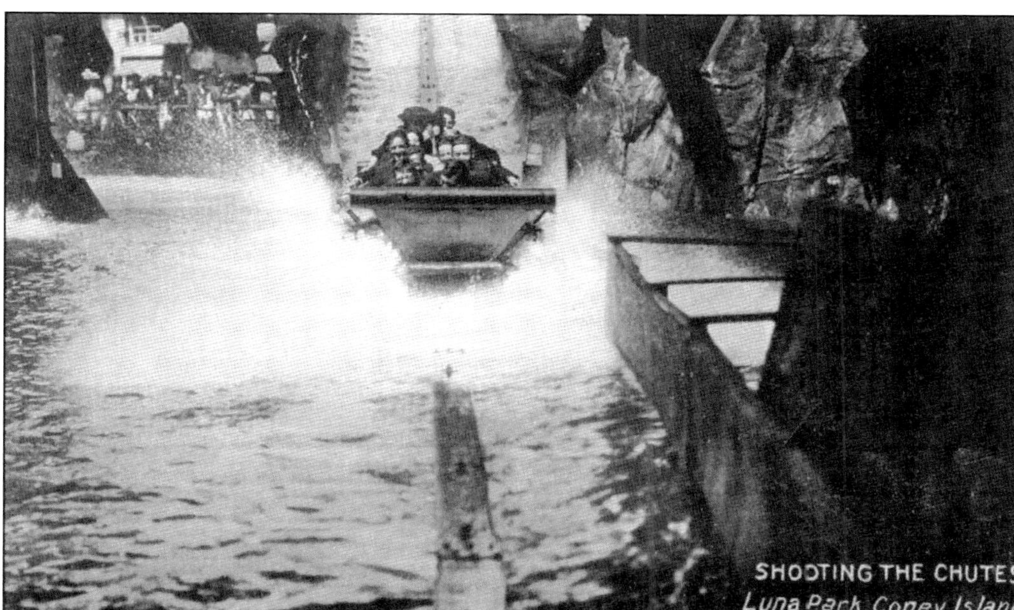

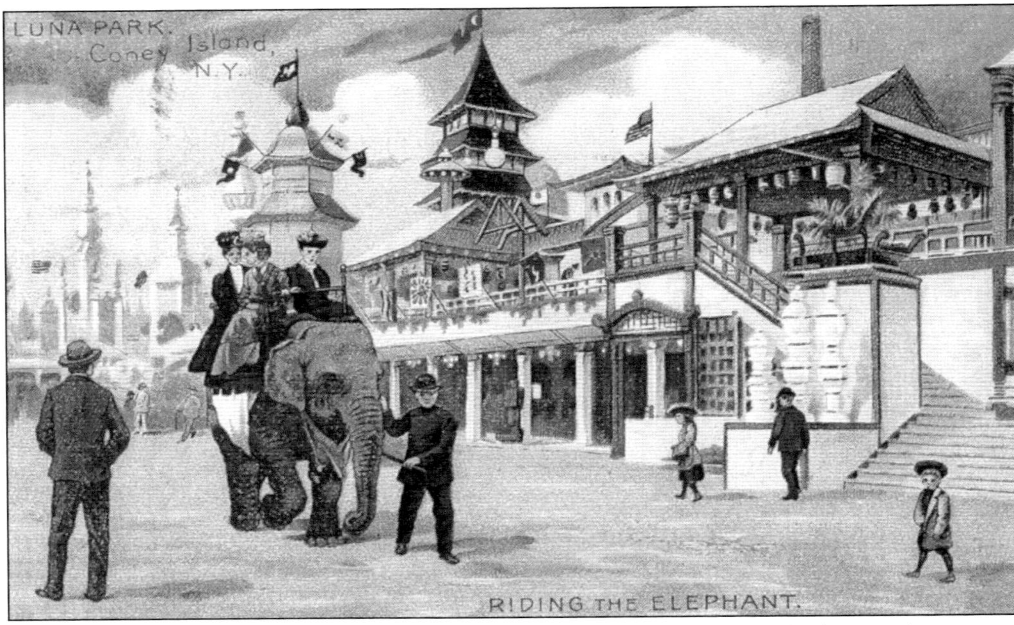

This postcard was mailed to New Market, New Jersey, in July 1912 with this simple message: "Great fun down here—think you would enjoy it." Visitors partaking in elephant rides intermingled with the general public on the promenade at Luna Park.

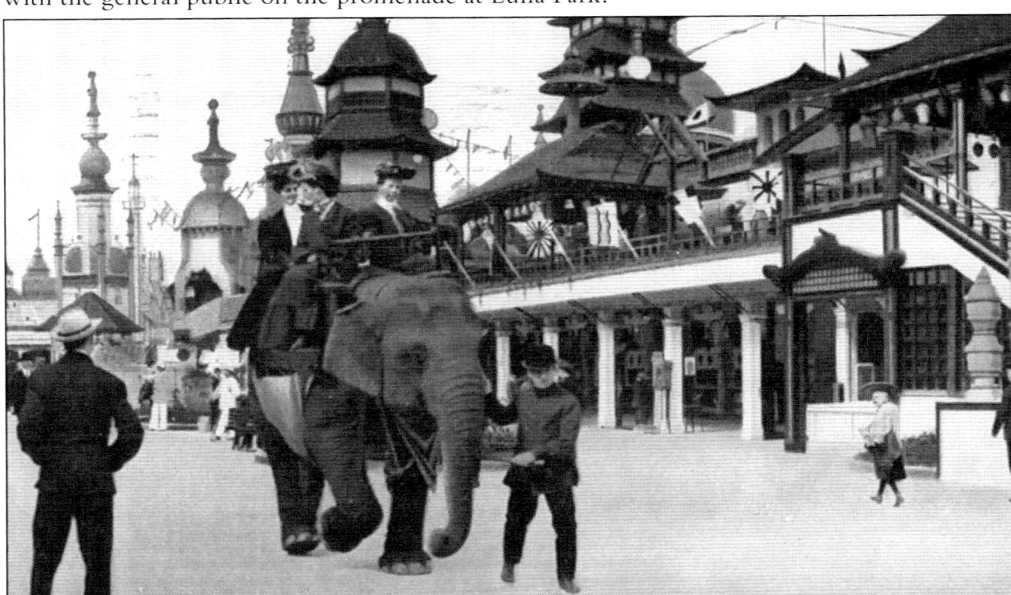

Luna Park co-owner Skip Dundy considered elephants to be good-luck charms after he found the junked remains of one of the Elephant Hotel's front legs when he and co-owner Fred Thompson were clearing the land for Luna Park, and Dundy became partial to elephant acts. For a while, he had four of his elephants slide down a specially made Shoot-the-Chutes into the lagoon. Note that both this postcard and the one above it appear to have been based on the same photograph.

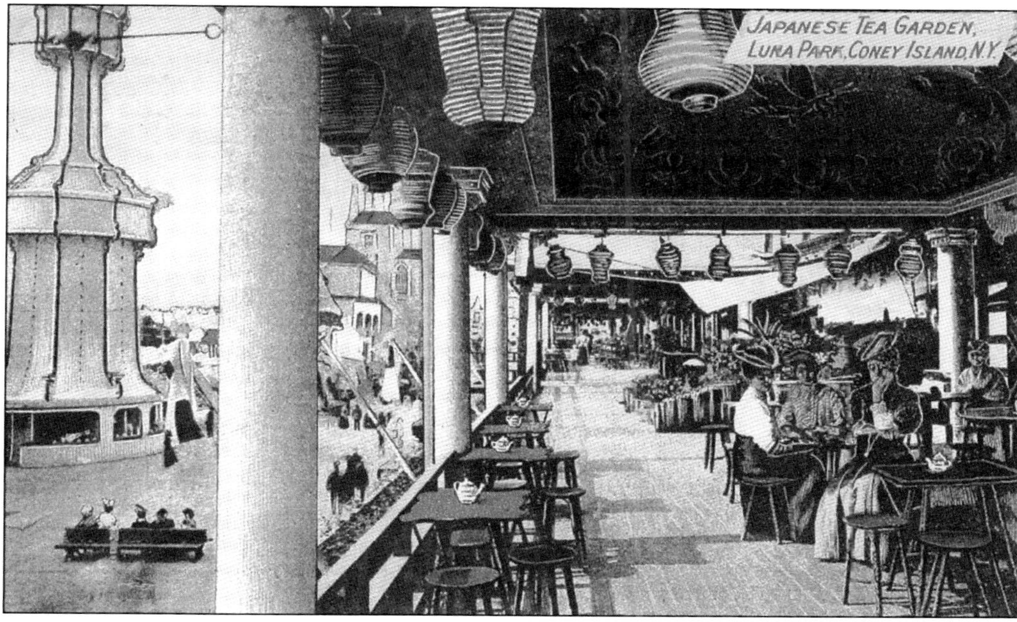

Each of the amusement parks in Coney Island had its own version of the Japanese tea house. The Japanese tea garden in Luna Park featured a 40-foot long roof garden, pictured here from two different vantage points. It ran the length of the second story of the Luna Park promenade.

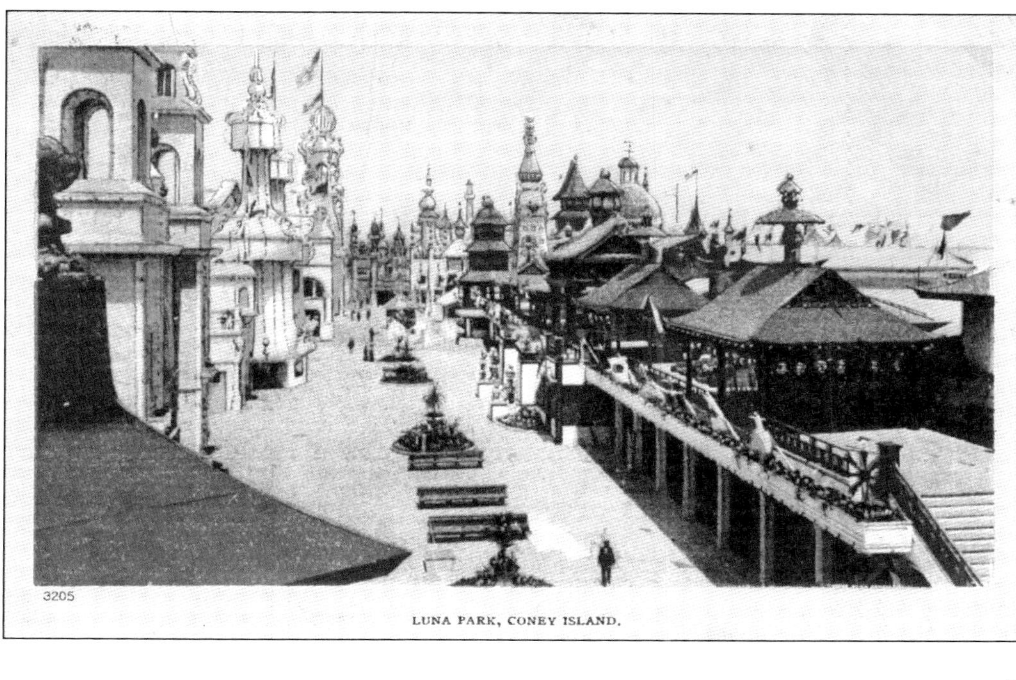

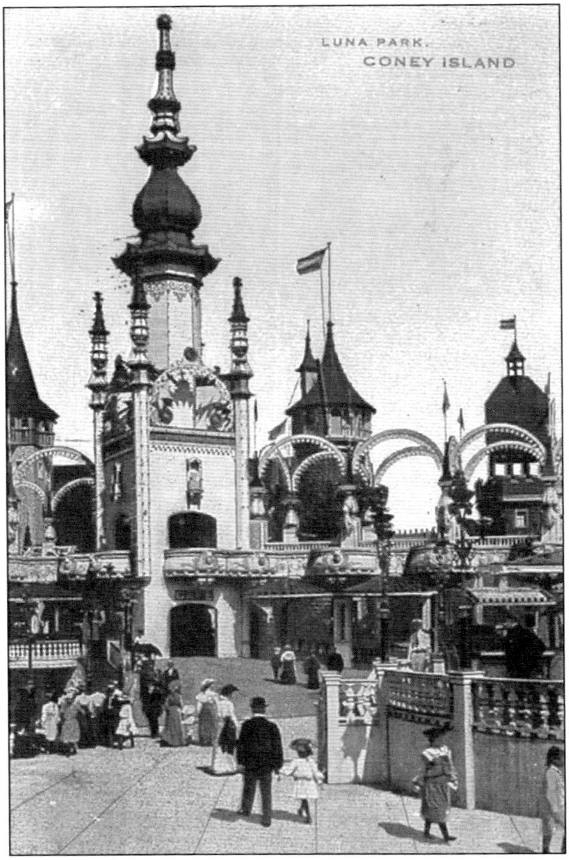

This Luna Park spire—one of many in the park—towered into the sky and featured a café underneath.

The Whip and Top ride opened at Luna Park in 1917. It was a large steel wheel that was tipped toward its heavier side, where it rested on its bottom edge. A roller coaster track spiraled around its outer rim, and as the four-car train circled the rim of the wheel, its weight changed the wheel's tilt, much like a slow-moving top. The wheel was more interesting to watch than to ride, and it only lasted for four seasons.

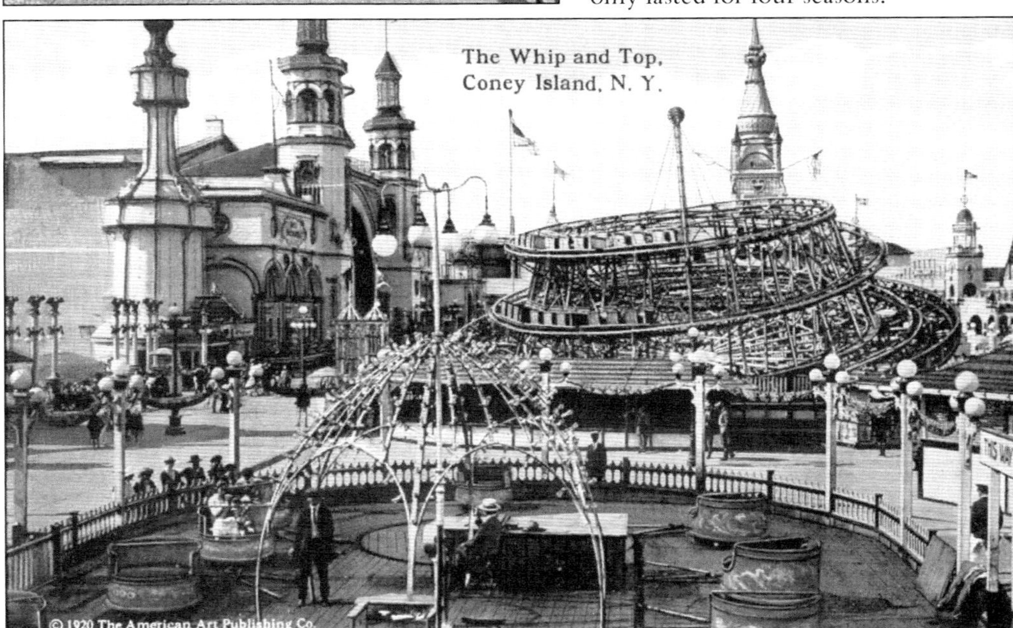

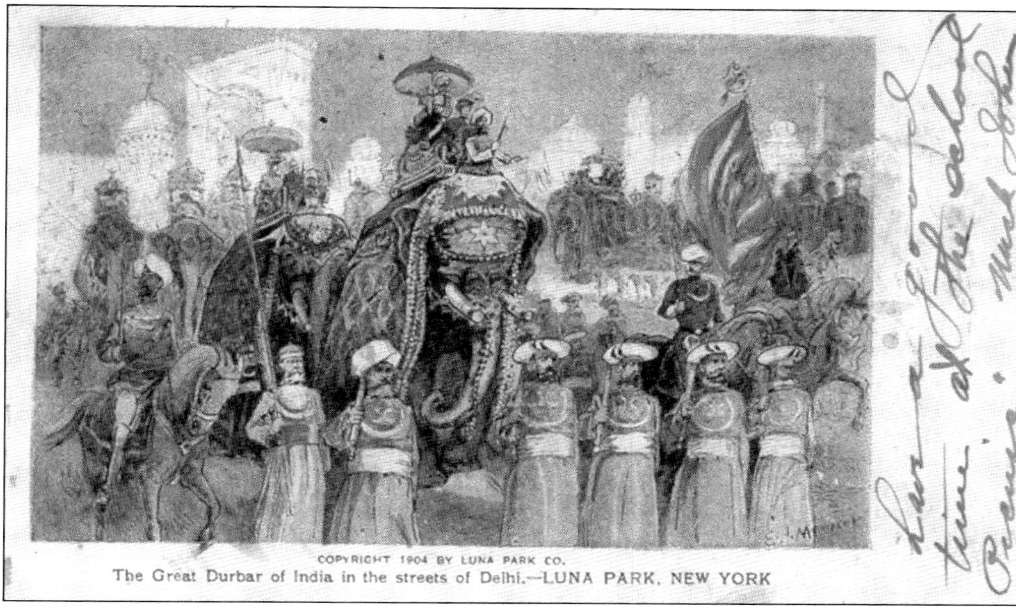

This private mailing card shows the "Great Durbar of India" in Luna Park's Streets of Delhi attraction. A parade of 300 India natives dressed in colorful costumes and riding elephants, camels, and horses created a unique experience for park visitors.

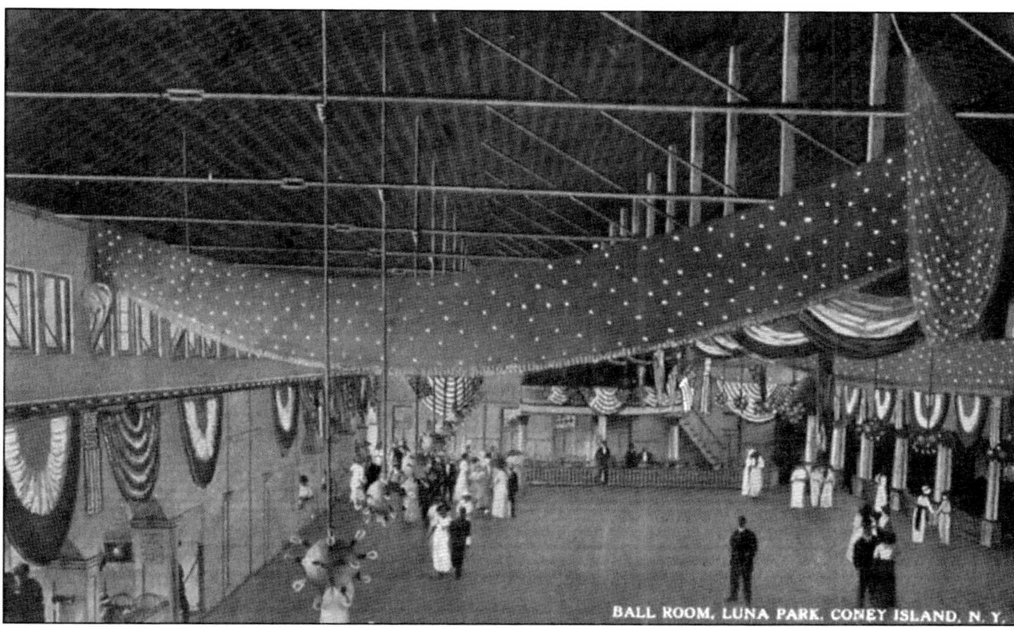

This postcard offers an interior view of the Luna Park Ballroom, which was situated between the Ostrich Farm and the German Village.

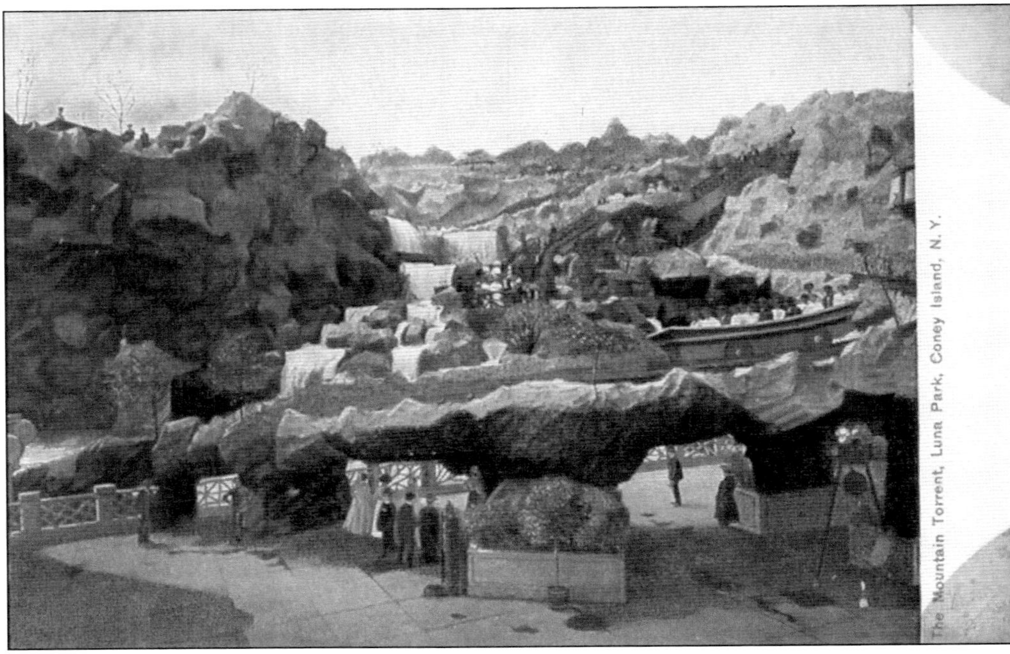

The Mountain Torrent, which debuted in Luna Park in 1906, became one of the park's most popular rides. The ride was a combination of a roller coaster and Shoot-the-Chutes. Passengers rode up an escalator or climbed its alpine paths to the top of an 80-foot-tall mountain that featured a series of cascading scenic waterfalls. They would then board cars, which raced down (and through) the mountain in a flume that had water flowing through it at a rate of 35,000 gallons per minute. The ride ended with a splash into the lake at the bottom of the mountain.

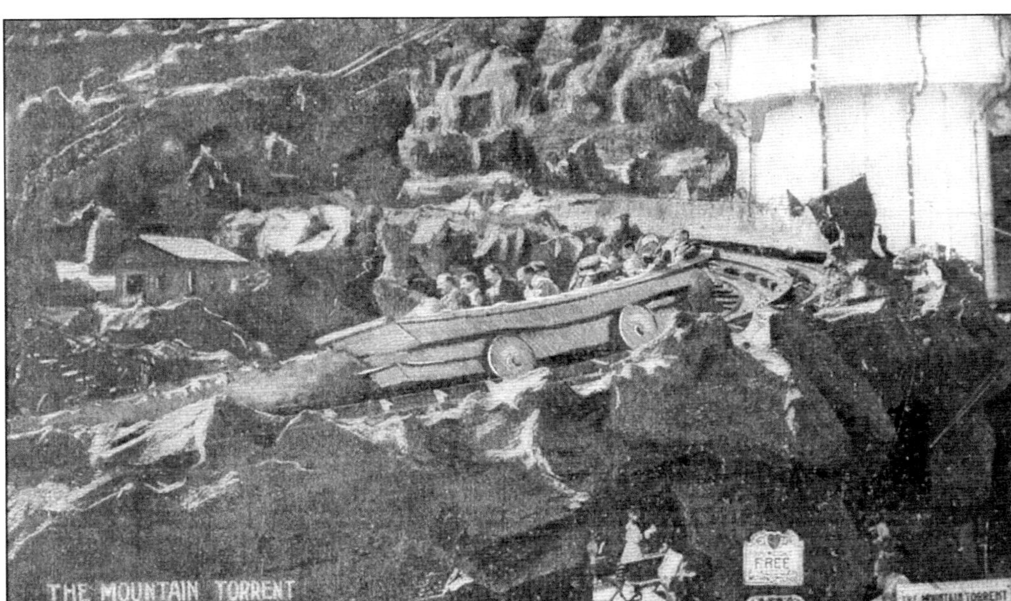

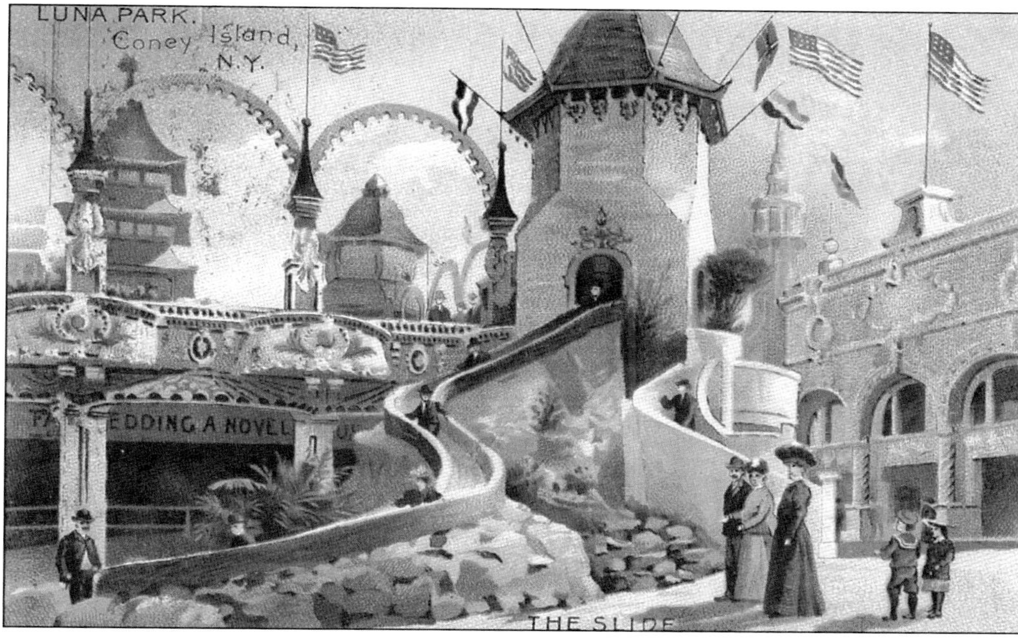

The Helter Skelter slide opened in 1906. It was essentially a slide for adults. Participants rode an escalator to the top of a huge chute made of rattan, then slid down the winding slide before landing on a mattress in front of a crowd of onlookers. Later, two chutes were set side-by-side so that couples could slide down together, but the paths split before coming together again near the bottom of the chutes.

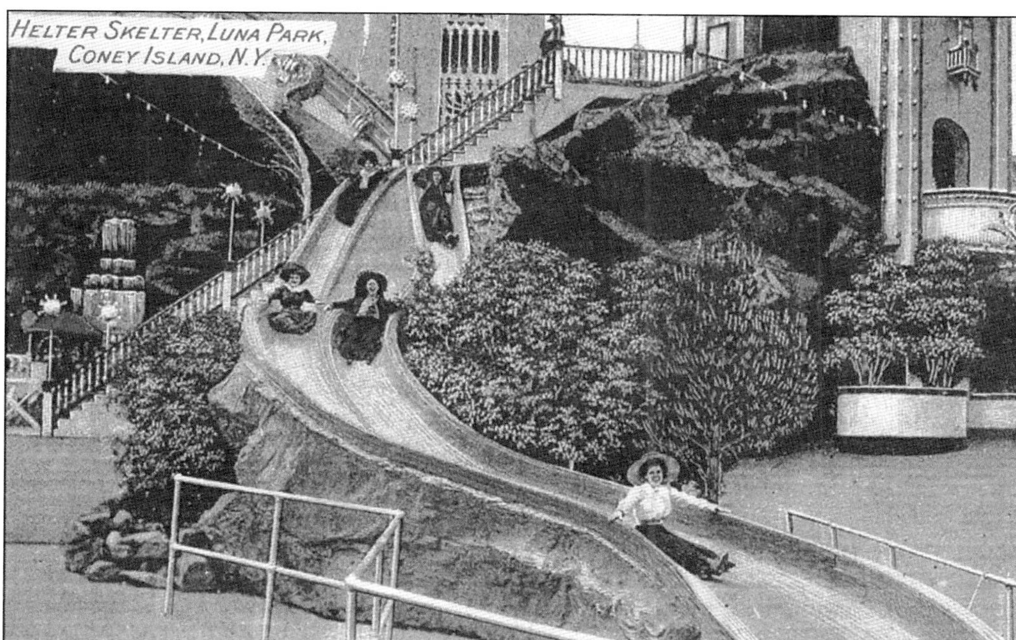

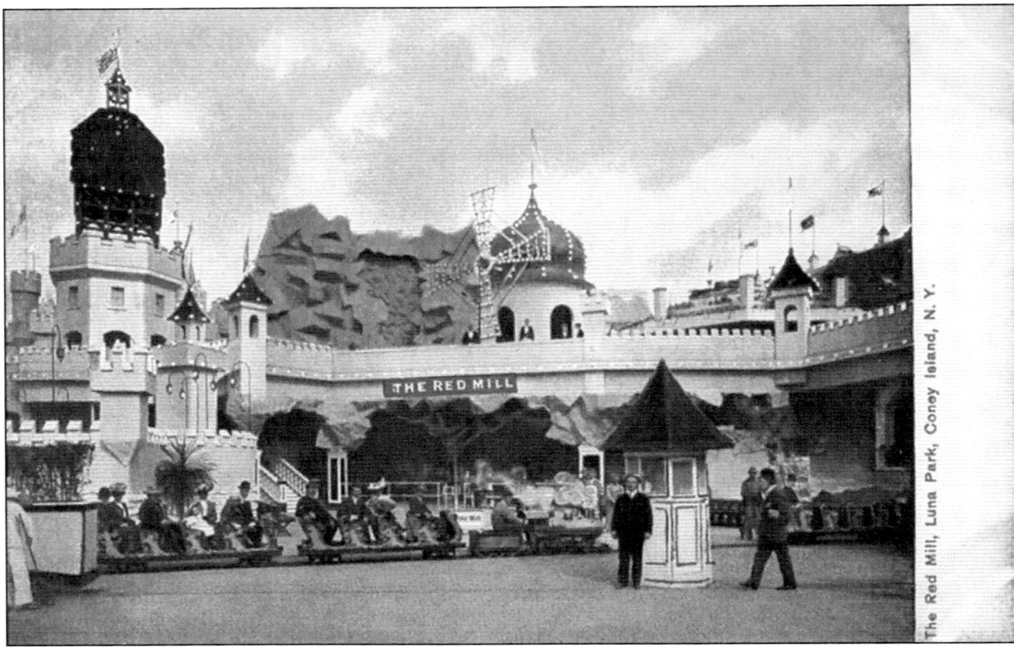

The Red Mill, a boat ride through tunnels, opened in 1907. It was rebuilt in 1913 with new scenery. Other rides that debuted at Luna Park in 1907 included Neptune's Daughter, Molly Coddle, Wiggle Woggle, and Night & Morning.

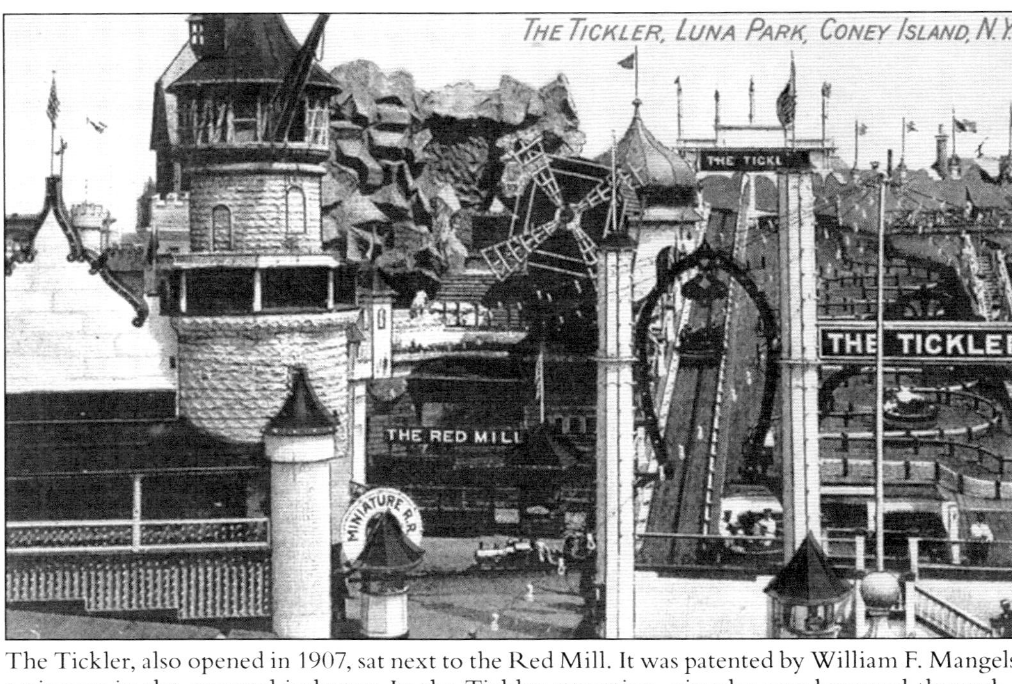

The Tickler, also opened in 1907, sat next to the Red Mill. It was patented by William F. Mangels, a pioneer in the carousel industry. In the Tickler attraction, circular cars bounced through a maze set on an inclined plane.

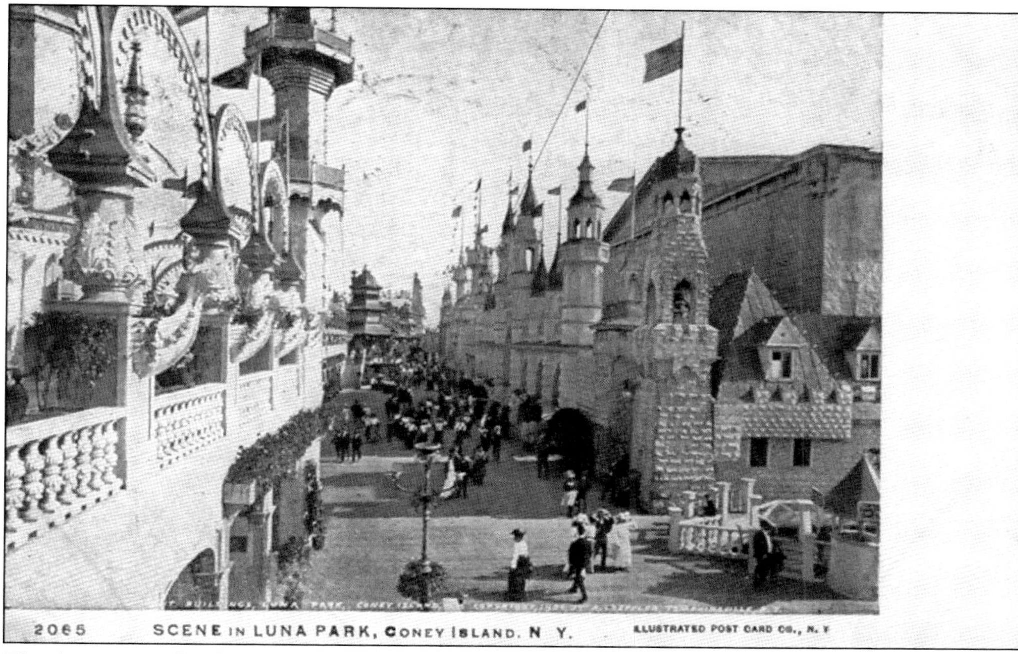

The image on the front of this 1906 undivided back postcard was taken in Luna Park. Park owner Fred Thompson had studied architecture, and—as evidenced by this photograph—the park was a showcase of his talent.

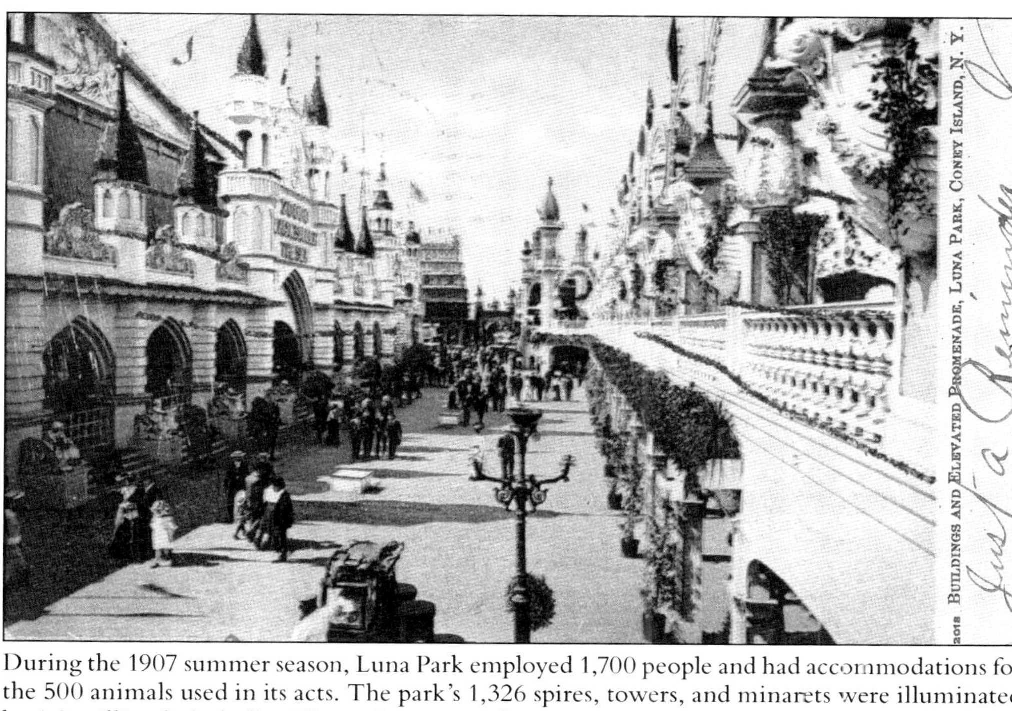

During the 1907 summer season, Luna Park employed 1,700 people and had accommodations for the 500 animals used in its acts. The park's 1,326 spires, towers, and minarets were illuminated by 1.3 million light bulbs. The park consumed more energy than an average American city.

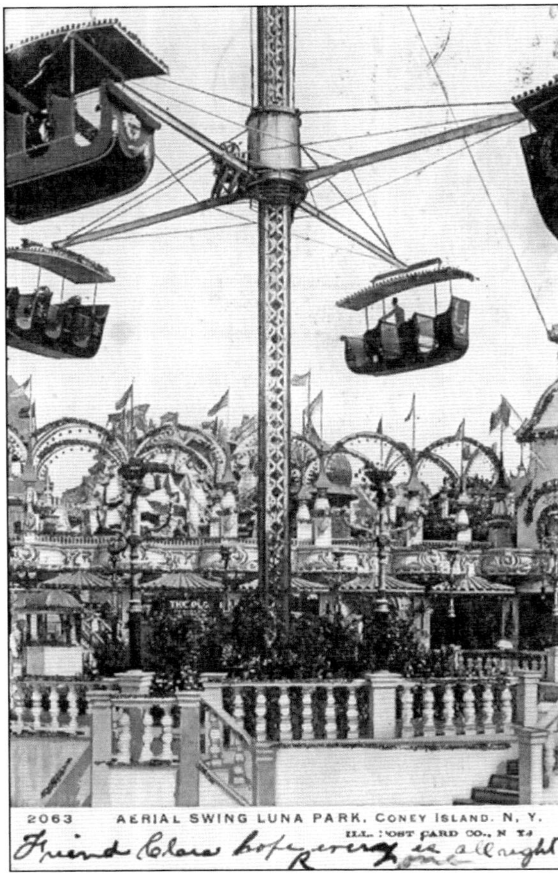

This glitter postcard shows Luna Park's Aerial Swing, which was also known as the Whirl the Whirl.

The circular Hippodrome arena to the right of the chutes was home to Carl Hagenbeck's trained wild animals. Near the foot of the tower, two circus rings built out into the lake were used to showcase regular performances by trained animals, equestrians, and clowns. There, trapeze and high-wire acts performed their feats at a height of nearly 200 feet.

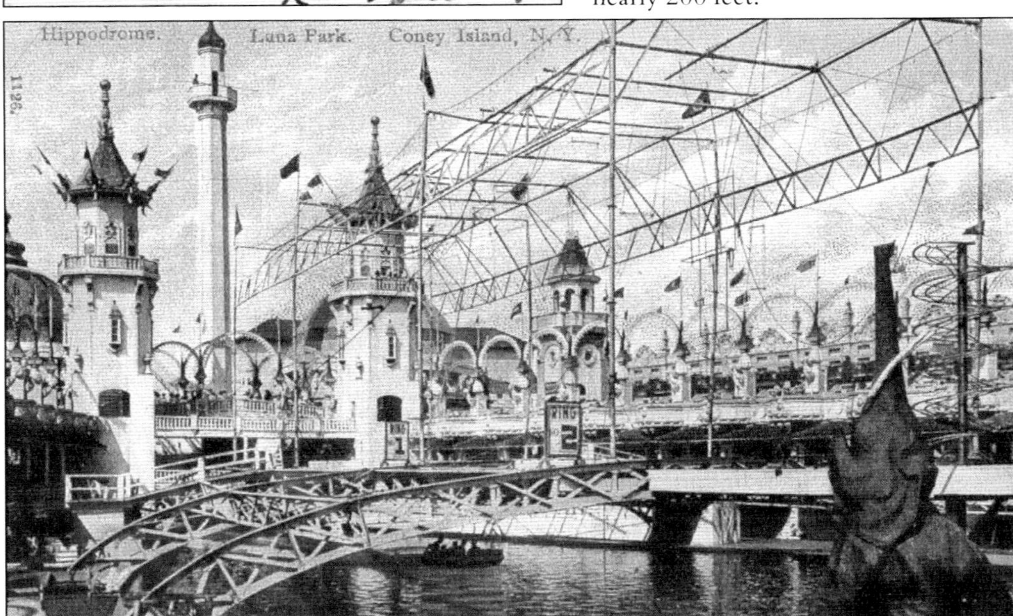

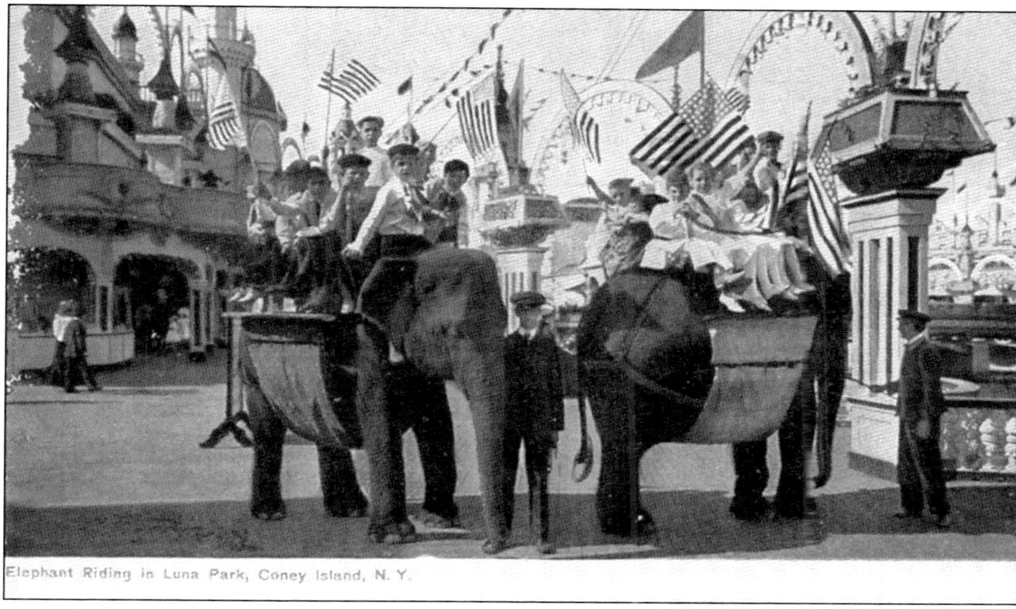

Luna Park owner Skip Dundy believed elephants brought good fortune, and for the most part, they did. In 1903, Topsy, a unfortunate elephant who supposedly killed a drunk trainer after he threw a lit cigar into her mouth, was murdered via electricity by Thomas Edison as part of a publicity stunt. Despite this horrific incident, elephants remained popular and carried an average of 9,000 people per week around Luna Park.

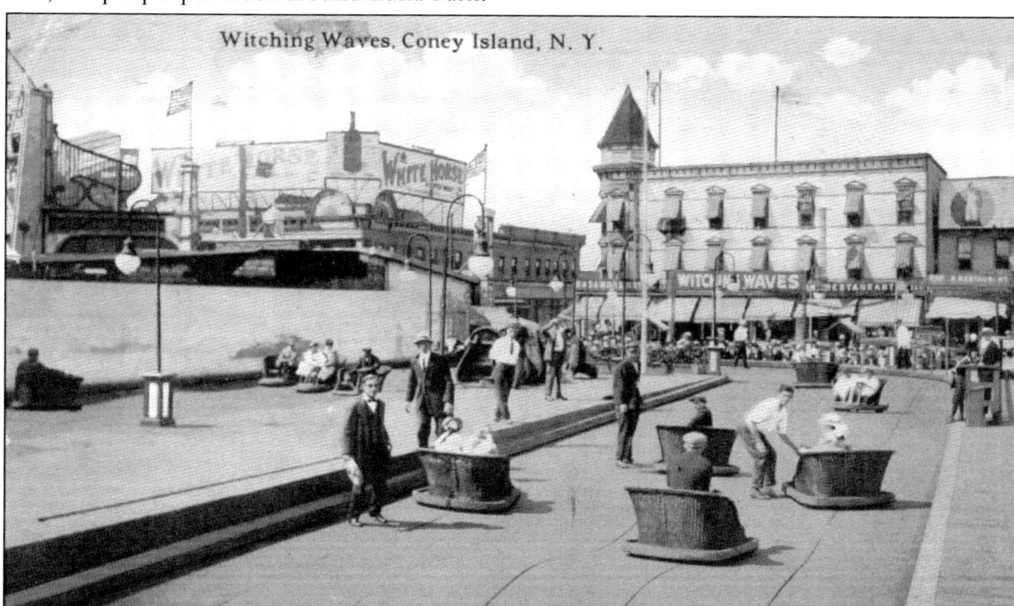

The Witching Waves, installed at Luna Park in 1907, used a system of reciprocating levers beneath the floor to generate a continuous wavelike motion. Steerable small cars that could seat two passengers were propelled forward by the undulating floor. It must have been fascinating to watch and became a popular, fun ride.

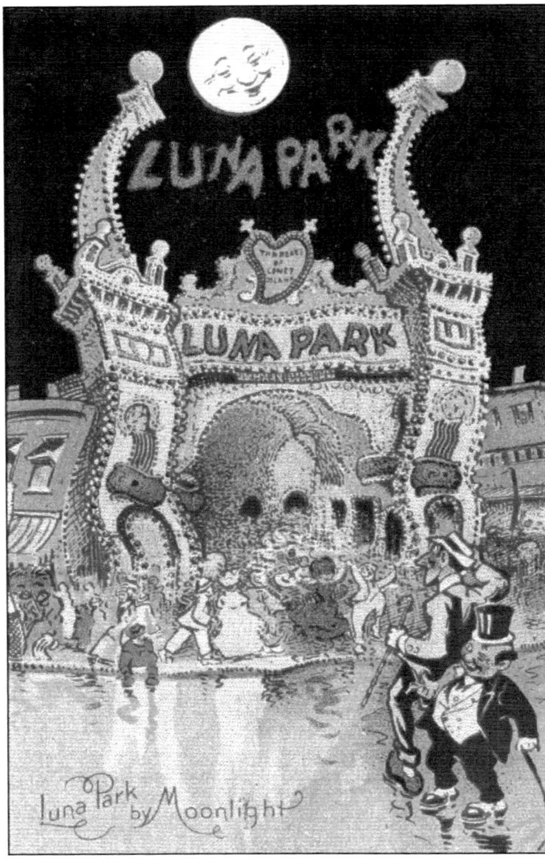

Moonlight Series No. 1 shows the entrance to Luna Park from the perspective of two red-cheeked gentlemen who appear to be "lit up" like the park.

While Fred Thompson was Luna Park's designer and showman, Skip Dundy handled the finances. The partnership worked well for them until Dundy died suddenly in 1907; Thompson continued running the park for a few years until he had to declare bankruptcy in 1912 and lost his beloved Luna Park to creditors. Between 1912 and 1945, Luna Park had various owners, including Barron Collier. Luna Park closed after the 1945 season, and the land was sold in 1946. A housing project was eventually built on the property.

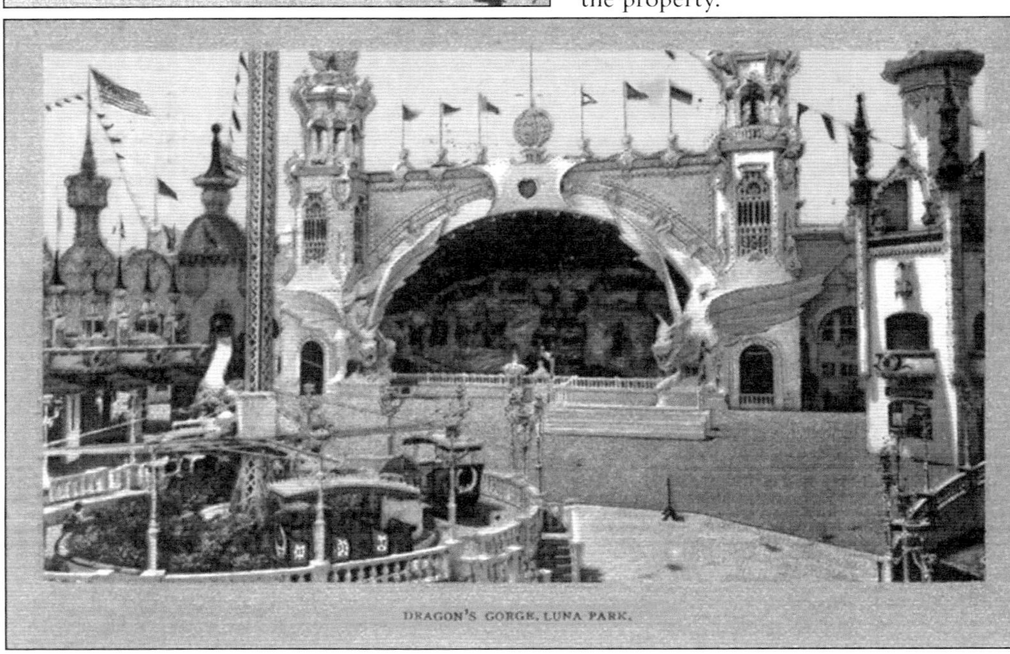

Four

Dreamland

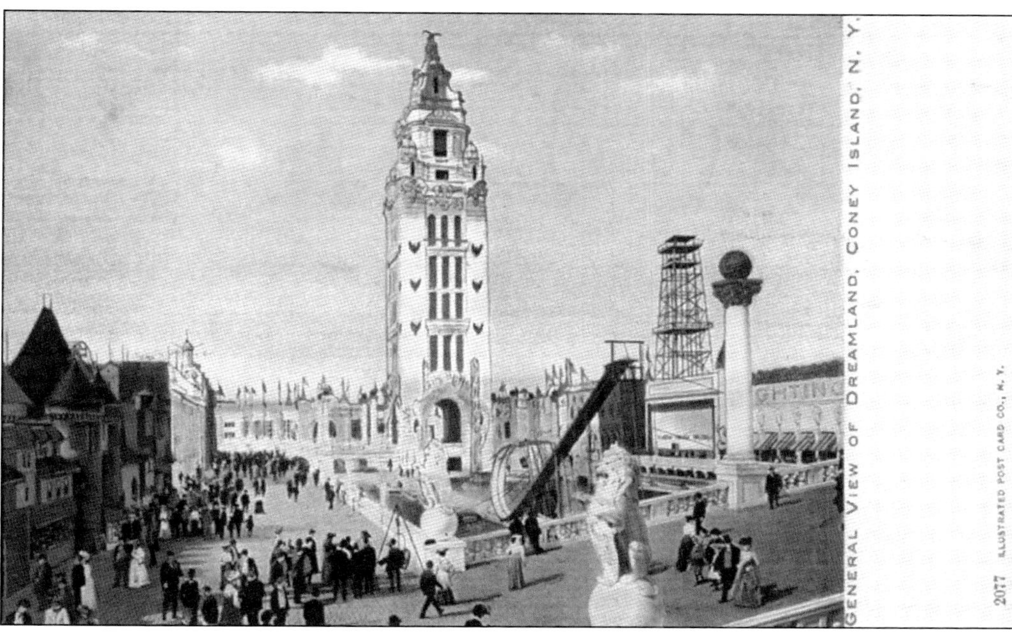

Former New York state senator William H. Reynolds opened Dreamland on May 14, 1904. He intended for Dreamland to be a high-class entertainment venue with elegant architecture, pristine white towers, educational exhibits, and rides. More than one million electric light bulbs were used to outline Dreamland's various buildings and illuminate the park.

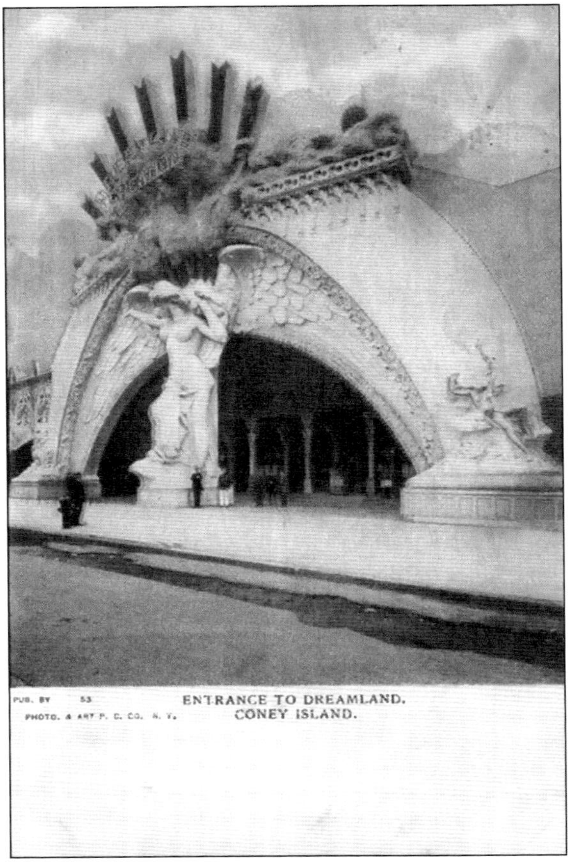

In 1905, Creation, a hit attraction from the 1904 St. Louis World's Fair, was housed in a huge domed building along Surf Avenue adjacent to the east promenade of Dreamland. The boat ride, which dramatized the biblical epic of the birth of the universe, had an entrance formed by the spread wings of a 40-foot-tall, bare-breasted female sculpture.

Just inside the Surf Avenue entrance at Dreamland was the baby incubator building, where Dr. Martin Couney cared for and displayed premature babies who had been entrusted to him by hopeful parents at a time when hospitals did not have incubators. When Couney first came to Coney Island in 1903, the medical establishment did not approve of his methods, so he created exhibitions at Dreamland and Luna Park. From the time Couney came to Coney Island until he retired in 1943, he saved the lives of over 5,000 infants. When Dreamland suffered a devastating fire in 1911, the babies there were rescued and moved to Luna Park.

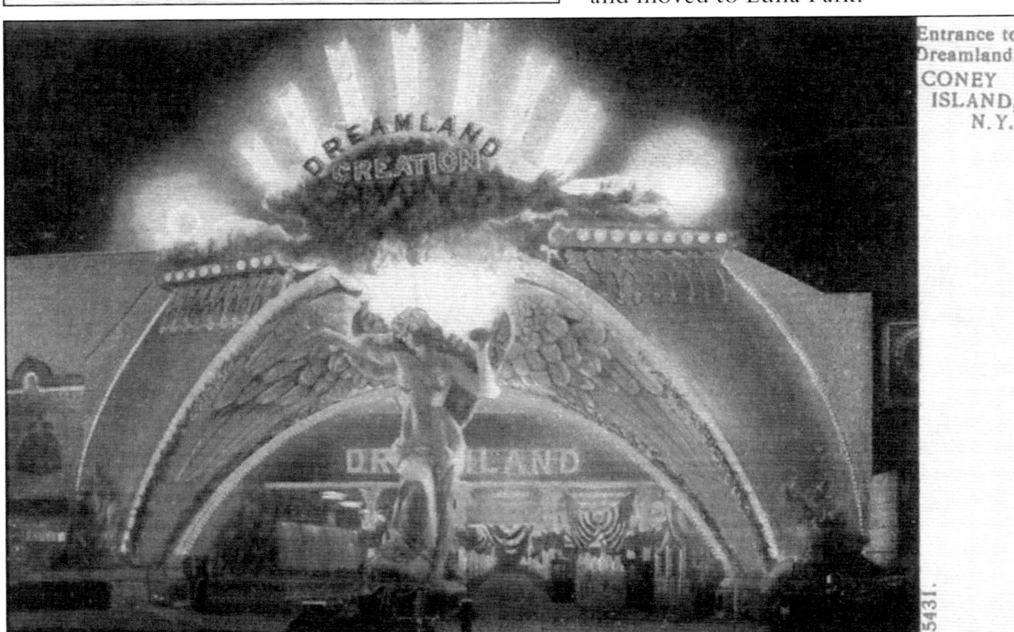

Visitors could ascend this tower—via two elevators to its observation deck—for a magnificent view of the surrounding area.

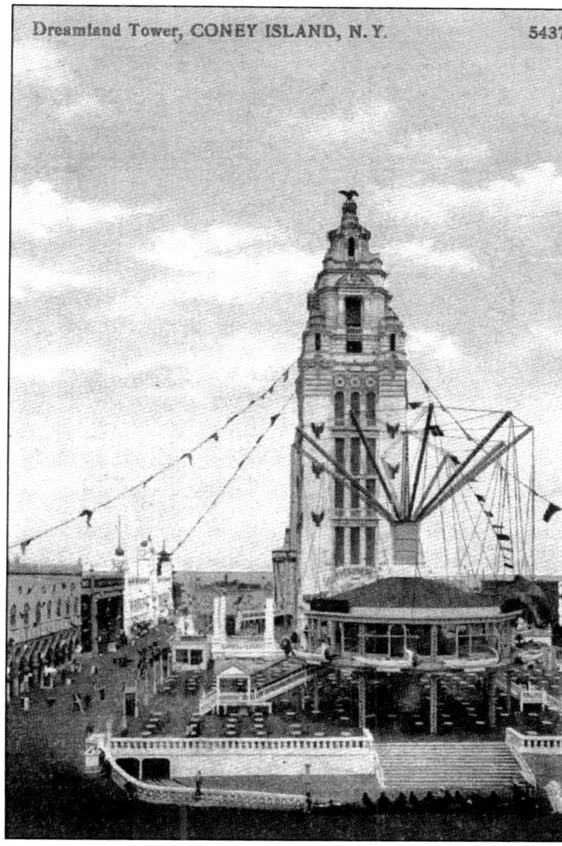

Animal shows were held daily at Bostock's Arena, situated at the entrance to Dreamland.

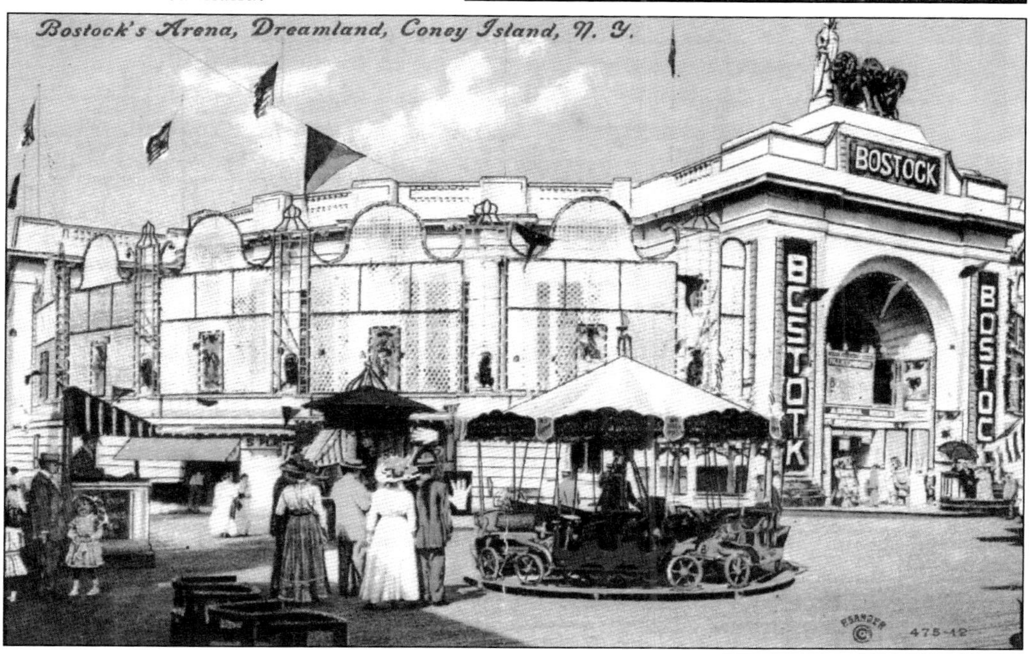

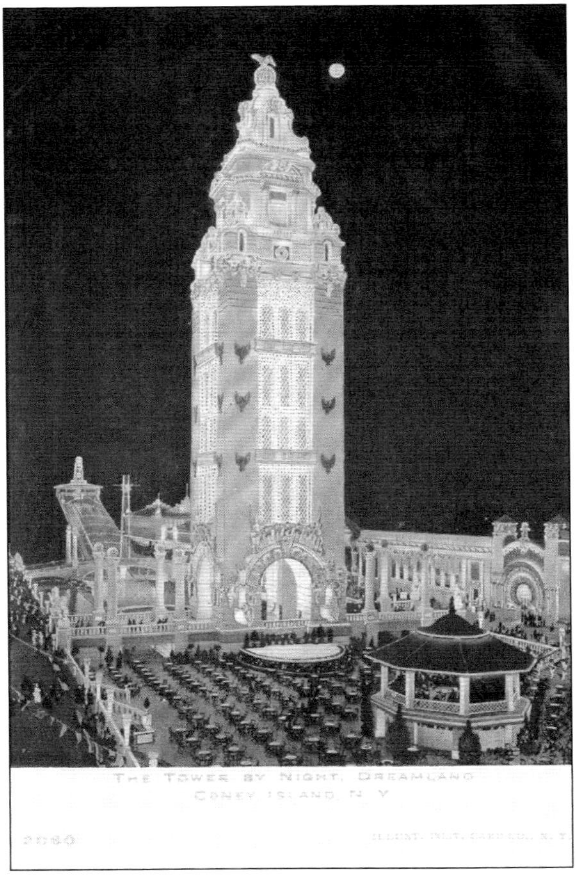

All of the buildings in Dreamland were painted pure white. The Beacon Tower glowed with 100,000 white lights at night. The 375-foot-tall tower provided a 50-mile view to patrons who rode to the top in its two elevators. The Beacon Tower was the centerpiece of Dreamland.

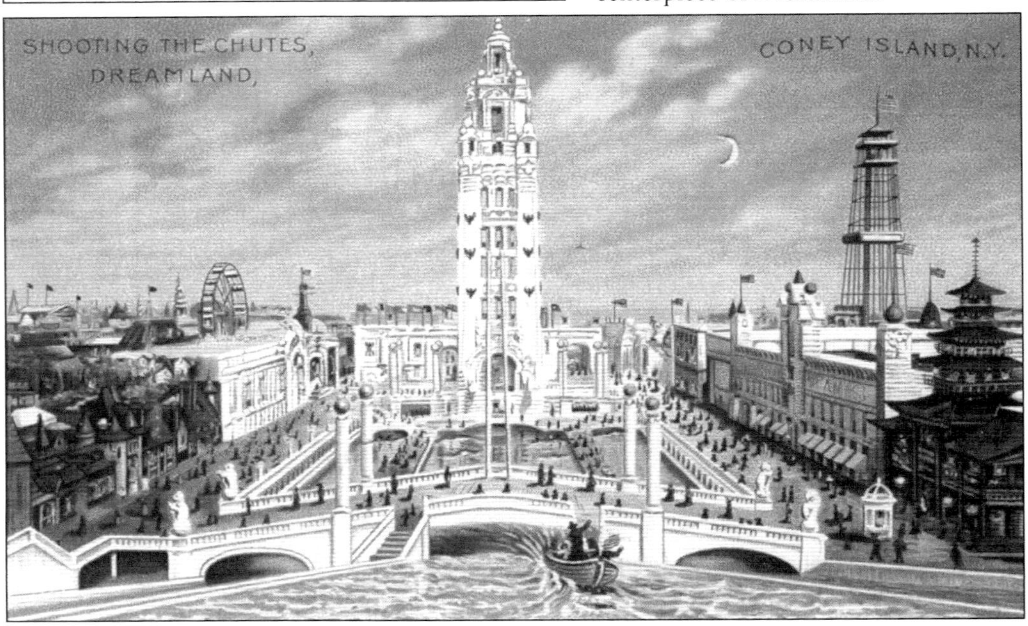

This image features the view from the top of Dreamland's Shoot-the-Chutes. This was the largest version of the water slide ride ever built, with two side-by-side chutes that provided a capacity of 7,000 people an hour. The chutes' 280-foot-long ramp extended over 175 feet beyond the beach and was supported by a high iron frame set above ocean pilings. A 360-foot-long moving staircase transported passengers to the top of the ride, where they boarded flat-bottomed boats that slid down a water-slicked chute that carried riders beneath a pedestrian bridge and into a large lagoon.

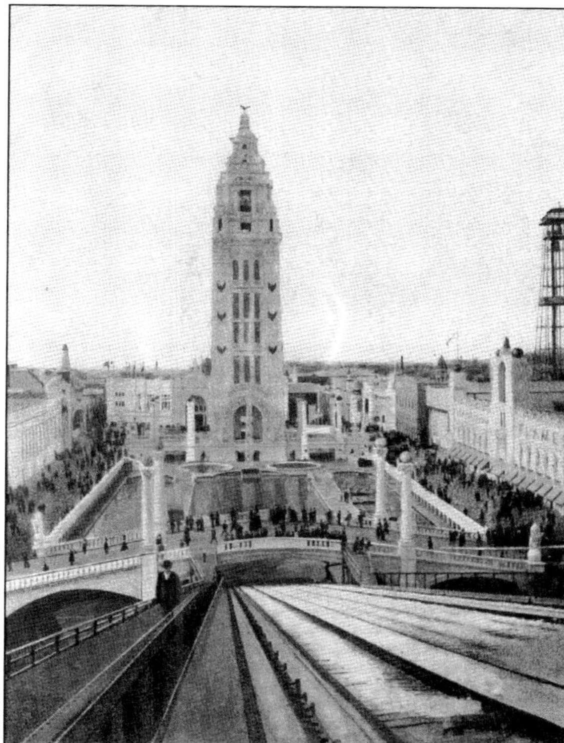

12712—*View from Dreamland from Chutes, Coney Island*

The postcard below offers a look at a boat coming down the chute. Each boat was manned by an oarsman who sat in the rear and guided the boat to a dock where passengers disembarked.

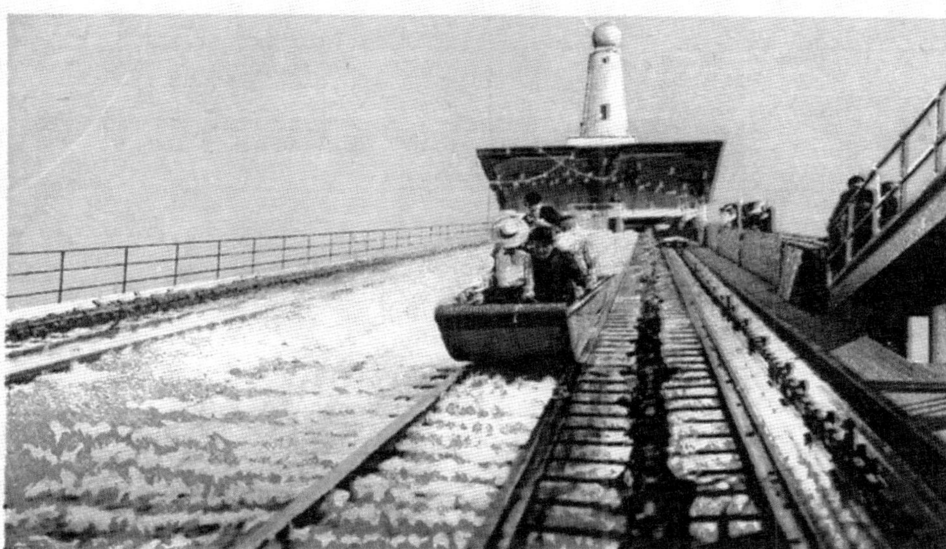

SHOOTING THE CHUTES. CONEY ISLAND.

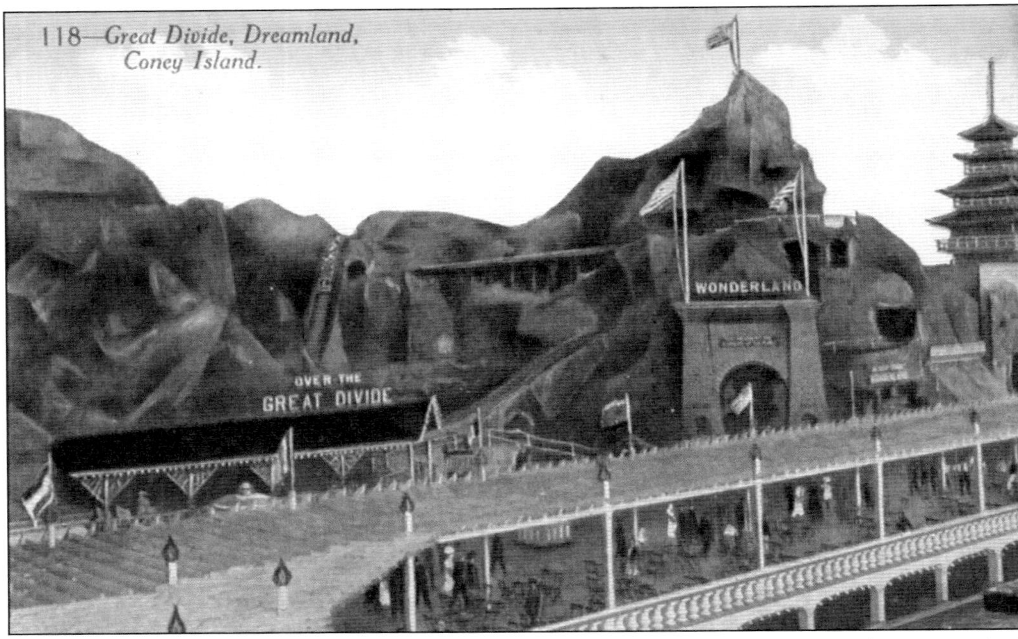

In Over the Great Divide, 20-passenger trains traveled over a portion of the "Rocky Mountains" on a 2,000-foot-long scenic railway. The electric railroad's two cars, which each had a motorman, traveled up to a height of 50 feet and then, thanks to gravity, traveled down along the mountain's winding trail. The journey included traversing a 40-foot bridge above a canyon and a volcano.

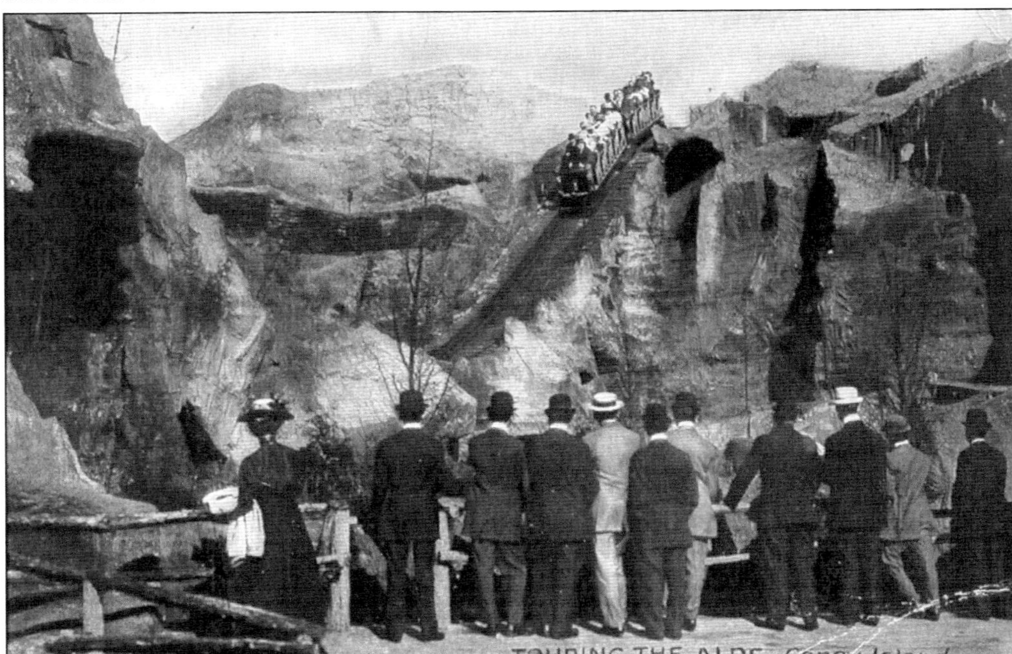

Touring the Alps was another part of Over the Great Divide; the entire attraction was destroyed in the fire of 1911.

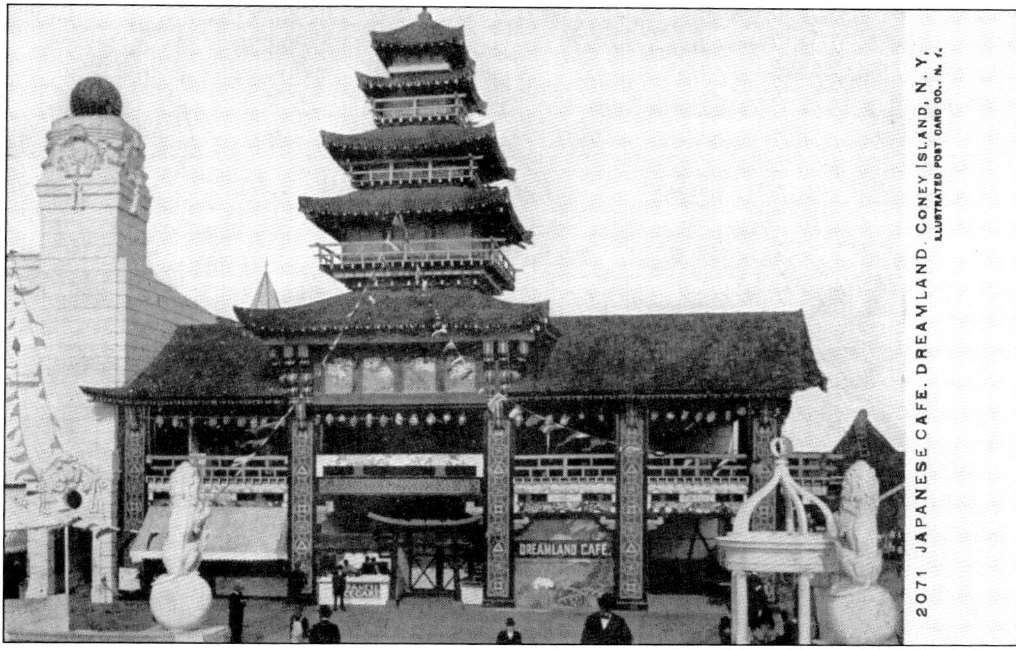

The Japanese Café at Dreamland featured an ornate two-story Japanese temple in which attendants served tea in the Japanese style.

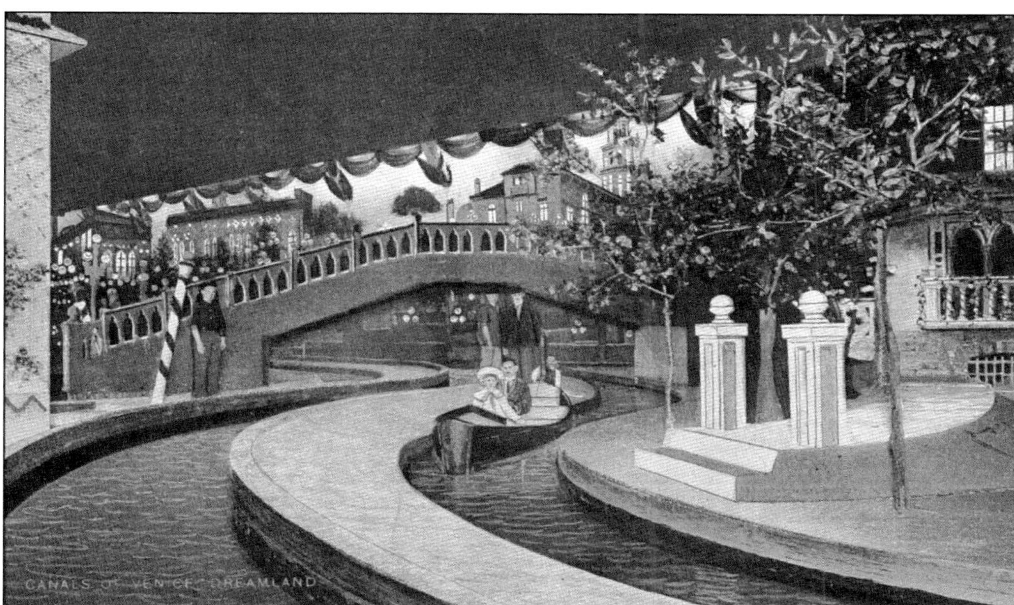

The Canals of Venice opened in Dreamland in 1903. Passengers toured the ride's canals in a gondola that passed scenery created to replicate the look of the famous Italian city.

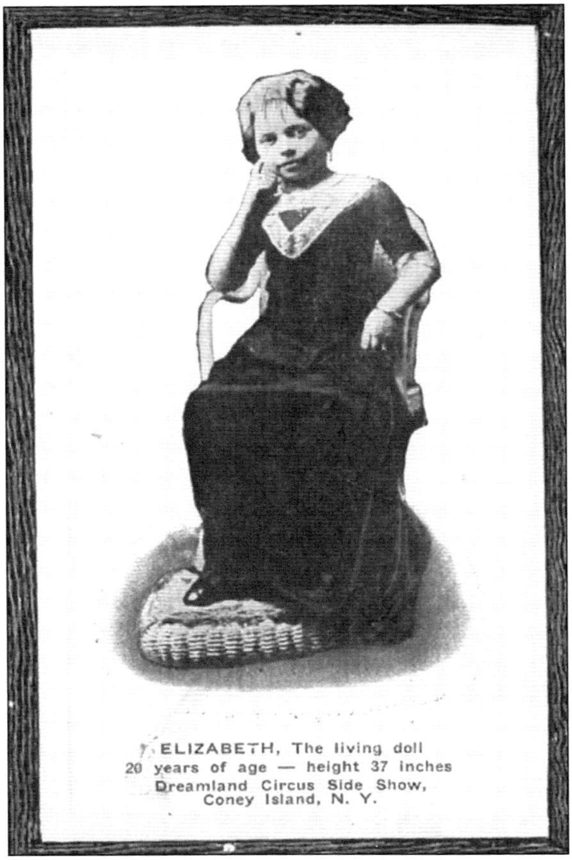

ELIZABETH, The living doll
20 years of age — height 37 inches
Dreamland Circus Side Show,
Coney Island, N. Y.

Samuel W. Gumpertz (1868–1952) is credited with bringing the first freak show to Coney Island. Gumpertz was hired by Dreamland owner William H. Reynolds to build and manage a "midget city" called Lilliputia for Dreamland's 1904 opening season. Gumpertz invited 300 little people from across the country to be the permanent residents of the experimental community. The postcard at left features 20-year old Elizabeth the Living Doll, who stood just 37 inches tall.

Lilliputia was built to resemble a small-scale version of 15th-century Nuremberg, Germany. The little people who resided there had their own parliament, fire department, and a beach complete with little lifeguards. Although they entertained patrons during the day, the residents of Lilliputia had their own lives and community when the park was closed—they even had their own Midget City Opera House.

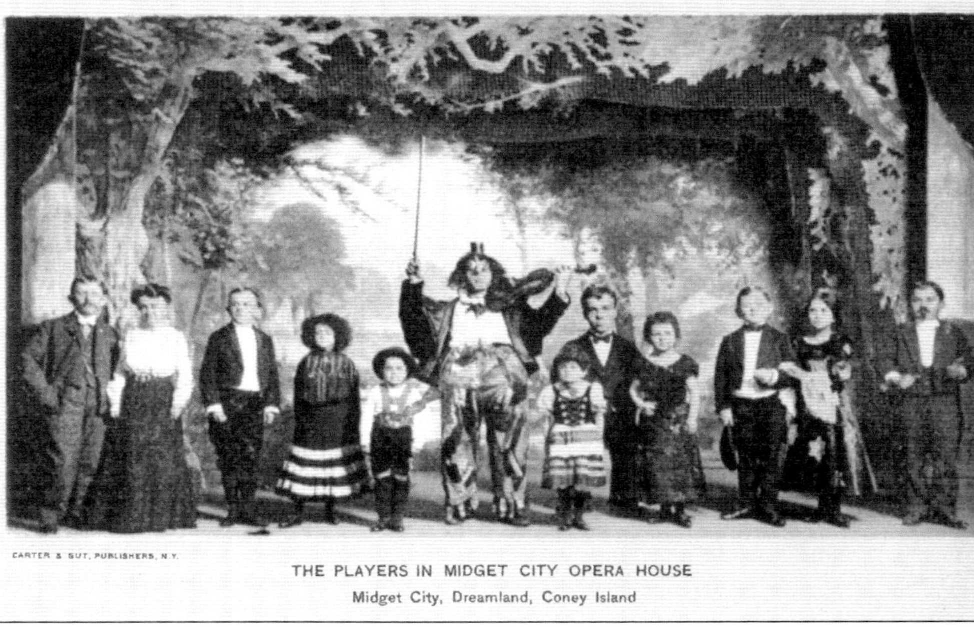

CARTER & SUT, PUBLISHERS, N.Y.

THE PLAYERS IN MIDGET CITY OPERA HOUSE
Midget City, Dreamland, Coney Island

Baron Paucci—"The Smallest and Most Perfect Man," according to the postcard at right—was a fan favorite at Dreamland for more than 15 years. An Italian man who stood only 27 inches tall, Paucci liked to dress in suits and drink champagne. Unfortunately, he had a bad habit of cursing during shows, and Lilliputia creator Samuel Gumpertz eventually had to fire him.

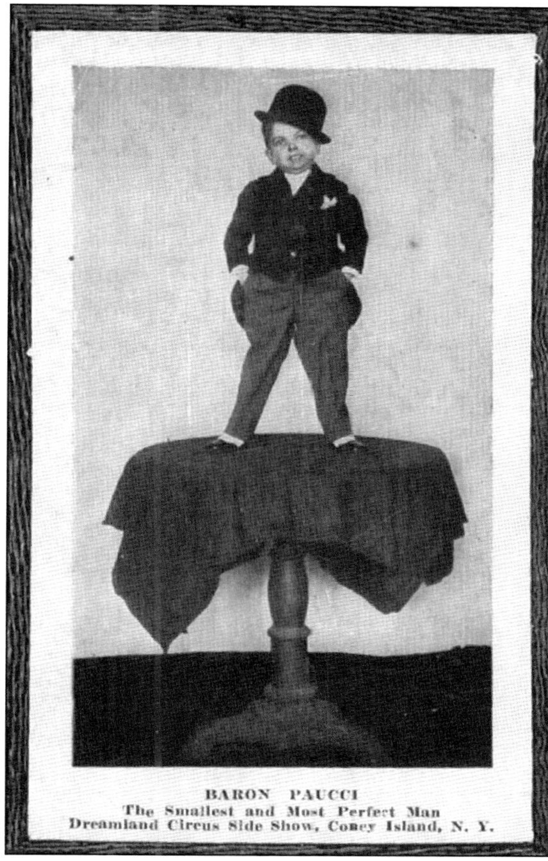

After Dreamland was destroyed by fire in May 1911, Gumpertz was free to devote more time to his first love: freak shows. Almost immediately after the fire, he assembled his Dreamland Circus Sideshow in a tent on Surf Avenue.

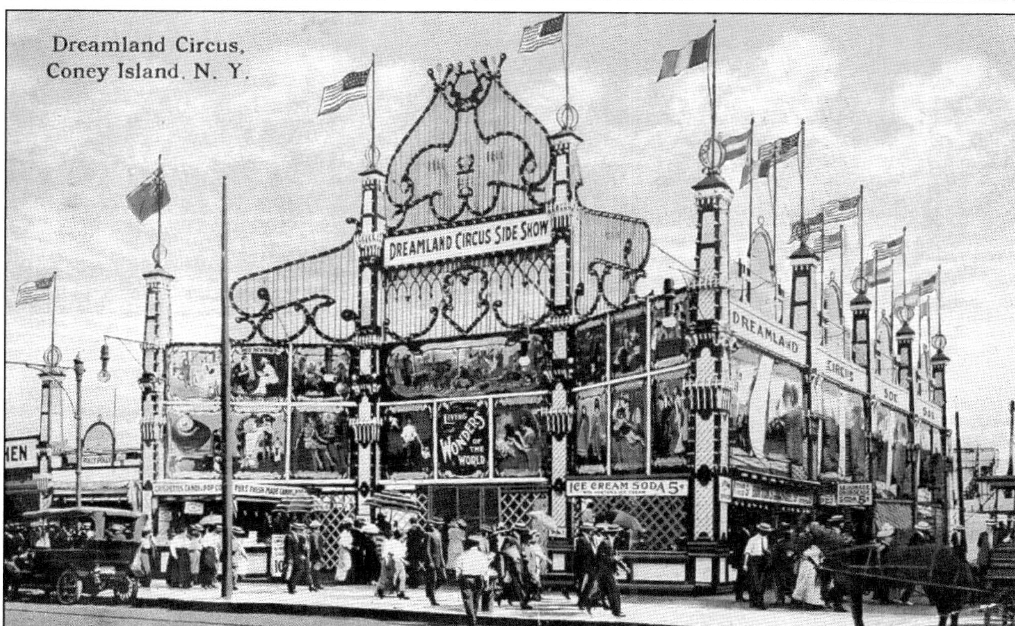

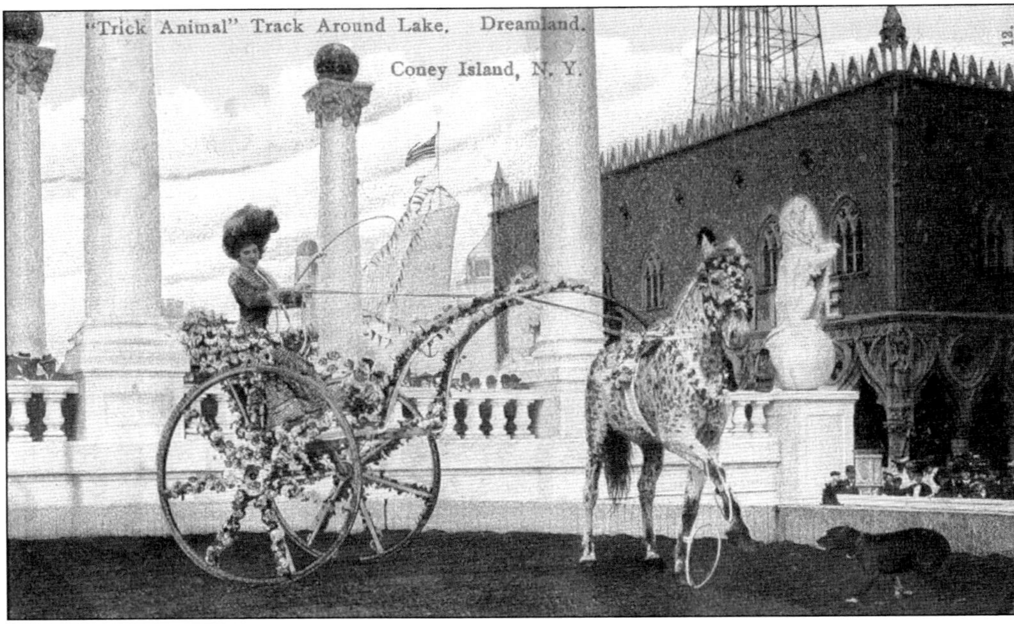

One of the attractions at Dreamland was a circus show—with animal acts including horses, dogs, and monkeys—that was performed on a track around the lake.

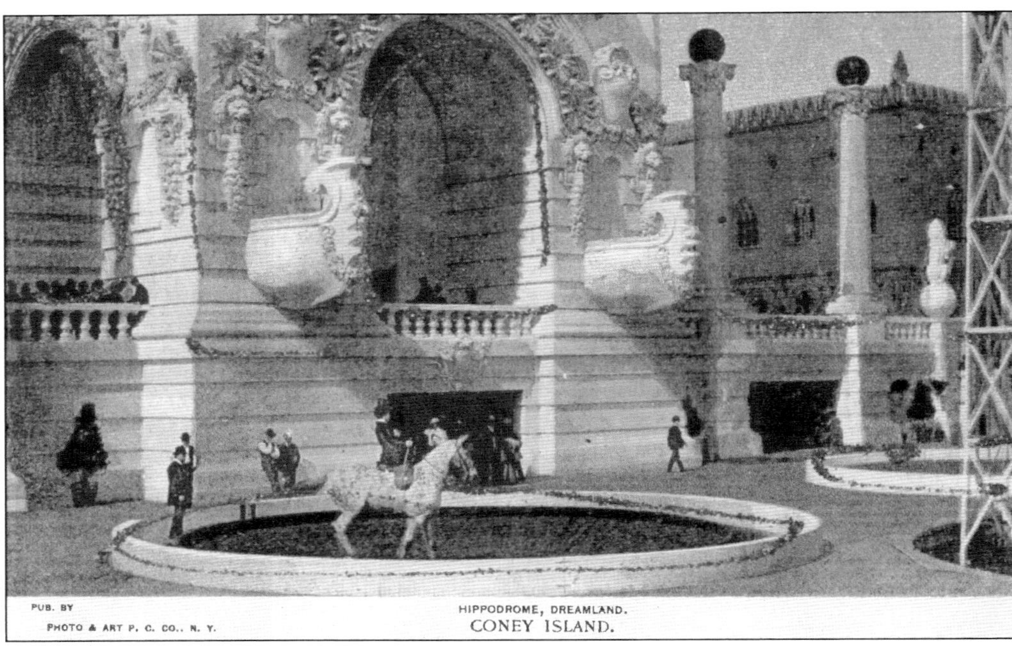

In the early 1900s, every Coney Island park had a Hippodrome, and the one in Dreamland (pictured) featured a Roman parade, chariot races, and ostrich races.

The Electricity House, aka the Palace of Electricity, housed the generators that lit the park's one million lights. Its facade was shaped like the armature of a dynamo and brilliantly illuminated at night.

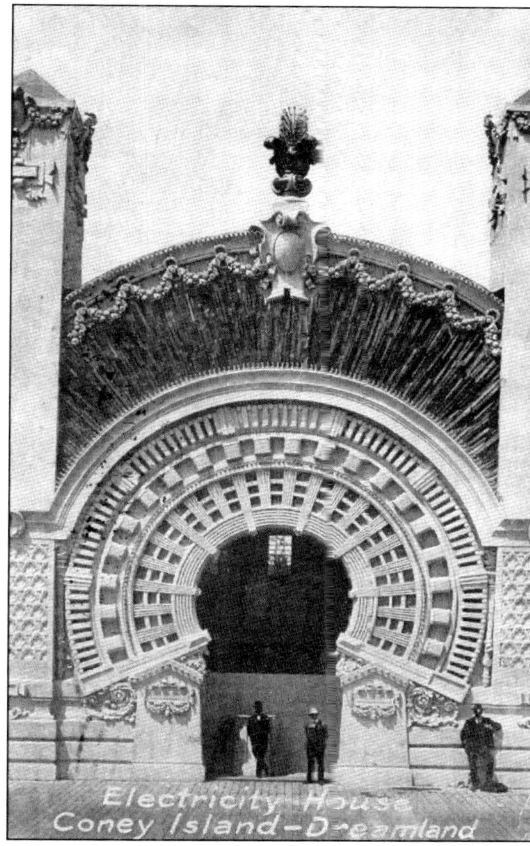

A miniature railroad built by the Cagney Brothers traveled a circuit beneath the promenade. Each of its three small cars—pulled by a small, oil-burning steam locomotive—held two passengers.

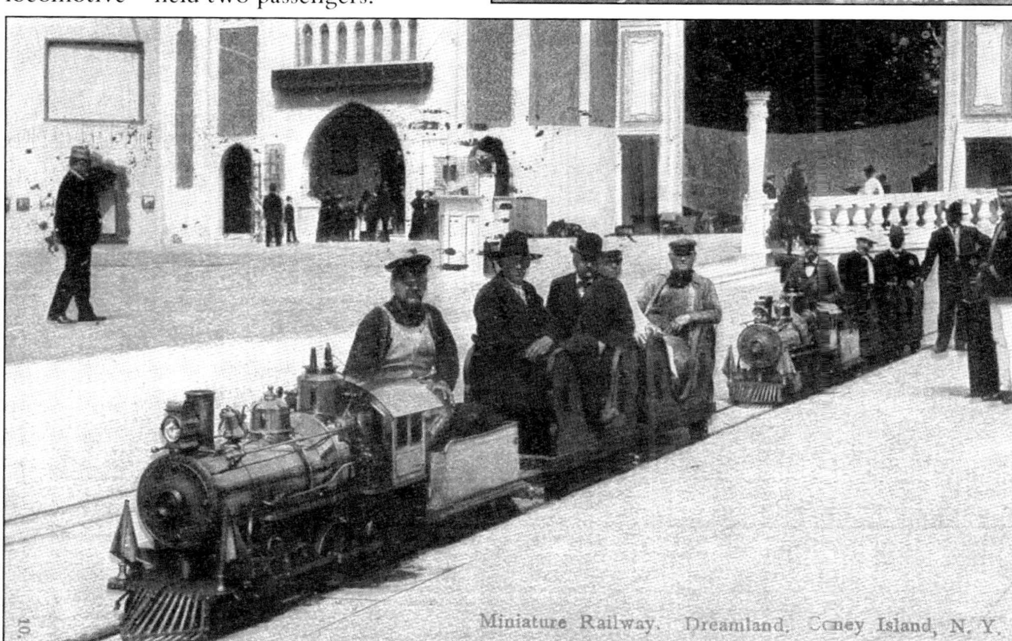

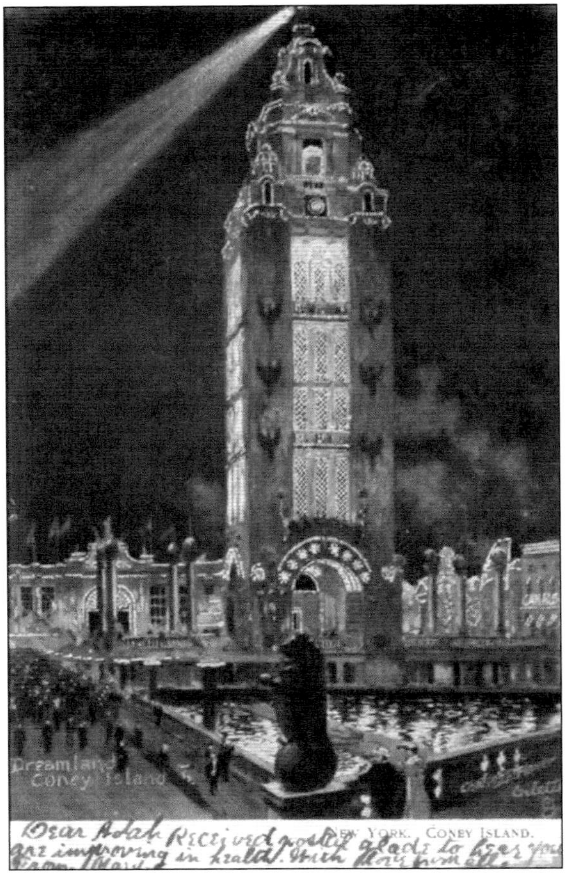

This postcard, which features an image of the Beacon Tower in Dreamland at night as painted by Charles E. Flowers, was included in the six-card Coney Island series published by Raphael Tuck & Sons in 1905.

This undivided-back postcard decorated with glitter shows Dreamland at night from the ocean. It is easy to see why the US Lighthouse Service had Dreamland turn off the searchlight on the Beacon Tower, as it could easily be confused with the beacon of the Coney Island (Nortons Point) Lighthouse on the west end of Coney Island.

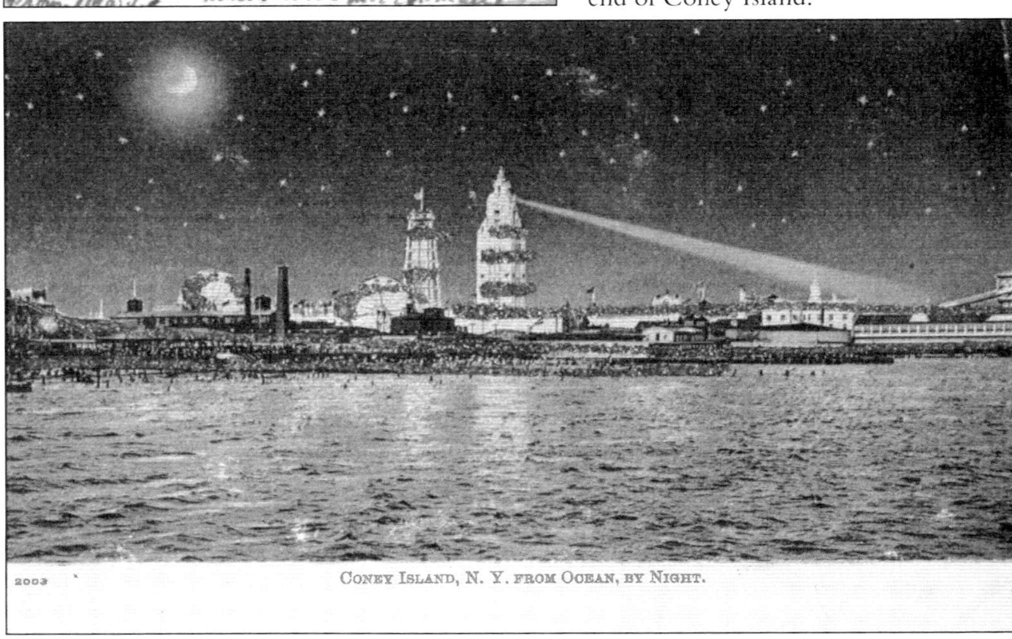

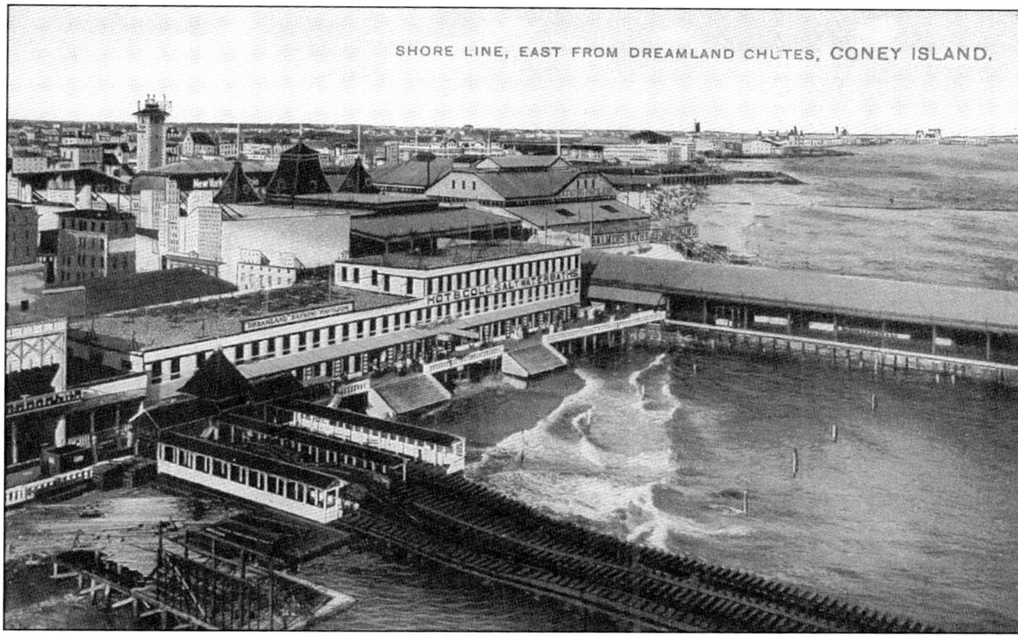

This postcard shows Dreamland's version of Shoot-the-Chutes, which was built out over the ocean. It also shows the Leap Frog Railroad (originally called Stern's Duplex Railroad), located on Dreamland Pier in 1905. The two trains each carried a set of tracks on the roof that enabled the cars to pass over each other as they met on a single track.

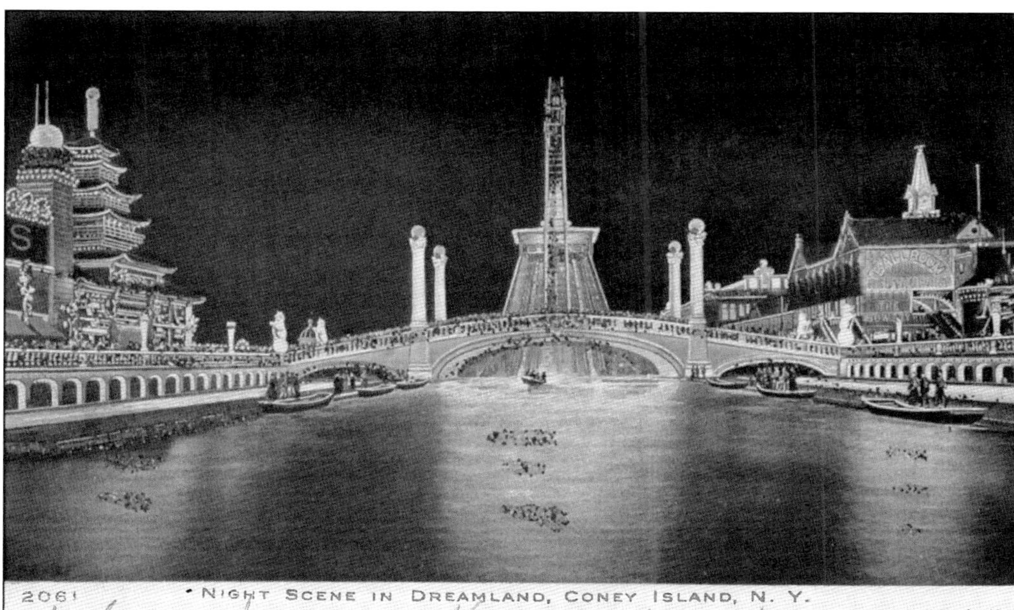

This night scene of Dreamland shows the Shoot-the-Chutes, along with the pedestrian bridge that crossed the lagoon, all lit up with white lights at night.

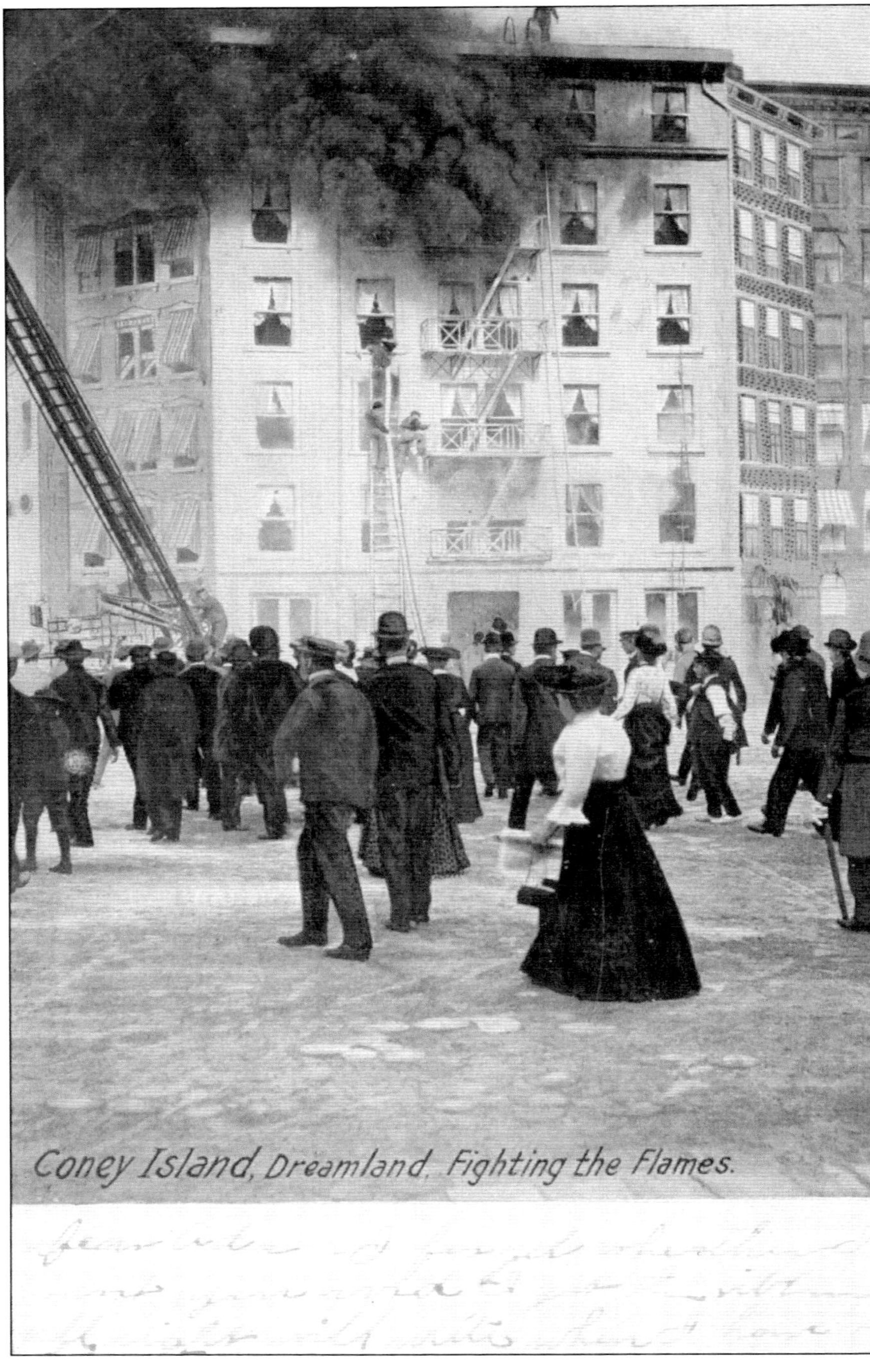

Dreamland's Fighting the Flames exhibit featured firemen who extinguished flames and rescued people from a six-story building each night. This attraction also had a competing version in Luna Park called Fire and Flame, where an entire city block was set ablaze each night. Dreamland's version had twice as many firefighters and fire engines. These exhibits were ironic, considering that fire played a major role in the demise of both parks.

Five

Surf Avenue

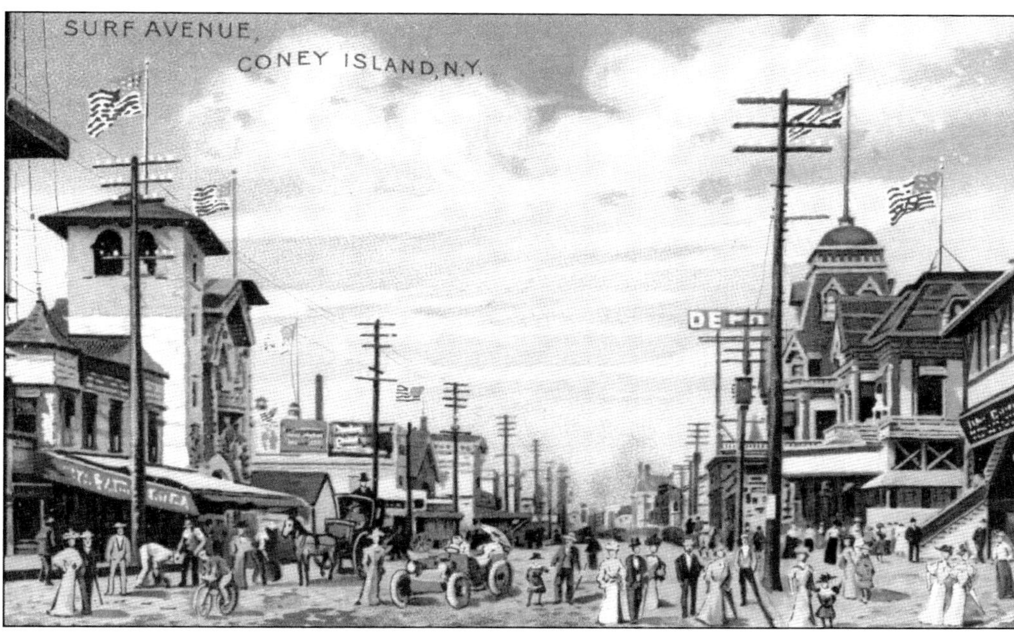

Surf Avenue is still the main drag in Coney Island. Back in its heyday, it was filled with amusements, restaurants, concessions, and shops. This postcard gives an idea of the crowds that were always filling the street and making their ways to the various attractions.

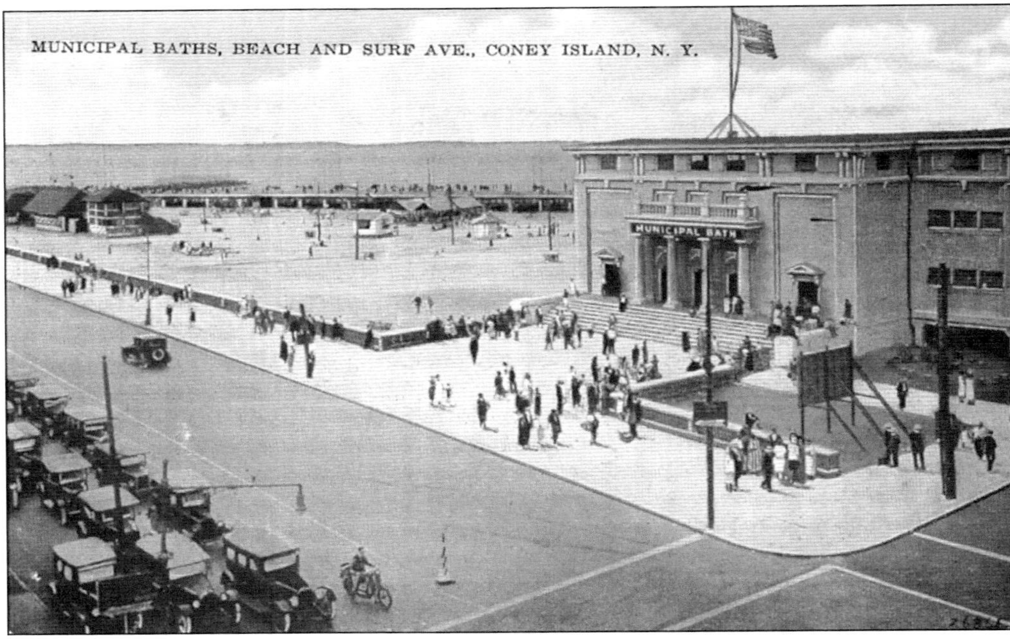

The Municipal Baths opened in 1911 at Surf Avenue and West Fifth Street. The bathhouse offered free admission, in addition to lockers, showers, and beach access. Because it was a concrete structure, it was not destroyed in the Dreamland fire of 1911. The building survived until 1954, when it was destroyed in order to make room for the New York Aquarium.

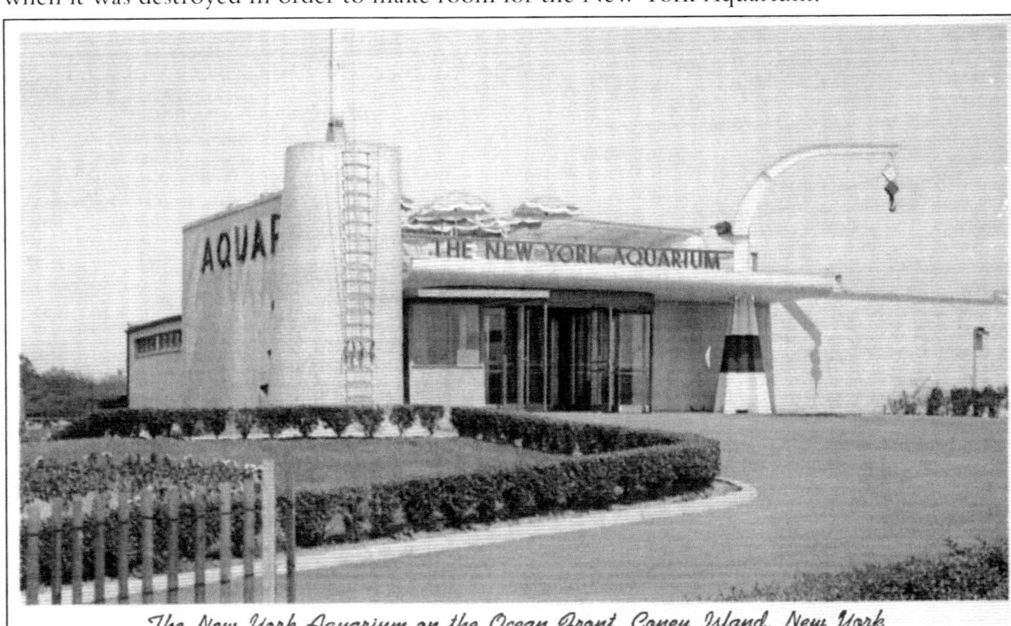

The world-renowned New York Aquarium opened in 1957 and now attracts 750,000 visitors each year. Unfortunately, the facility sustained severe damage during Superstorm Sandy in October 2012. Miraculously, most of the aquarium's fish and mammals survived the storm, and the aquarium reopened to the public in May 2013.

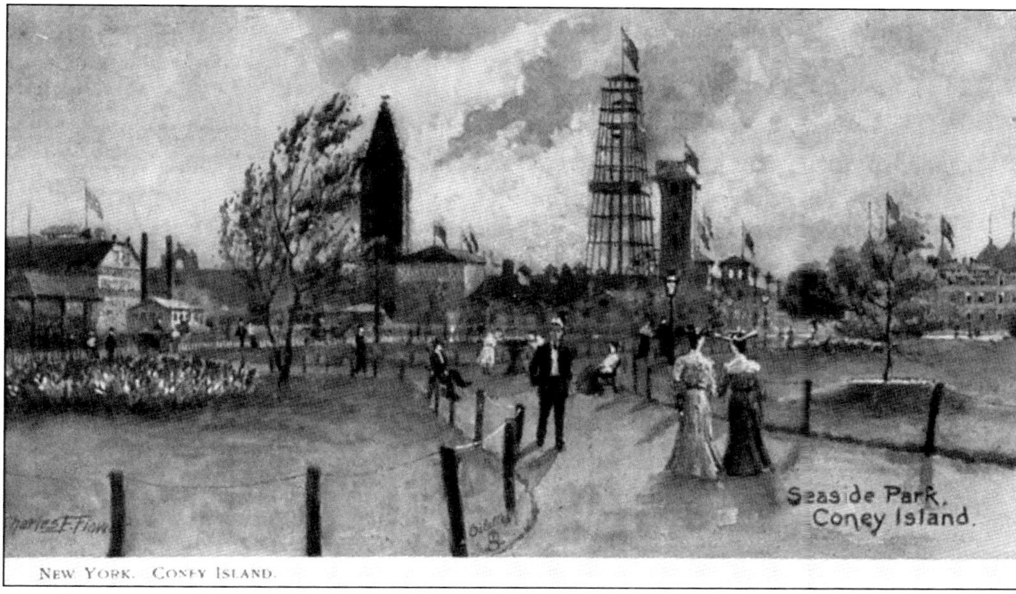

Seaside Park, now known as Asser Levy Park, is located north of Surf Avenue at West Fifth Street. It was the site of the first Coney Aquarium, which was built in the 1870s. This painting by Charles E. Flowers was part of the six-card Coney Island series published by Raphael Tuck & Sons in 1905. The Iron Tower is visible in the background.

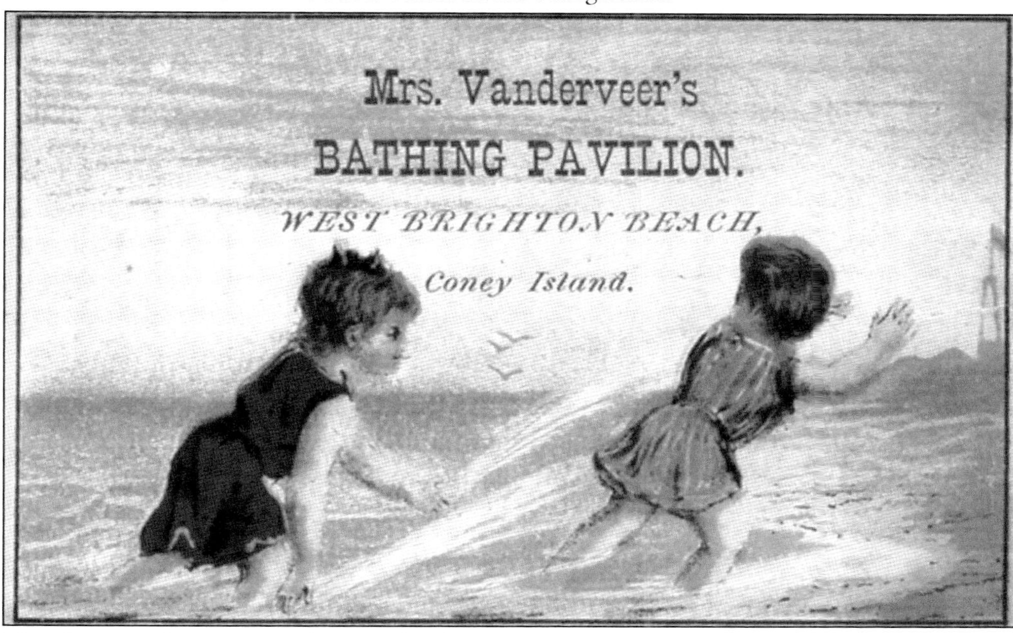

The clam was the most popular treat for diners on Coney Island until it was surpassed by the hot dog. The restaurant at married couple William and Lucy Vanderveer's Ocean Concourse Hotel served grilled clams with butter for a penny apiece in the late 1800s. The Ocean Concourse Hotel was built in 1875 at West Fifth Street and Surf Avenue. After William's death, Lucy continued to run the hotel and bathhouse. This advertisement was probably used to entice those who came down from Brooklyn for the day.

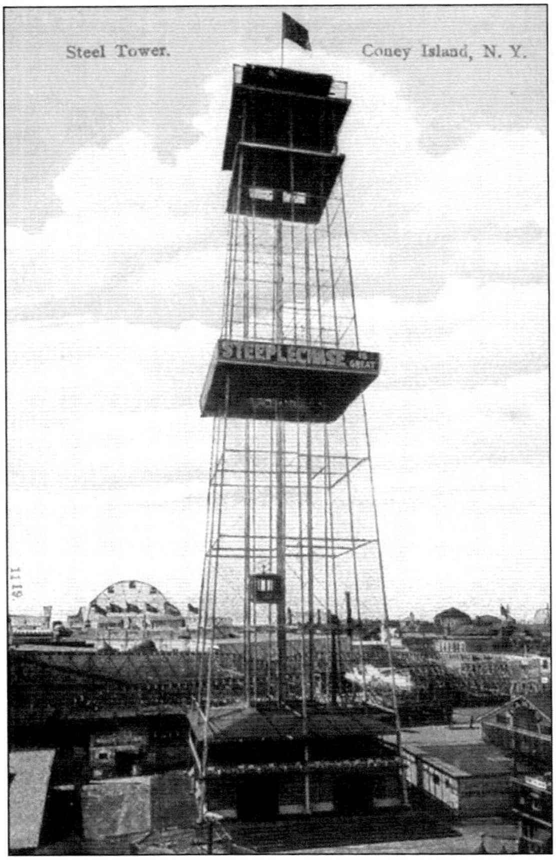

The 300-foot-tall Iron Tower (mislabeled on this postcard as "Steel Tower") was moved from the 1876 Centennial Exhibition in Philadelphia to Culver Plaza in 1881. It was the tallest structure in New York at the time and featured two steam elevators that would carry visitors to the observation deck. The tower collapsed in the 1911 Dreamland fire.

Pike's Peak Railway, designed by L.A. Thompson and built by Stephen Jackman in 1906 on Surf Avenue and West Fifth Street, stood next to Dreamland. It consisted of a 138-foot-tall mountain with railway cars that circled around the mountain. It was destroyed in the 1911 Dreamland fire.

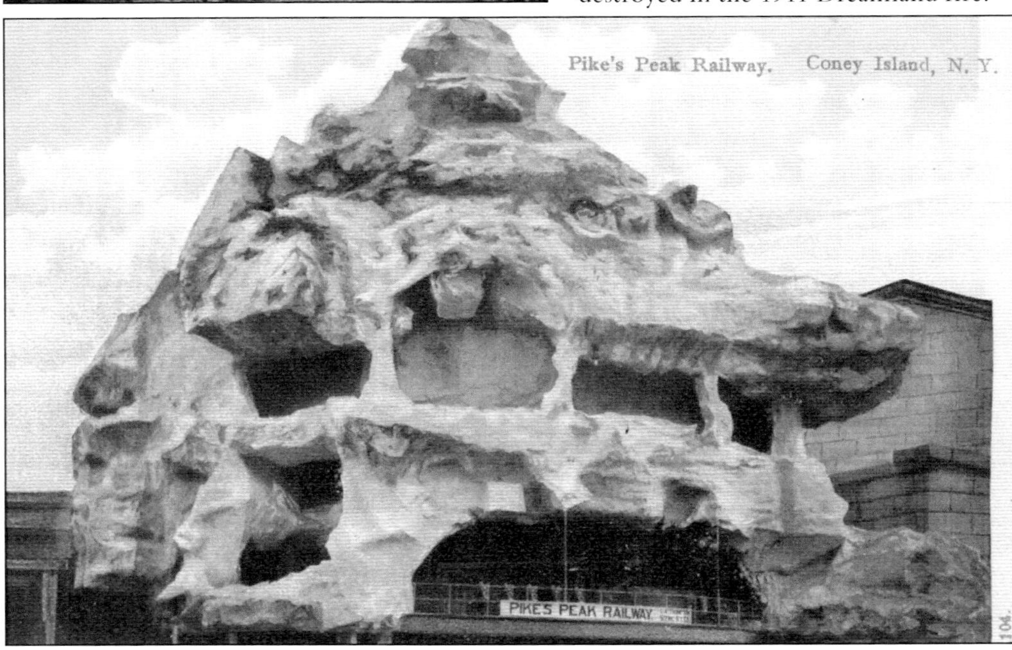

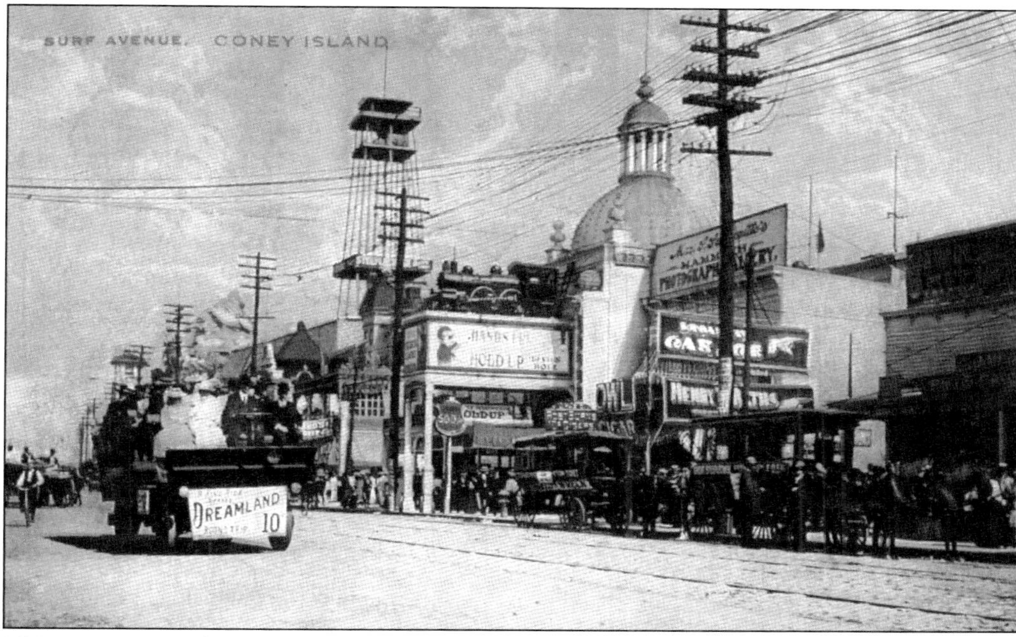

This street view of Surf Avenue shows the Iron Tower in the background and the top of Pike's Peak in the distance.

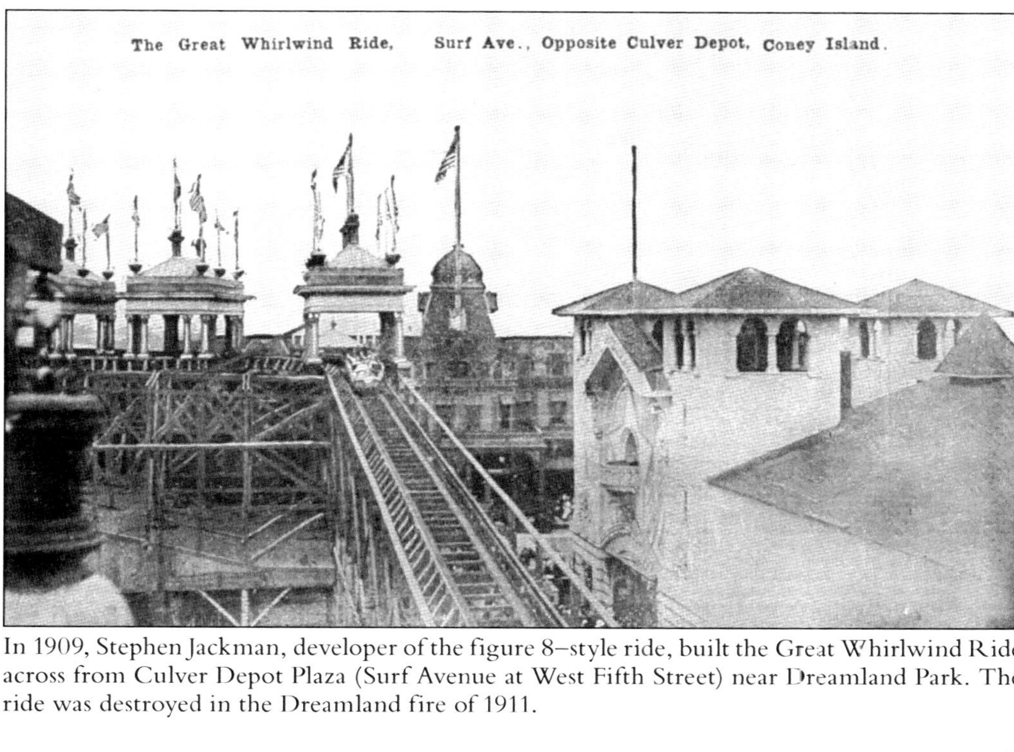

In 1909, Stephen Jackman, developer of the figure 8–style ride, built the Great Whirlwind Ride across from Culver Depot Plaza (Surf Avenue at West Fifth Street) near Dreamland Park. The ride was destroyed in the Dreamland fire of 1911.

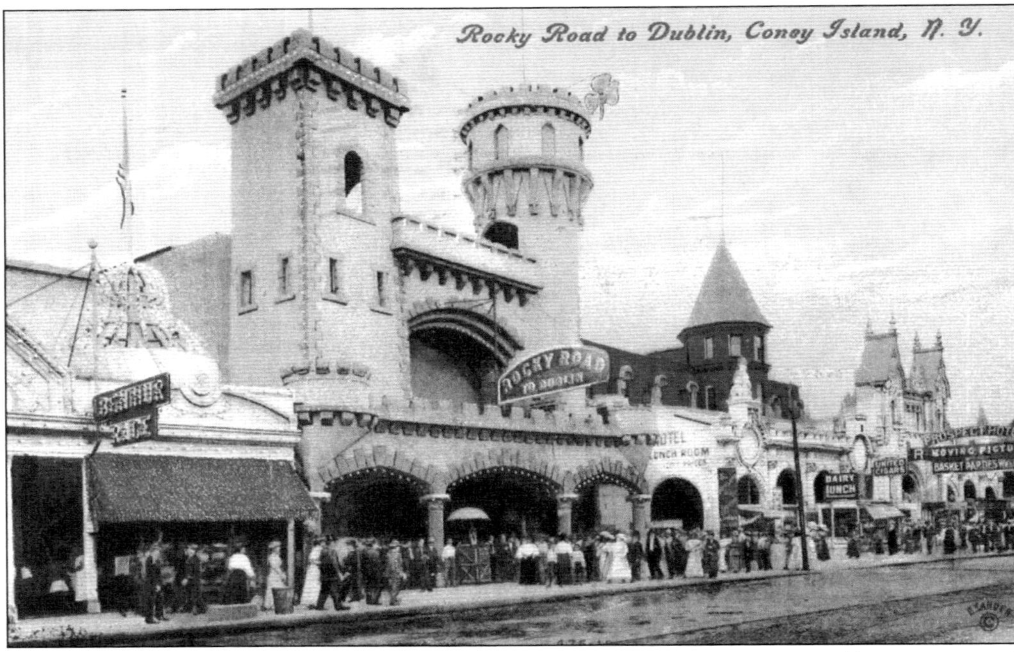

The Rocky Road to Dublin was the third electric scenic railway built by William F. Mangels (1867–1958). It was located on Surf Avenue at West Sixth Street from 1906 to 1923.

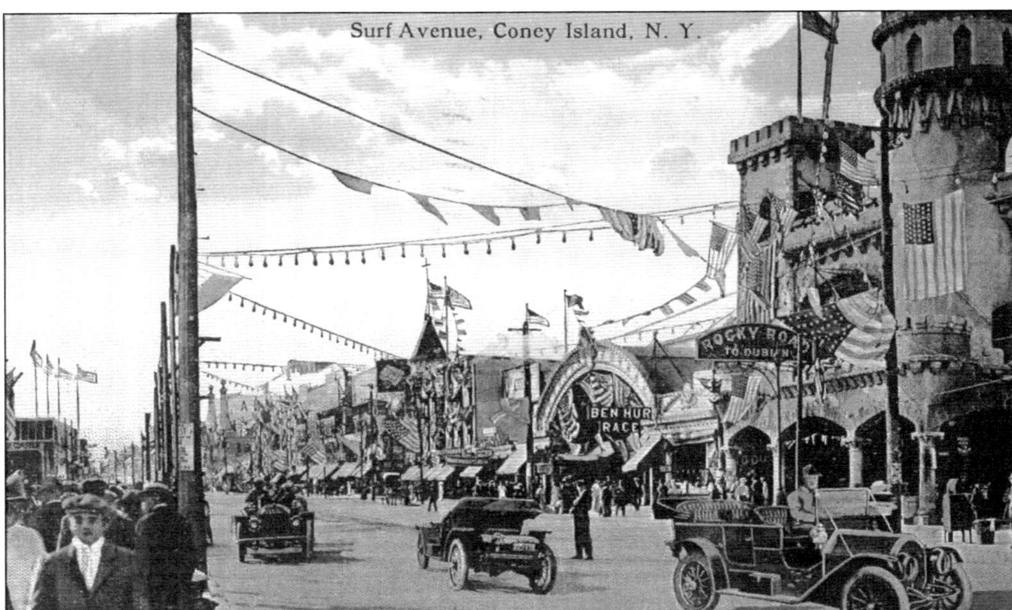

The entrance to the Ben Hur Chariot Race, which opened in 1908 in Dreamland's Hippodrome arena, was next to Rocky Road to Dublin.

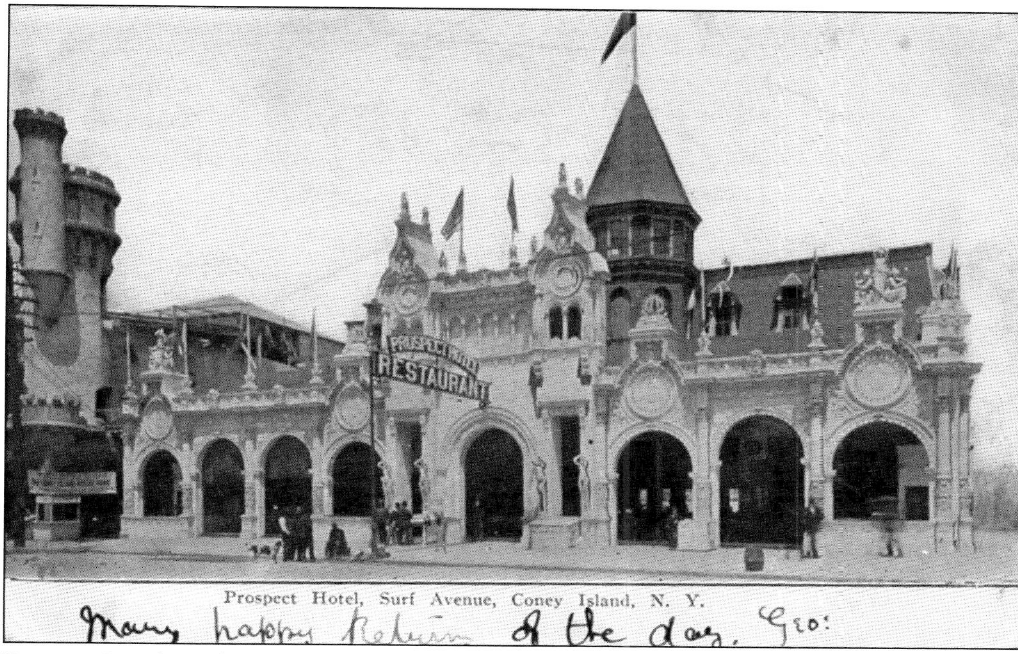

Prospect Hotel was located on the north side of Surf Avenue at West Sixth Street, next to the Culver Terminal. For all the hotels that once populated Coney Island, visitors can be hard-pressed to find a hotel room there today.

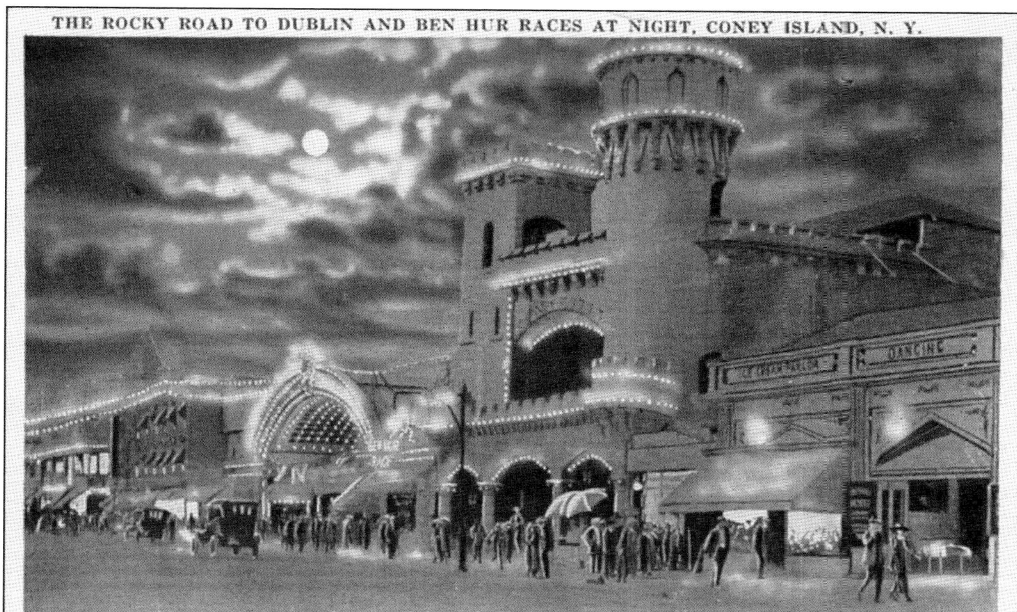

This card shows the entrances of the Rocky Road to Dublin and Ben Hur Chariot Race at night. The Ben Hur races continued until 1923.

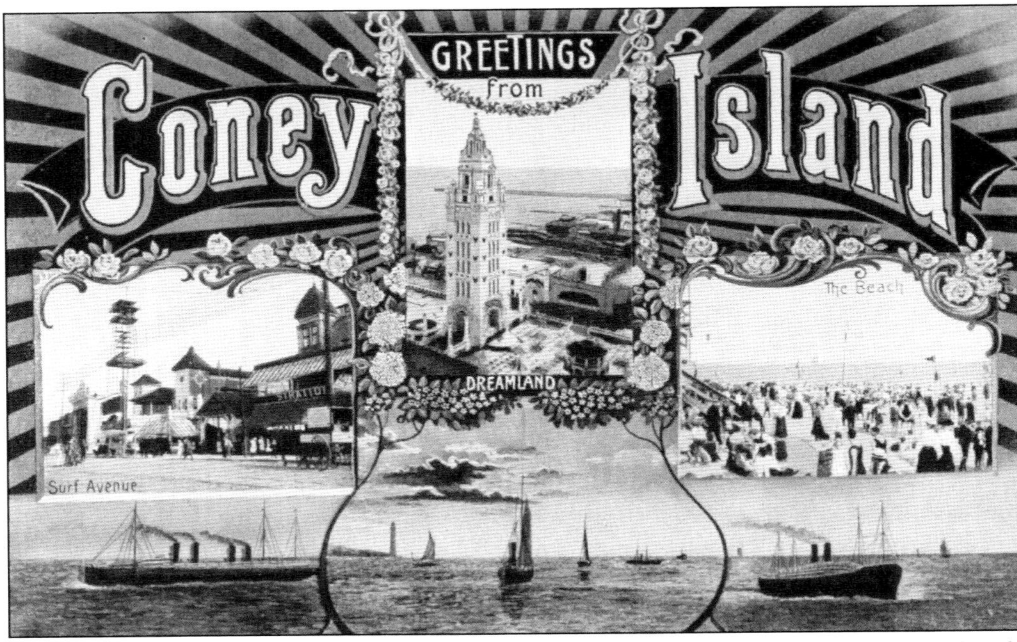

Greetings from Coney Island—this postcard shows Surf Avenue, Dreamland, and the beach, with steamboats along the bottom of the image.

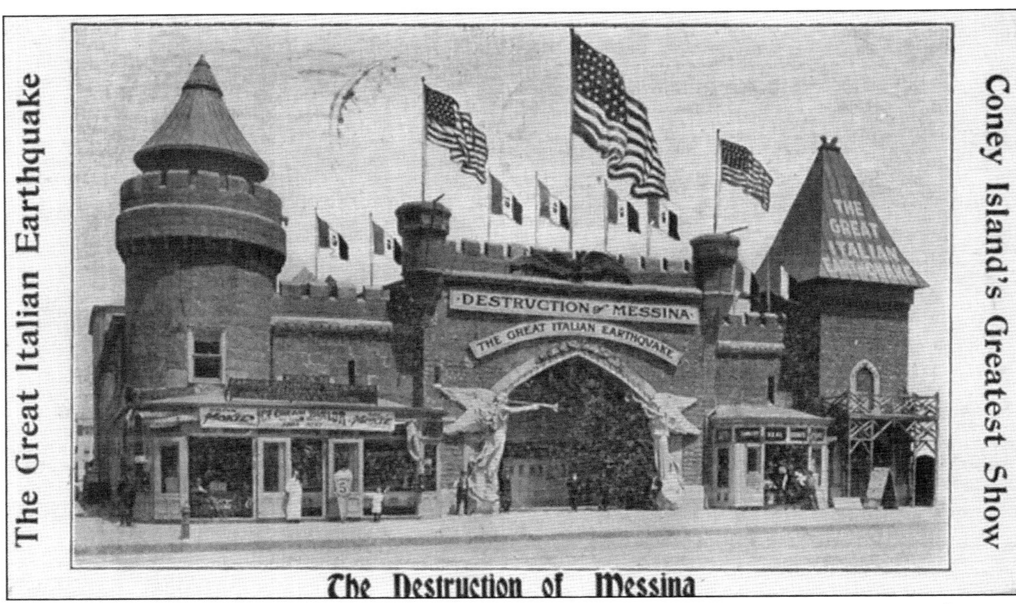

The Great Italian Earthquake was also known as the Destruction of Messina. Disaster reproductions were popular and constantly changed with the times. This building also housed a production featuring the Johnstown Flood, which killed more than 2,000 people in Pennsylvania in 1889.

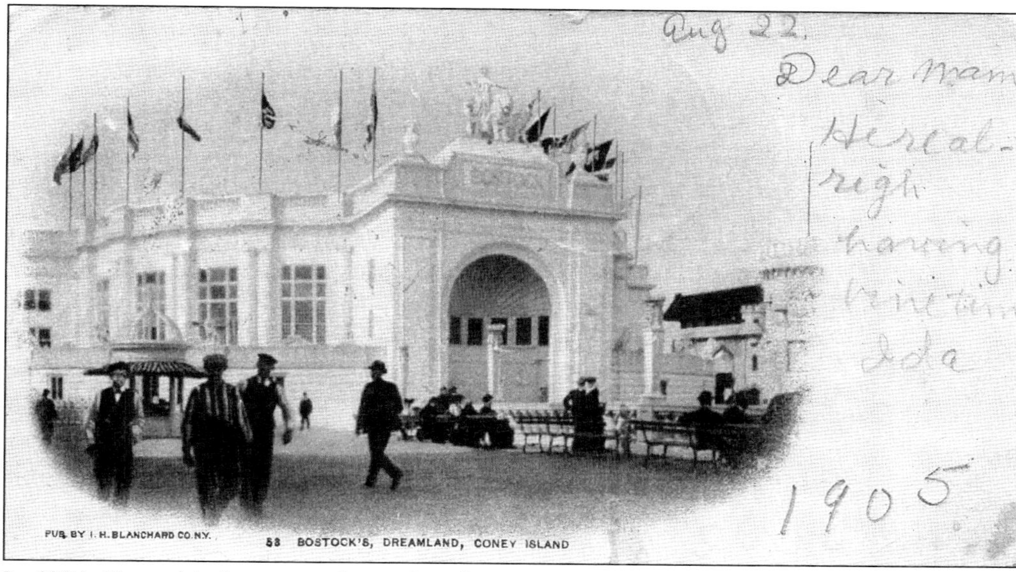

In 1904, Bostock's Arena was located at the entrance to Dreamland. For publicity, the park hired Broadway actress Marie Dressler to sell peanuts and popcorn. Dressler was said to be in love with Dreamland's dashing, one-armed lion tamer, Capt. Jack Bonavita. He lost his arm after one hand was severely clawed by a lion; the infection spread throughout his arm, requiring its amputation.

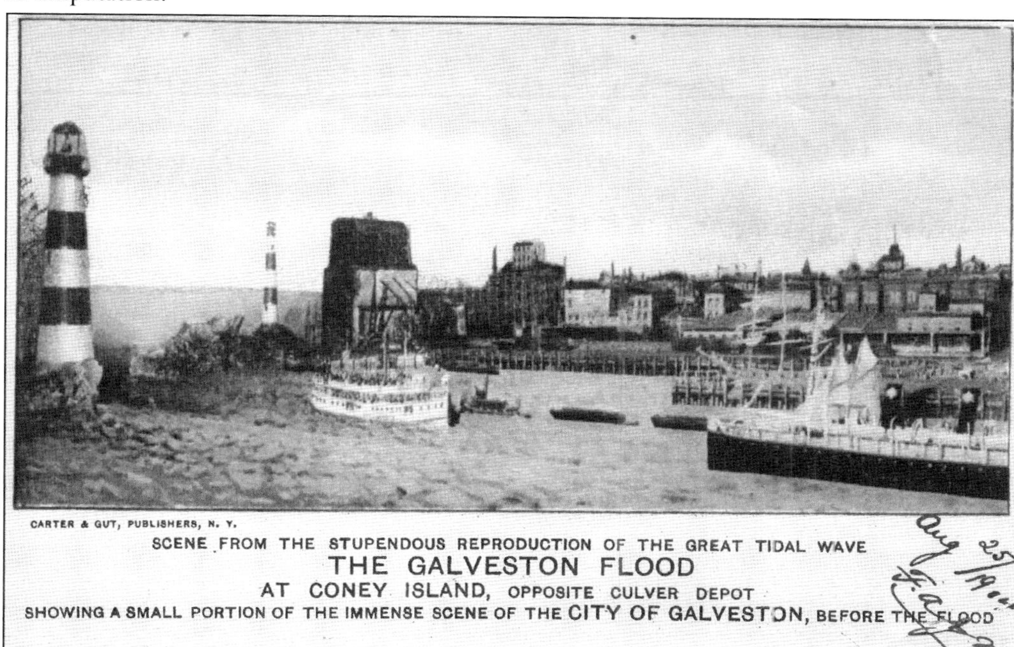

Coney Island loved to re-create disasters, and the morbid curiosity of the general public kept them coming. One of the earliest disasters re-created at Coney Island was the Galveston Flood, which went into production in 1902. The September 1900 flood, prompted by a hurricane, was a devastating catastrophe for the Texas resort town. Winds of 125 mph and a 15-foot-high flood nearly leveled the entire town and killed more than 6,000 people.

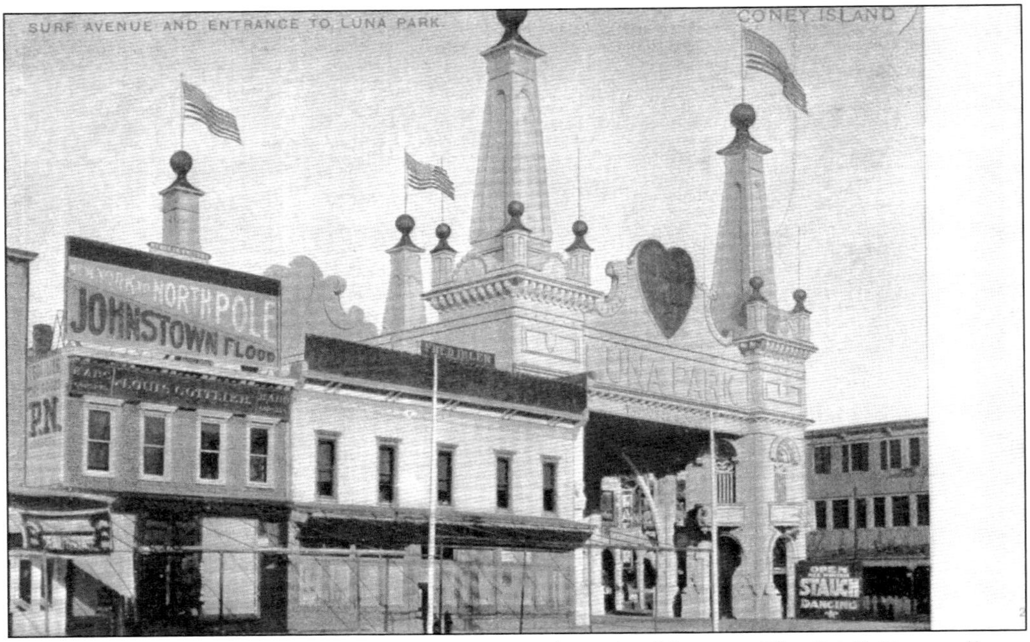

This card shows the original entrance to Luna Park on Surf Avenue. The B&B Carousell was moved to this area in 1939. It has since been refurbished and relocated to the new Steeplechase Plaza on the Boardwalk.

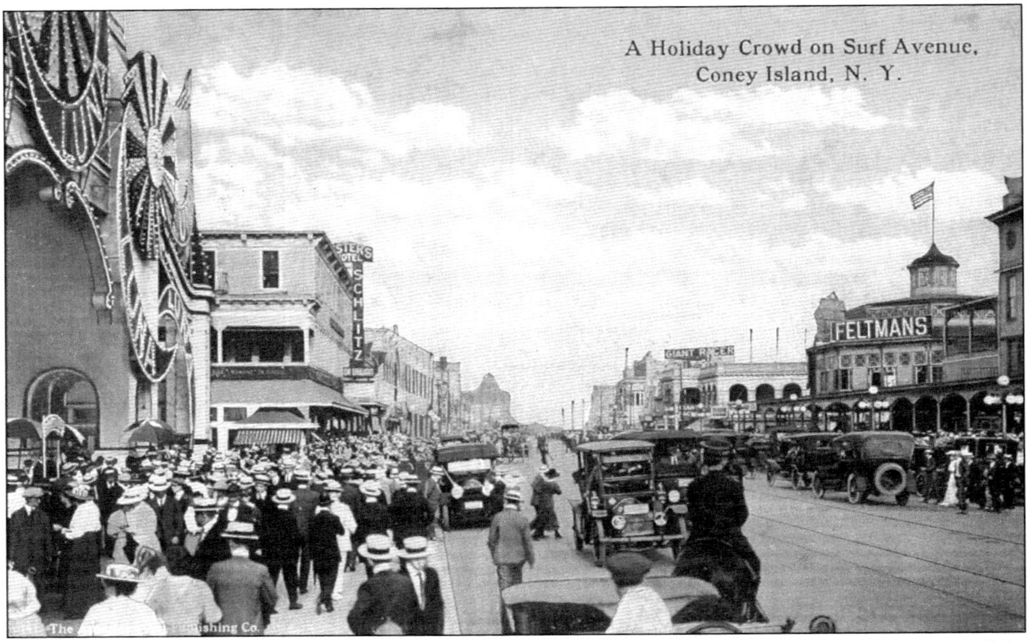

A holiday crowd walks east down Surf Avenue. Luna Park's new entrance—constructed in 1905—is at left, and Feltman's restaurant complex is at right.

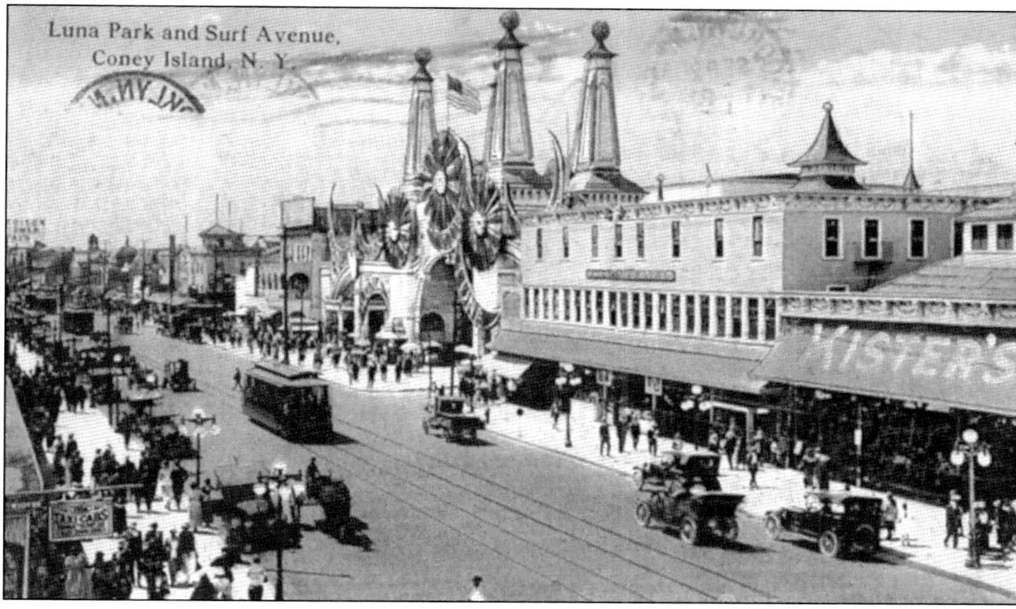

In 1896, Fred Kister had this three-story building built on the north side of Surf Avenue. He opened Kister's Restaurant on the first two floors, while the third floor was converted into apartments. When Luna Park opened in 1903, the main entrance was right next to Kister's building. Kister's son, George, inherited the property in the 1920s and operated various amusements there. The building was demolished in 1979 after a series of fires.

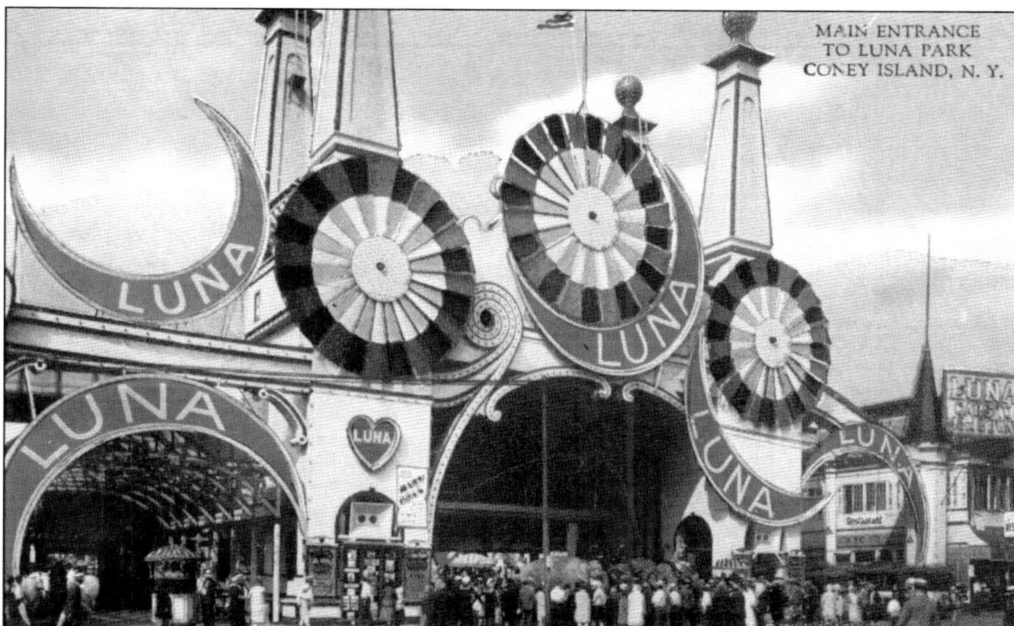

Luna Park's main entrance along Surf Avenue was widened and given an Oriental/Turkish look featuring crescent moons embossed with the word "Luna" and three red-and-gold pinwheels set above the central archway. The Japanese promenade, located to the left as one walked down Luna Court, was moved aside to open a broader walkway to the Electric Tower.

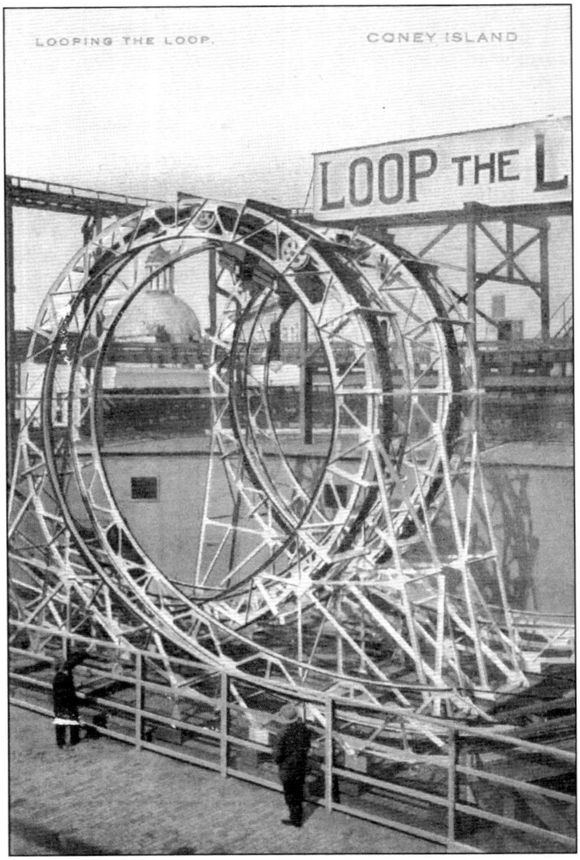

Surf Avenue and West Tenth Street is the most famous corner in Coney Island. It was home to the first roller coaster, L.A. Thompson's Switchback Railroad, in 1884. Ten years later, the coaster was replaced with Wharton's World's Fair Ice Slide. One year later, the Streets of Cairo took over the corner. The Loop the Loop was located there from 1901 to 1910. The Giant Racer occupied the corner until 1927. Since 1928, it has been the home of the Cyclone roller coaster.

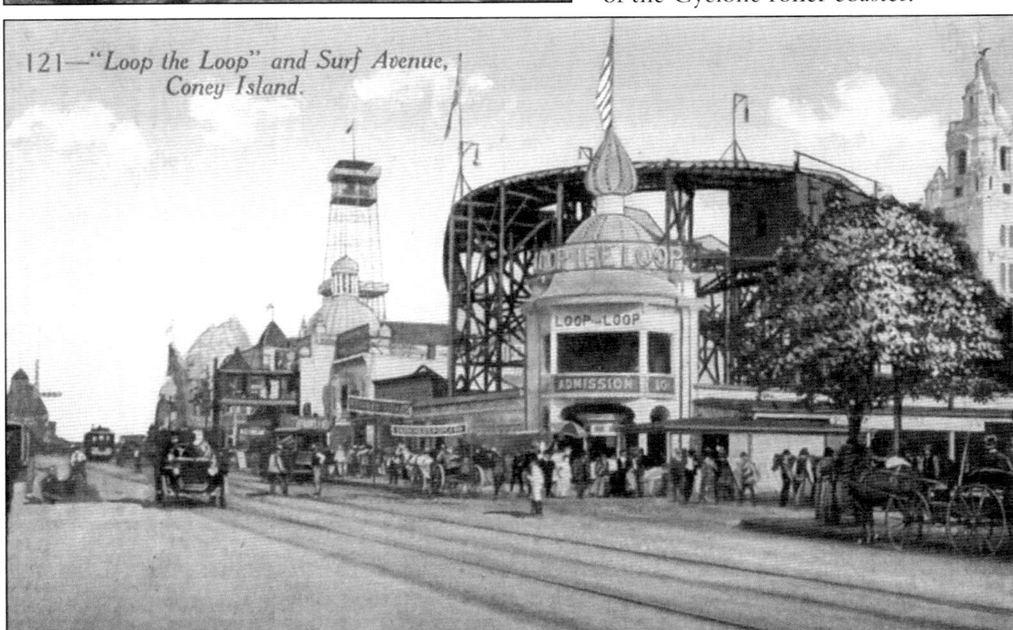

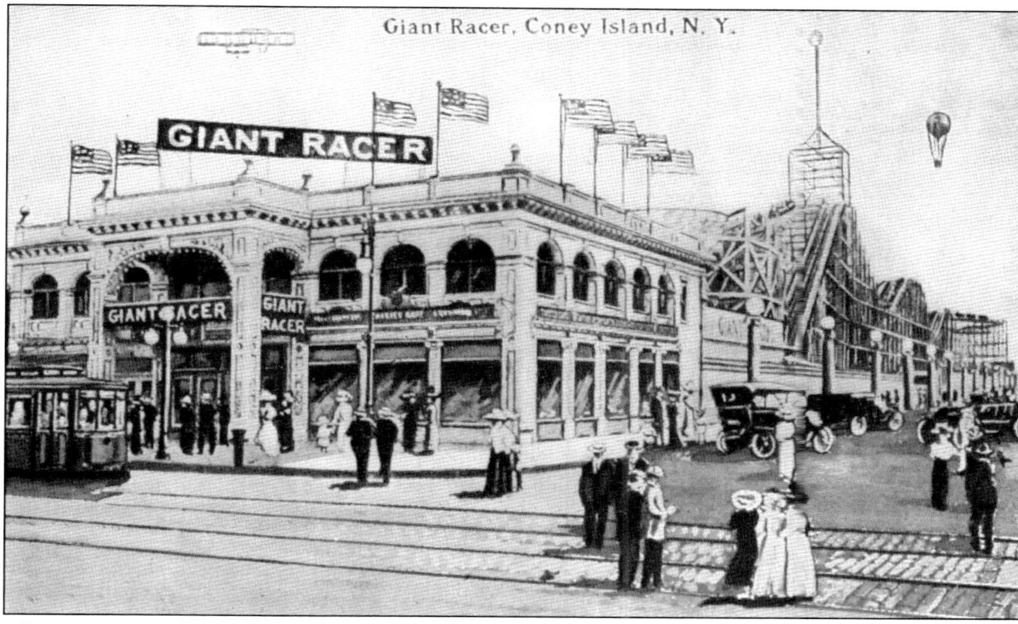

The Giant Racer was a double steel-track racing coaster built by Chris Feucht in 1911 and located just off Surf Avenue and West Tenth Street. It was moved 50 to 70 feet north to Surf Avenue in 1916. After several fatal accidents, it was dismantled in 1926 and replaced by the Cyclone.

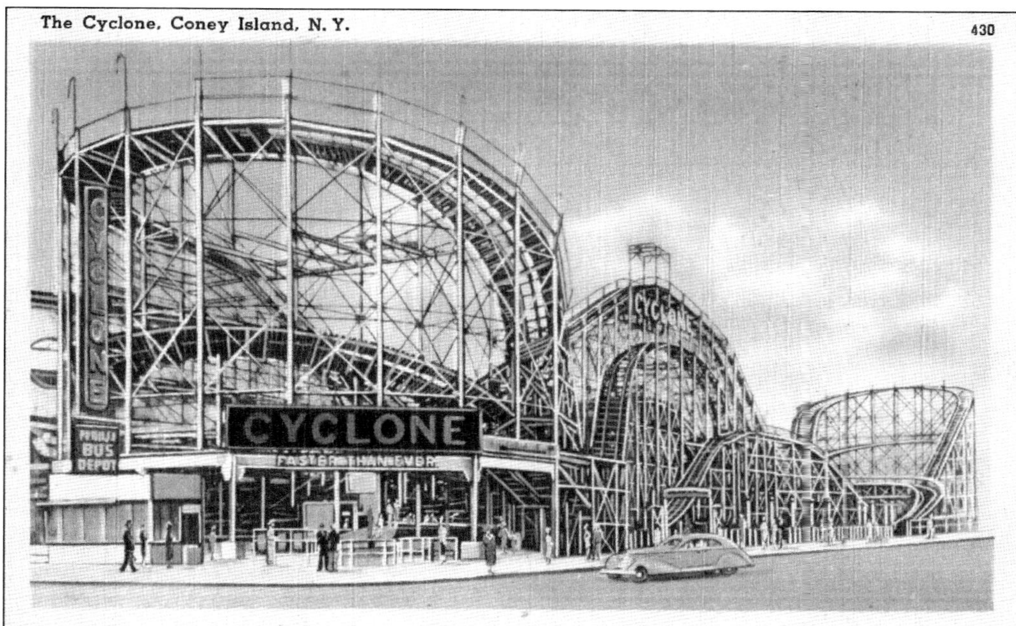

The Cyclone is a historic wooden roller coaster that opened in June 1927 at Surf Avenue at West Tenth Street. It reaches speeds of 60 mph, and the first drop falls more than 85 feet. The Cyclone was declared a New York City landmark in 1988 and a National Historic Landmark in 1991. It has had numerous owners, most notably the Dewey Albert family, who invested millions in its upkeep. Since 2011, the new Luna Park has taken over the operation of the Cyclone.

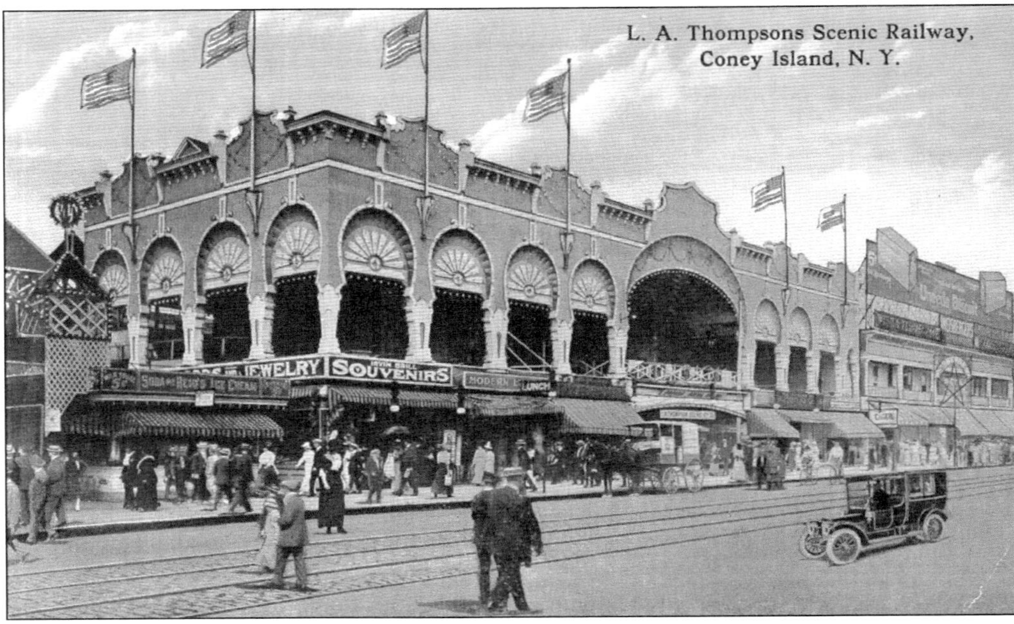

The description provided on the back of this postcard says, "The Scenic Railway is located on Surf Avenue opposite Feldmans [*sic*], being one of the most extensive and popular concessions at Coney Island. The swift and exhilarating ride is enjoyed by old and young and is always crowded by the merry-makers."

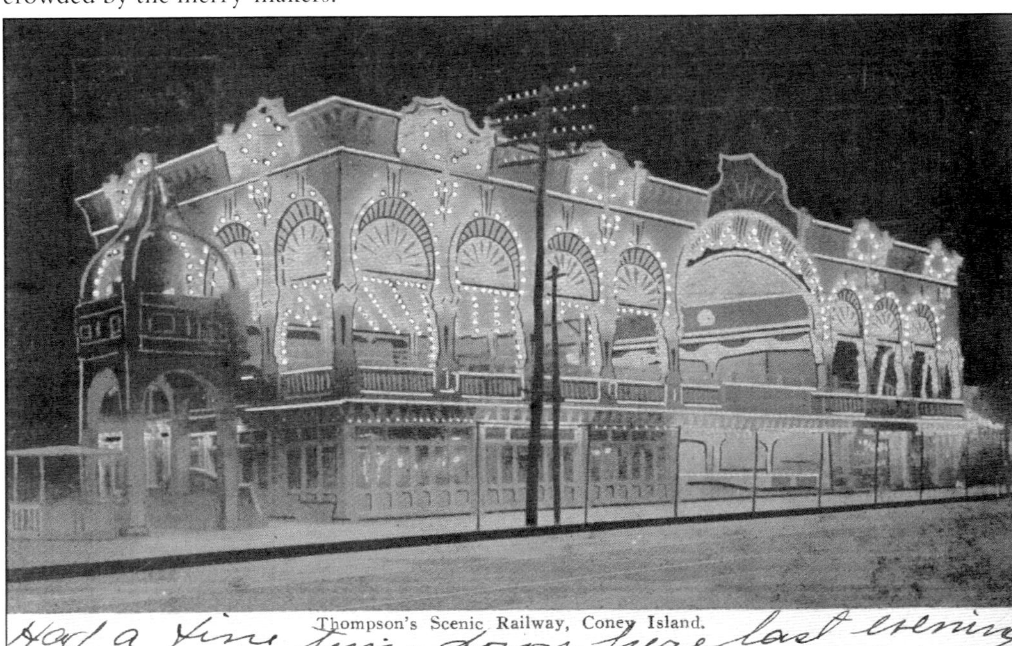

In 1884, LaMarcus Adna Thompson (1848–1919) created the Coney Island roller coaster called the Switchback Railway and became known as the "father of gravity." The Scenic Railway (pictured) was one of his many creations—he had over 25 patents related to roller coasters. He founded the L.A. Thompson Scenic Railway Company in 1895.

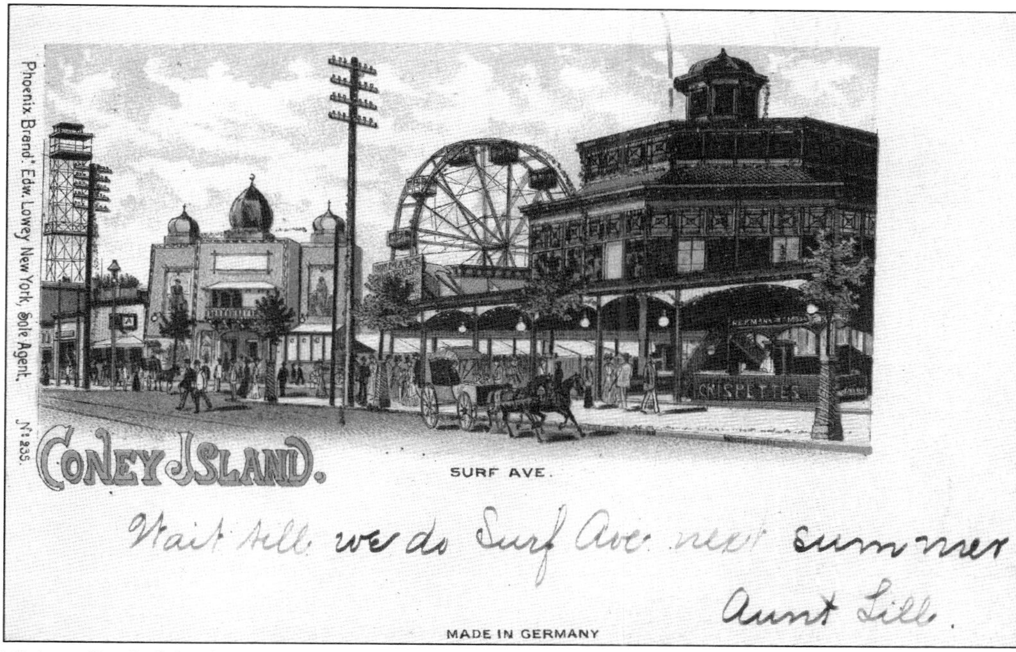

This undivided-back postcard featuring Surf Avenue was mailed in 1905. Between the Iron Tower and the Ferris wheel sat an attraction called the Streets of Cairo, where exotic dancer Fahreda Mahzar, who performed under the stage name Little Egypt, became very well known.

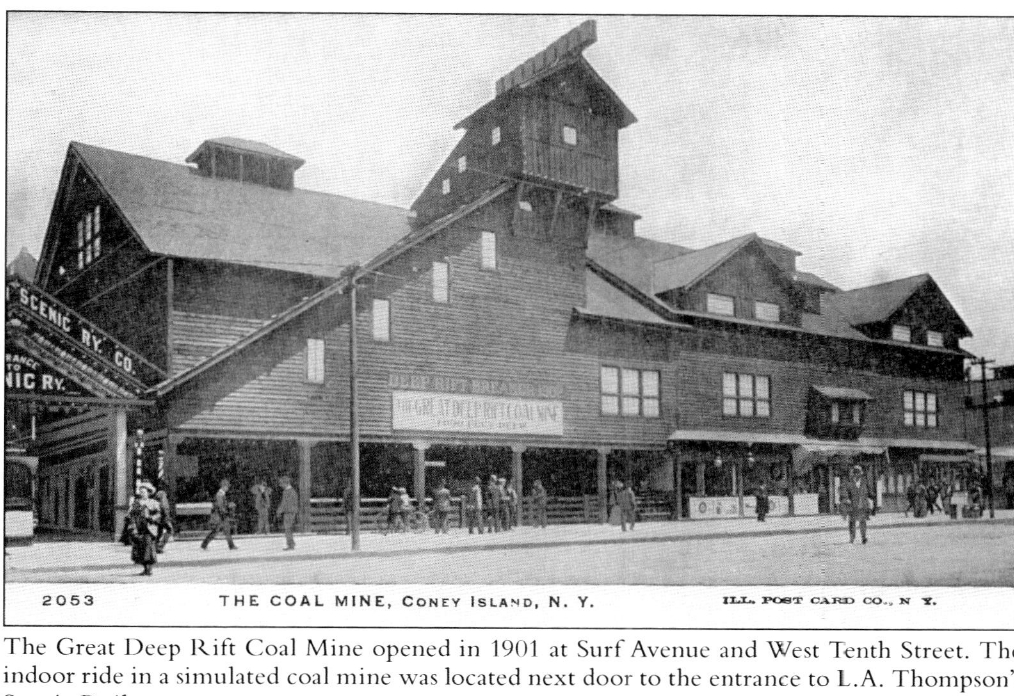

The Great Deep Rift Coal Mine opened in 1901 at Surf Avenue and West Tenth Street. The indoor ride in a simulated coal mine was located next door to the entrance to L.A. Thompson's Scenic Railway.

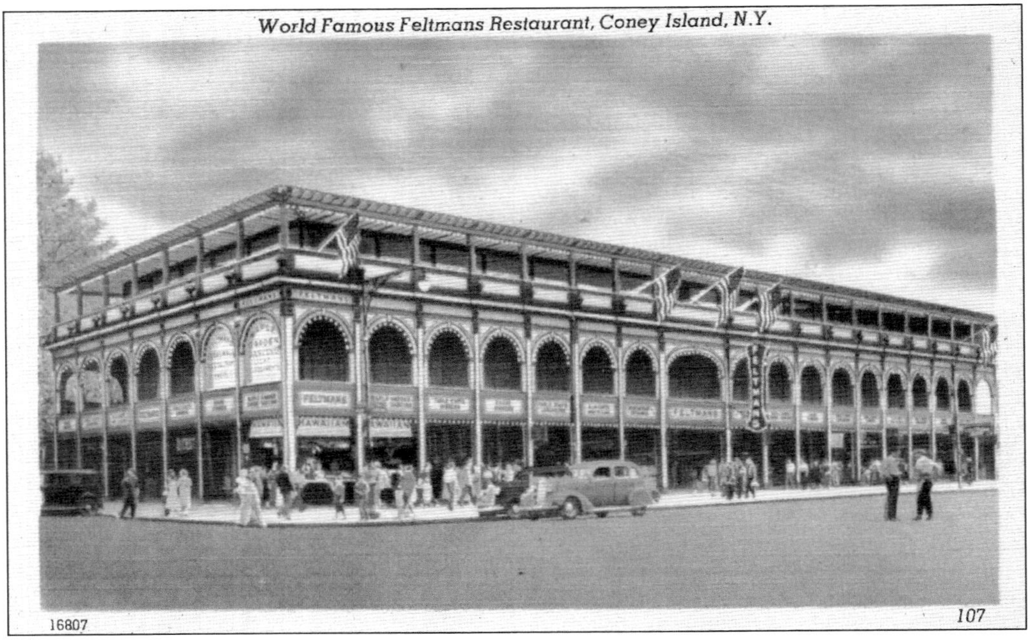

German immigrant Charles Feltman (1841–1910) is credited with inventing the hot dog (which he called the Coney Island Red Hot). He came to Coney Island in 1867 and delivered freshly baked pies with his wagon. Four years later, he acquired property along West Tenth Street from Surf Avenue to the beach and built his first restaurant, Feltman's. It evolved into an entertainment complex that consisted of nine restaurants, a roller coaster, a carousel, a ballroom, and a beach pavilion.

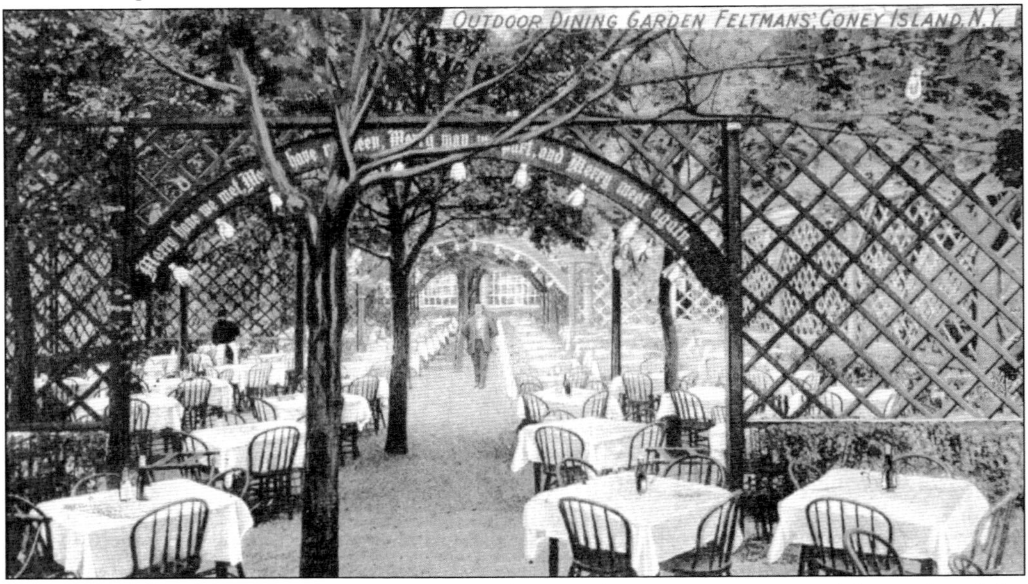

In the late 1800s, Feltman's became very popular with horse-racing patrons. They enjoyed the thick steaks and Bavarian beer in the outdoor dining garden that was shaded by maple trees. German bands entertained the crowds with music each night. Feltman's seating capacity, for the whole venue, was 10,000 persons.

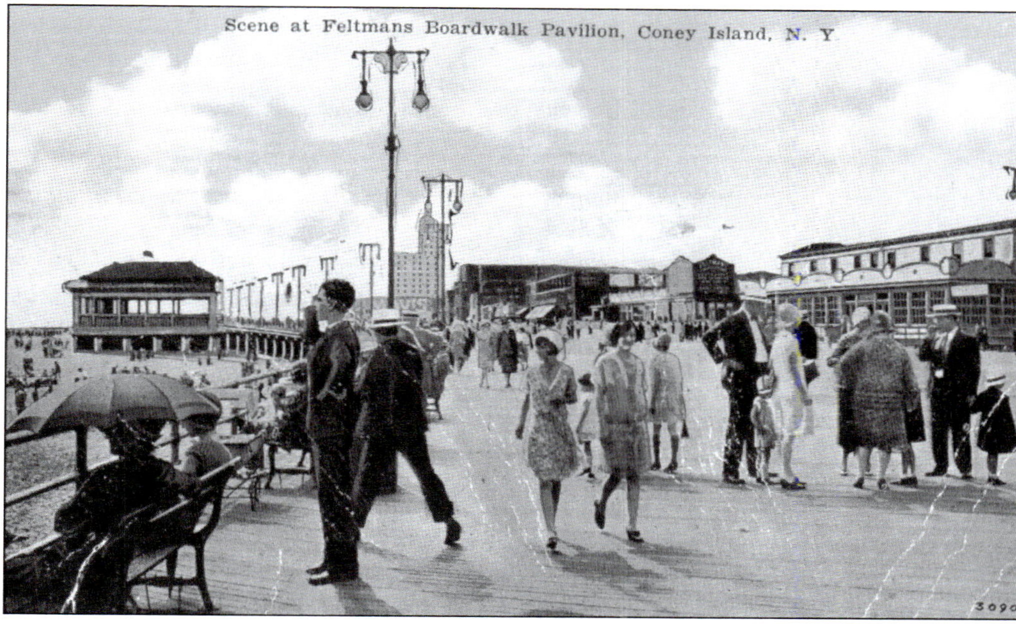

Hot dogs cost 10¢ at Feltman's, and owner Charles Feltman set his all-time record after serving 40,000 hot dogs in a single day. The Boardwalk Pavilion was built after Feltman died in 1910. His sons continued to run Feltman's for many years, but the Depression took its toll in the 1930s, and his sons decided to sell the complex in 1946. The property later became home to Astroland.

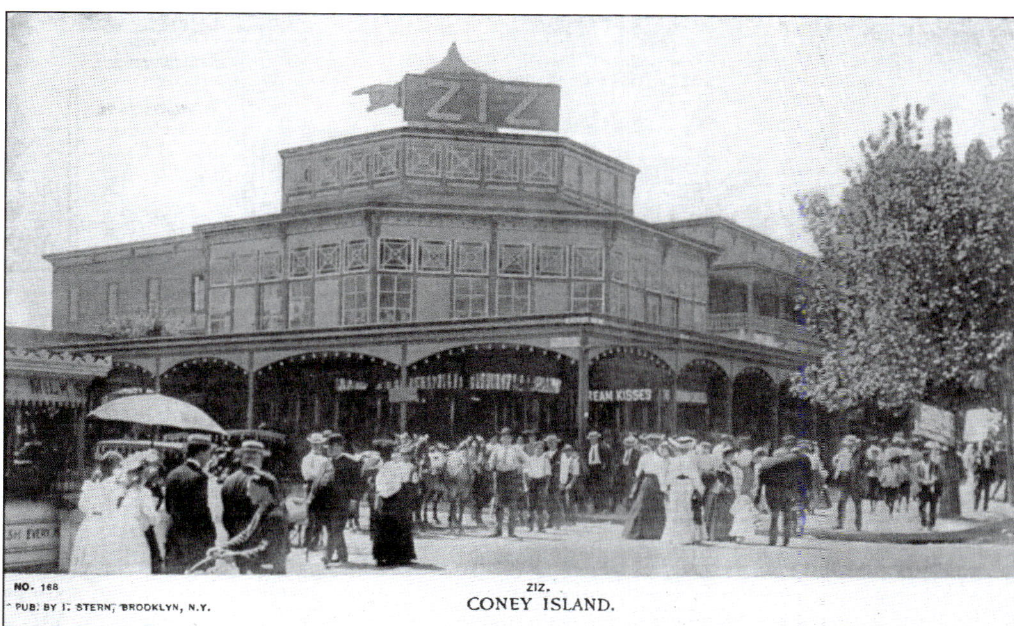

In 1905, the Ziz "mile a minute" roller coaster opened in the Feltman's restaurant entertainment complex. It was a scenic railway and ran through the grove of trees on the Feltman's property.

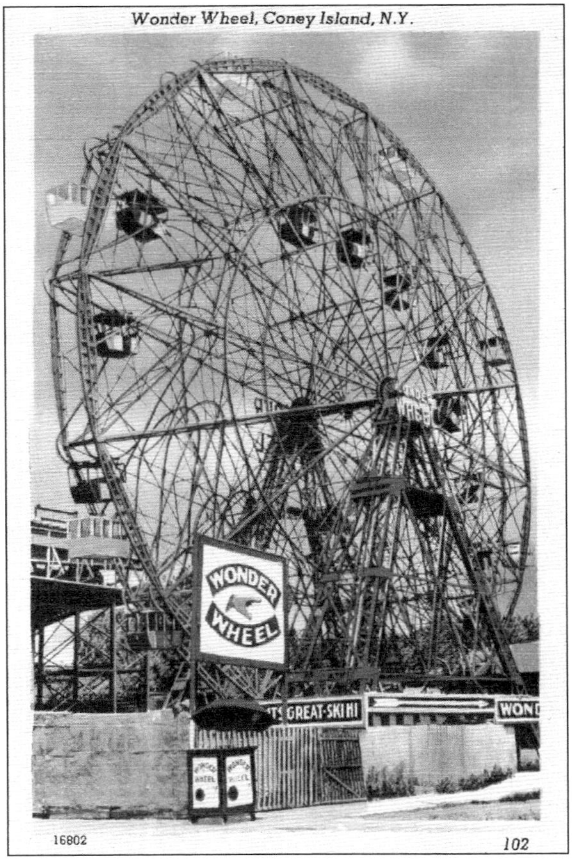

Deno's Wonder Wheel Amusement Park features 21 thrilling rides, two arcades, live entertainment, and food. The world-famous Wonder Wheel, a New York City landmark built in 1920, is still the pride and joy of Coney Island. At 150 feet tall, it is one of the largest Ferris wheels in the world. It has swinging and fixed cars and can carry up to 150 people at a time.

The Tunnels of Love ride on Surf Avenue is shown here with the Wonder Wheel in the background.

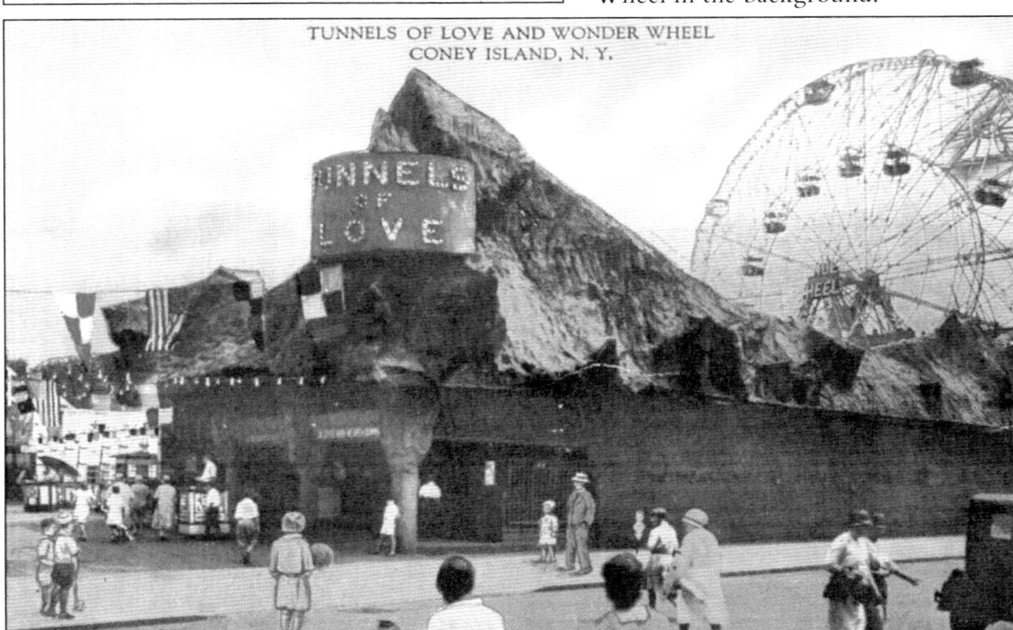

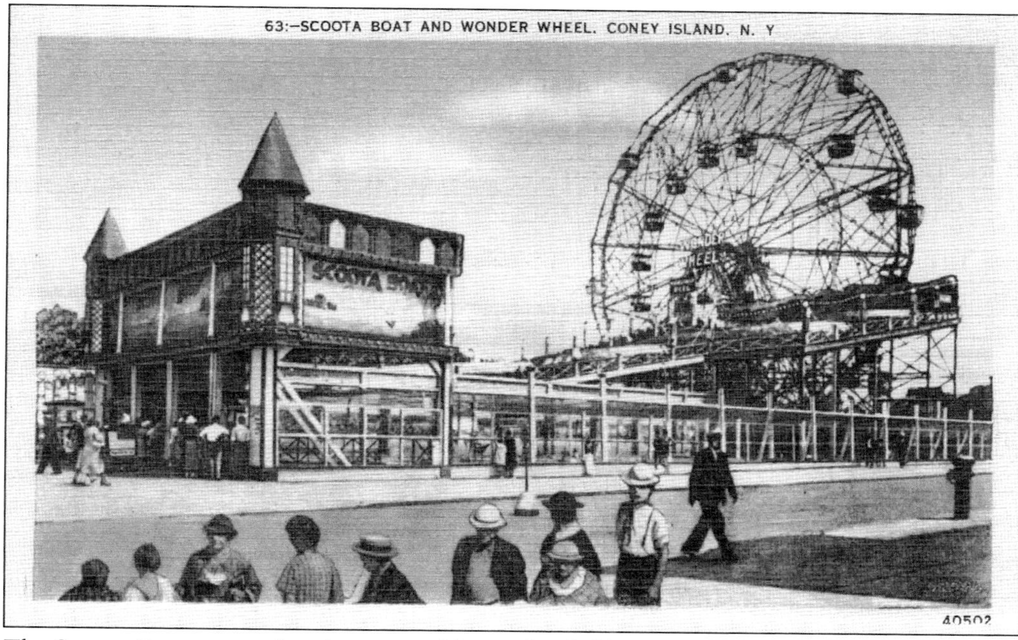

The Scoota Boats were electric-powered boats that held two passengers and, like the Tunnels of Love, appealed to young, romantic couples.

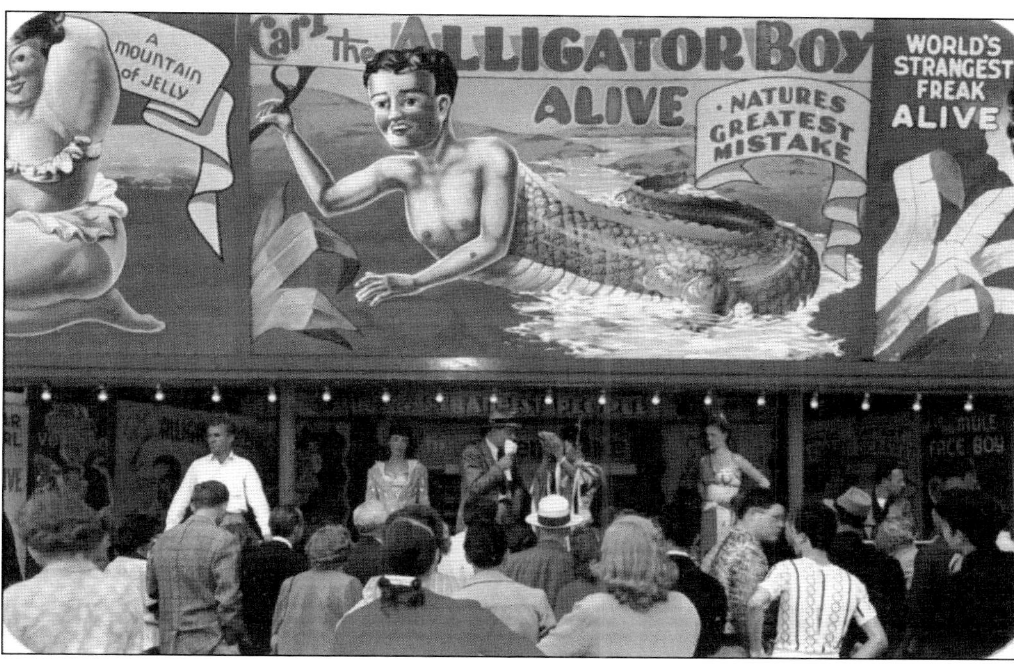

Carl the Alligator Boy was a huge sideshow attraction in his day. Other popular sideshow freaks included Lionel the Lion-faced man; Violetta, the limbless woman; Zip, the pinhead; and many others.

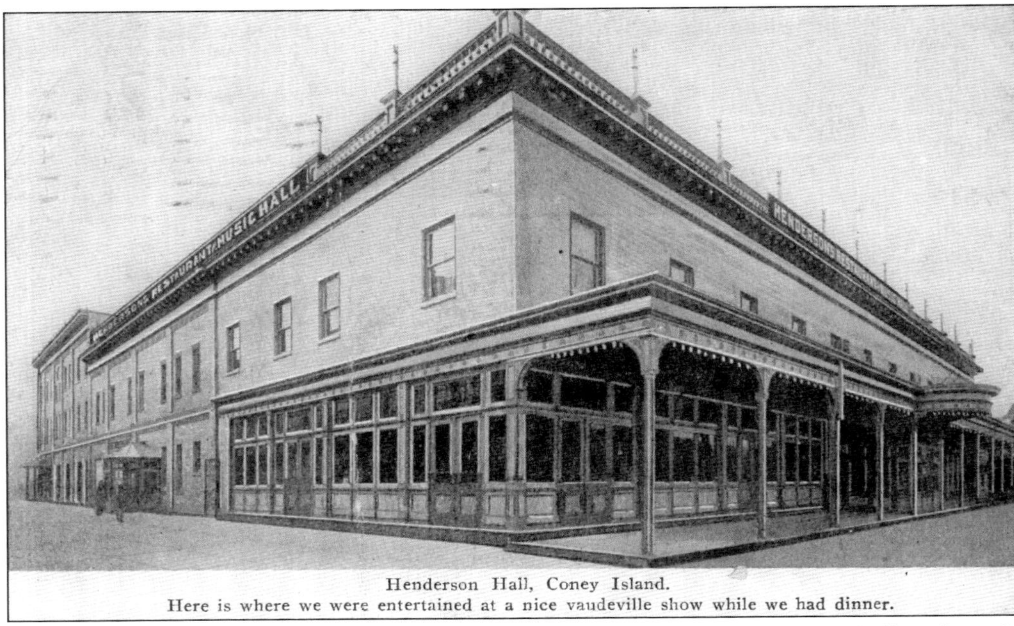

Fred Henderson built Henderson's Hall in 1881 as a restaurant and dance hall. When the building burned in the 1903 Bowery fire, Henderson rebuilt it with brick at the corner of Surf Avenue and Stillwell Avenue. The western facade (pictured) was lost when Stillwell Avenue was widened in 1923.

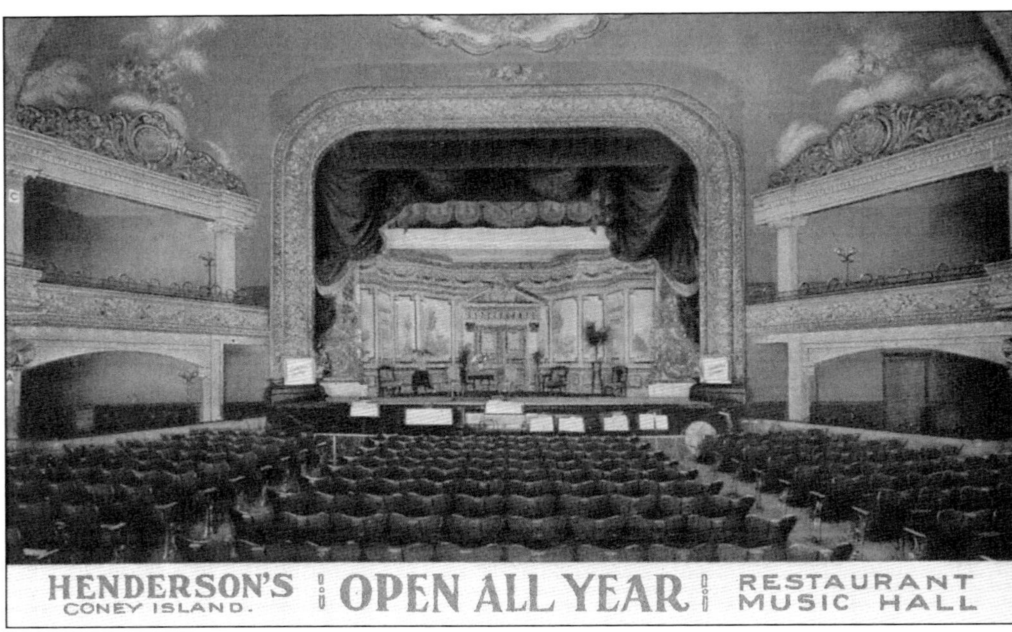

In its earliest years, Henderson's Music Hall featured musical and vaudeville acts such as Al Jolson, Sophie Tucker, and the Marx Brothers. Harpo Marx first joined his brothers on stage at Henderson's.

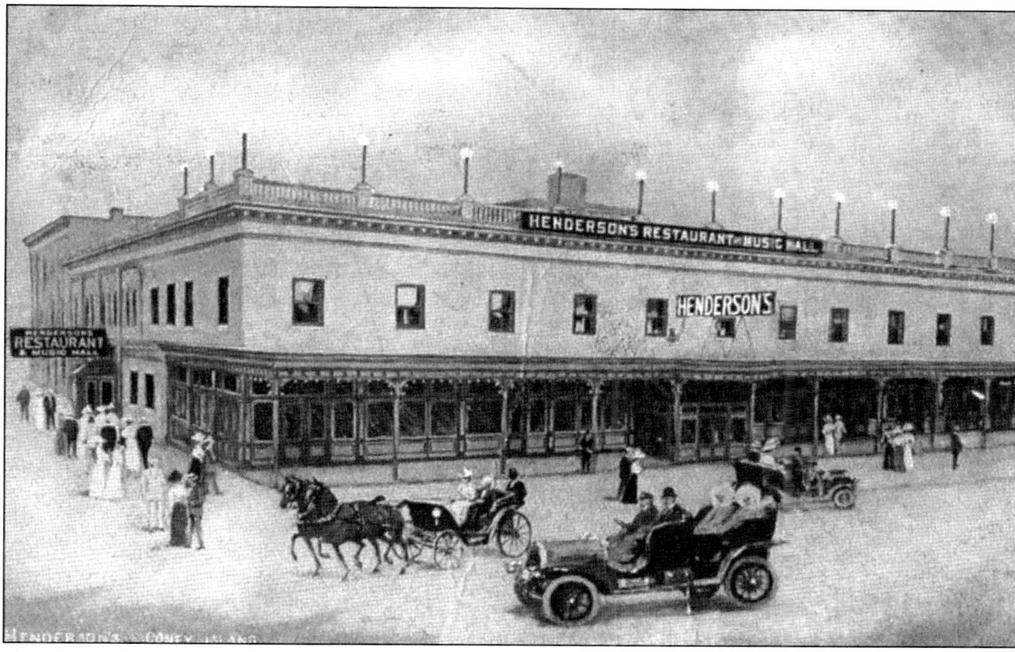

Henderson's Music Hall closed in 1926. The building housed Lilly Santangelo's World in Wax Musee until 1984. The second floor was restored in 2004 and housed the Velocity Nightclub until 2007. After more than a century of use, the building was, unfortunately, demolished in 2010.

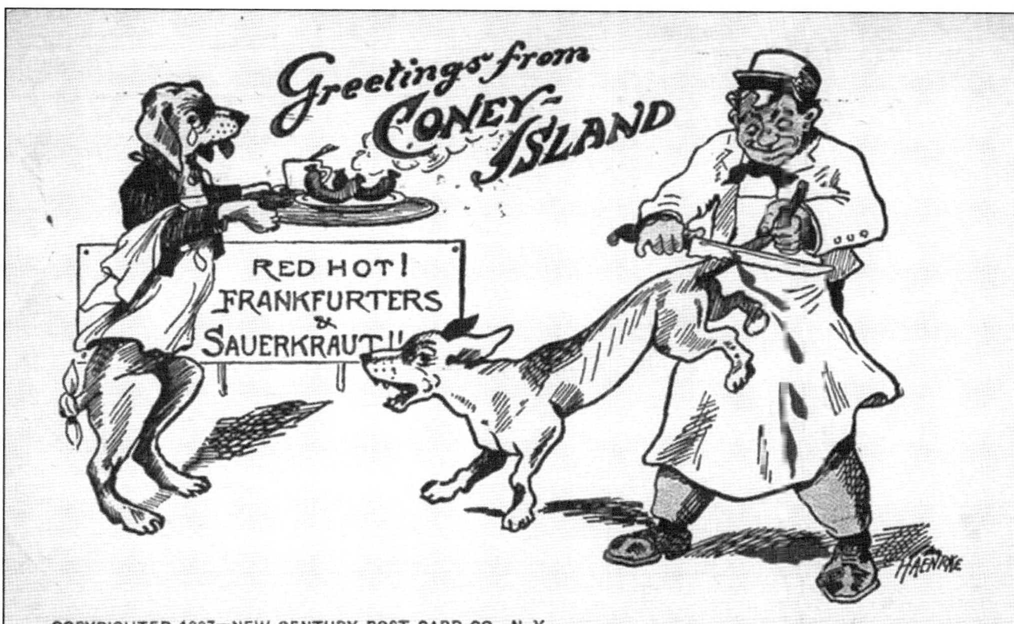

This "Greetings from Coney Island" postcard, created in 1907 by the New Century Post Card Company in New York, shows a dog on his hind legs dressed as a waiter holding a tray. The dog has a bandage on his tail and is shedding a tear while watching another dog lose his tail to the butcher's knife. A sign in the background says "Red Hot! Frankfurters & Sauerkraut!!"

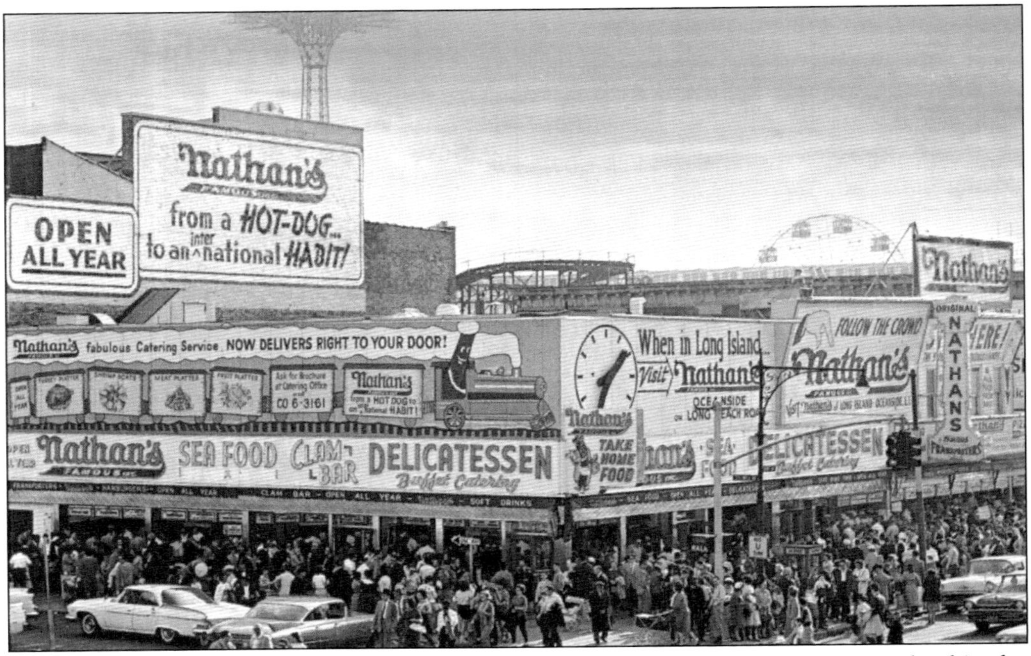

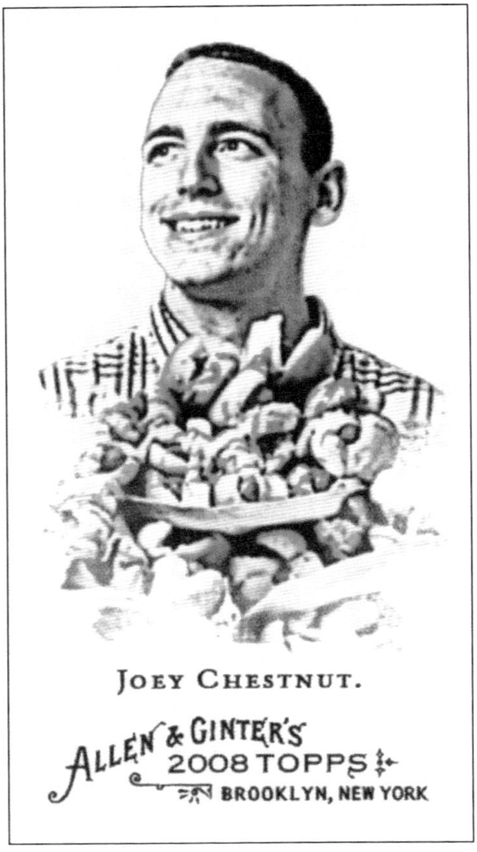

Nathan Handwerker visited Coney Island in the summer of 1915 and saw a "help wanted" sign at Feltman's restaurant. He took the job, saved his money, and within a year started selling his famous 5¢ hot dogs. In the early 1920s, the subway extension enabled millions of New Yorkers to come to Coney Island for only a nickel; Nathan's Famous was and still is located on the corner of Surf and Stillwell Avenues, directly across from the subway station.

The Nathan's Famous Hot Dog–Eating Contest has been held at the original Nathan's location in Coney Island on the Fourth of July each year since 1972. Joey Chestnut, of San Jose, California, holds the competition record for eating 69 Nathan's Famous hot dogs (and buns) in 10 minutes, and he has won the contest for seven straight years, from 2007 through 2013.

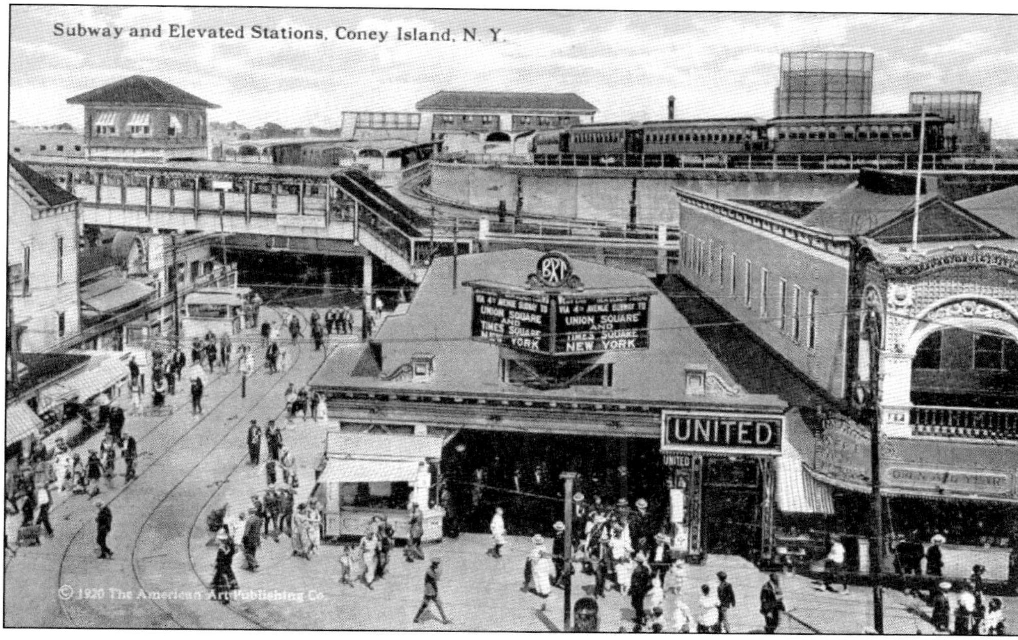

In 1915, the Sea Beach Railroad was converted to a subway line. This was followed by upgrades to the other former excursion roads and the opening of the new West End Terminal in 1919, thus ushering in Coney Island's busiest era. The terminal (pictured above) was built on an elevated structure to consolidate the terminals of most the former steam railroad lines. The train station at Coney Island shows several levels; the subway ran on the lower level, and elevated trains rode on the upper levels. Today, the intersection of Stillwell and Surf Avenues on Coney Island is home to one of the largest subway stations in the world. The station, originally opened in 1919 and rebuilt and reopened in 2004, provides access to the D, F, N, and Q trains. The postcard below shows the Albemarle Hotel, which opened on Surf Avenue in 1911.

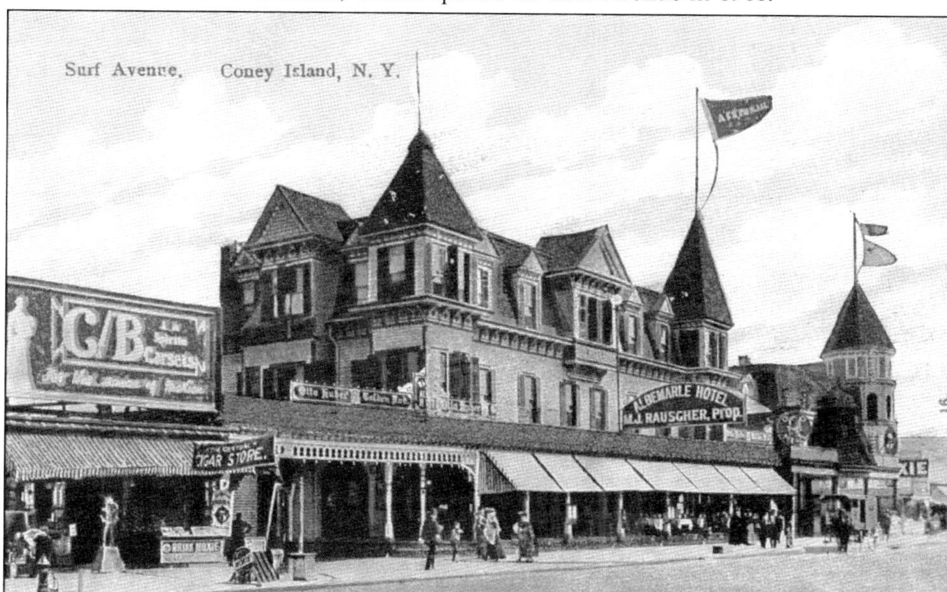

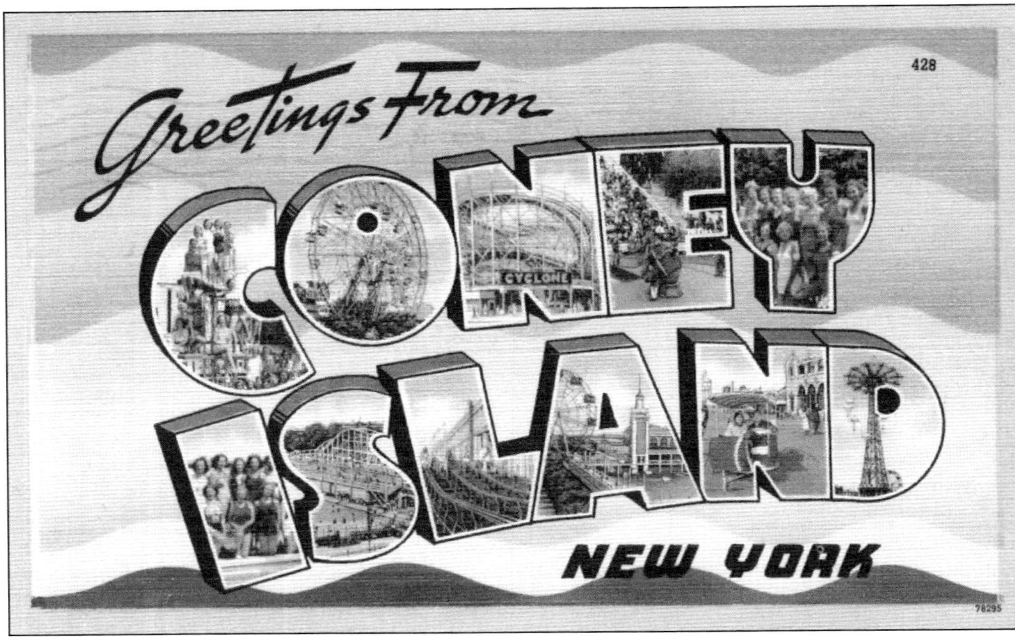

This "linen" postcard was sent in 1949.

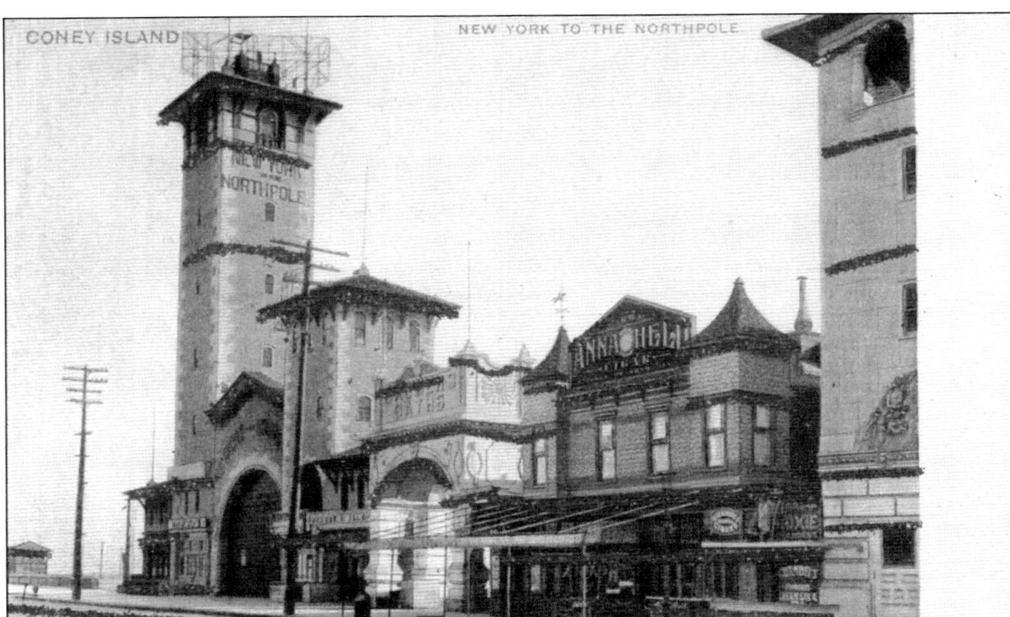

This Surf Avenue attraction, New York to the North Pole, was only around for the 1906 season. It was first replaced by a ride called Deep Sea Divers and then, in 1911, by a German carousel.

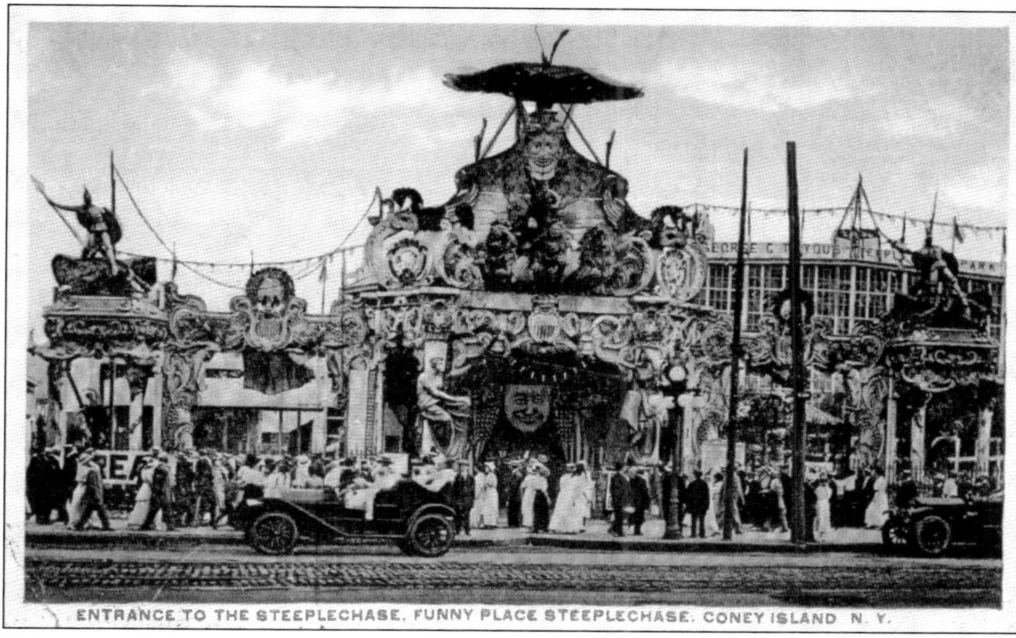

This postcard shows the entrance to Steeplechase Park on Surf Avenue.

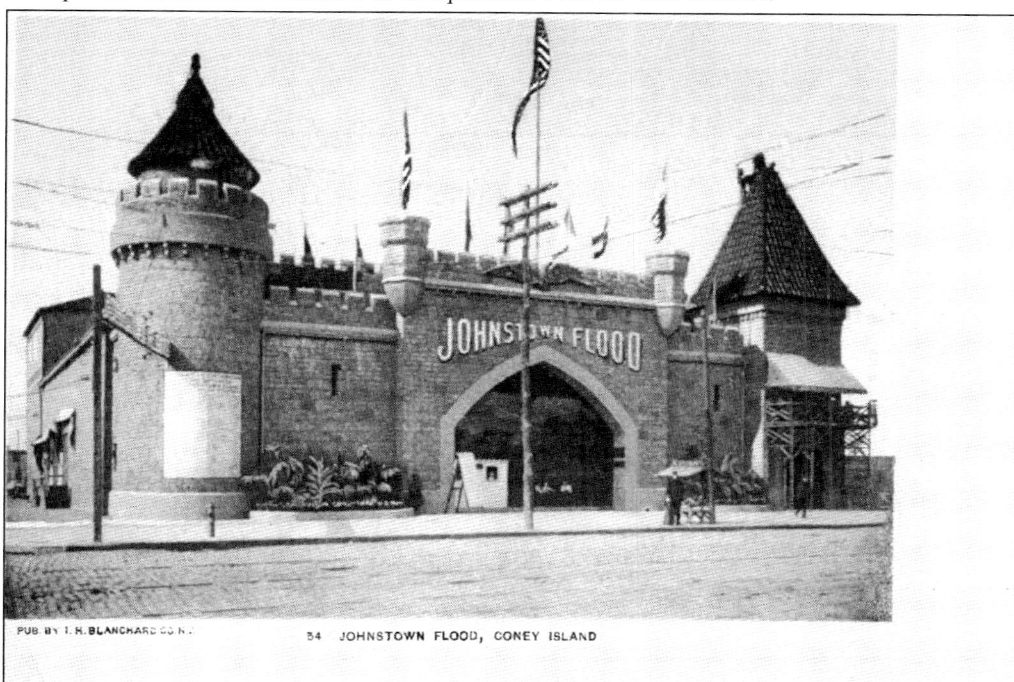

The Johnstown Flood was a popular disaster show attraction on Surf Avenue. In May 1889, after eight inches of heavy rain, a dam located 14 miles upstream burst and sent 20 million tons of water down into the valley toward the unsuspecting Pennsylvania town of Johnstown. The wall of water took almost an hour to reach Johnstown; by the time the flood was over, at least 2,200 people were dead.

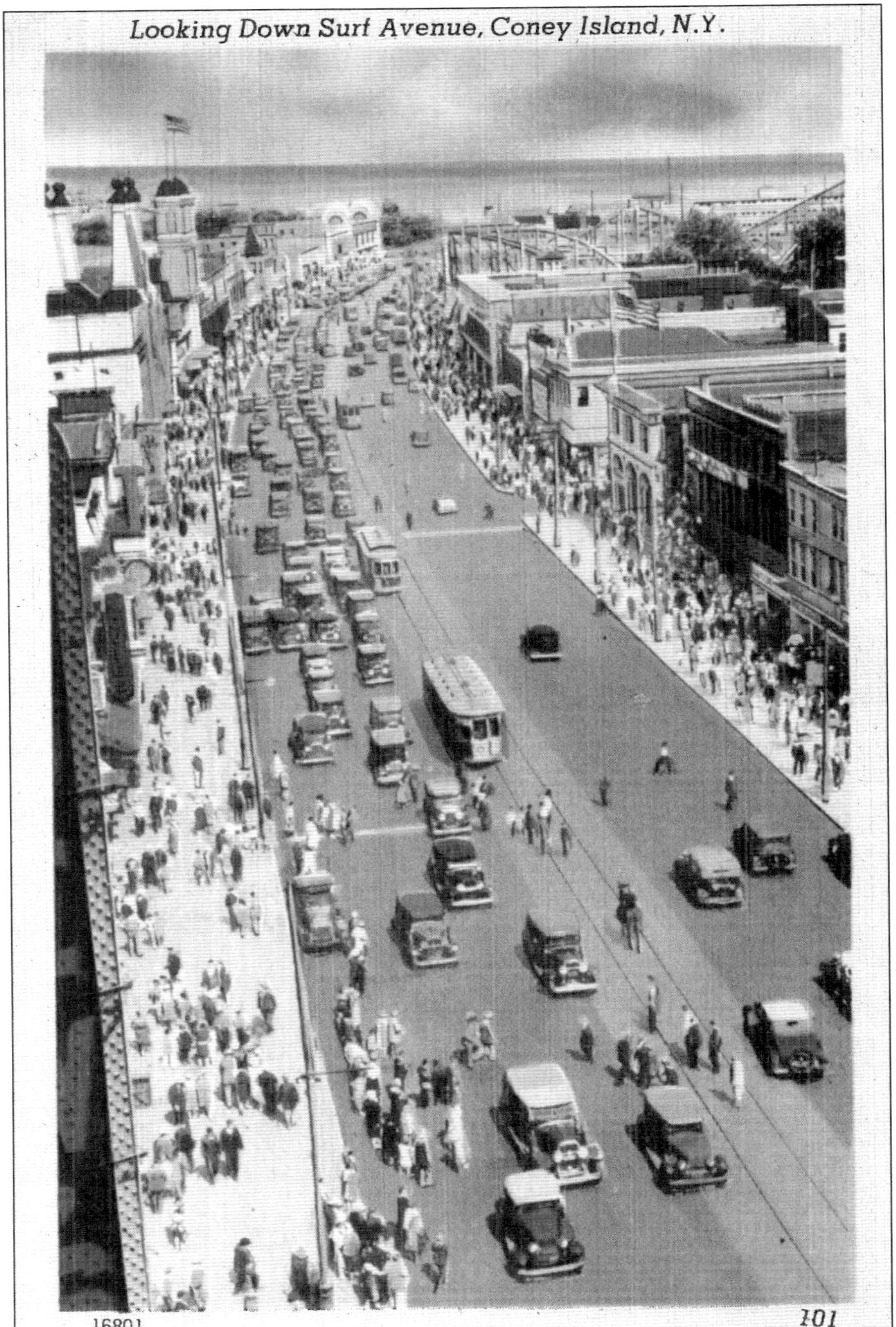

This aerial view of Surf Avenue shows the route of the annual Mermaid Parade. The parade was founded in 1983 and is organized by Coney Island USA, a nonprofit organization dedicated to "defending the honor of American popular culture." Every year on the summer solstice, hundreds of people participate in the parade and hundreds of thousands come to watch as it flows down Surf Avenue from West Twenty-first Street to West Tenth Street, then south to the Boardwalk.

Six

The Bowery

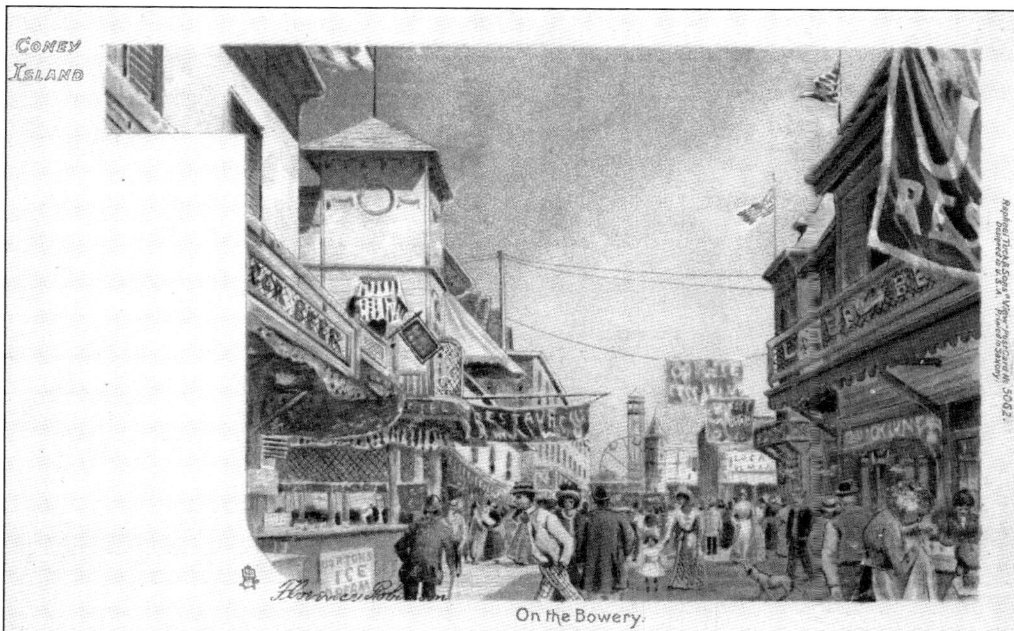

This private mailing card offers a view of the Bowery, originally named Ocean Walk Avenue. George C. Tilyou created the Bowery in the 1890s to help guide customers to his Steeplechase Park. This narrow street still exists today, but it is no longer filled with amusements, bars, restaurants, and shops.

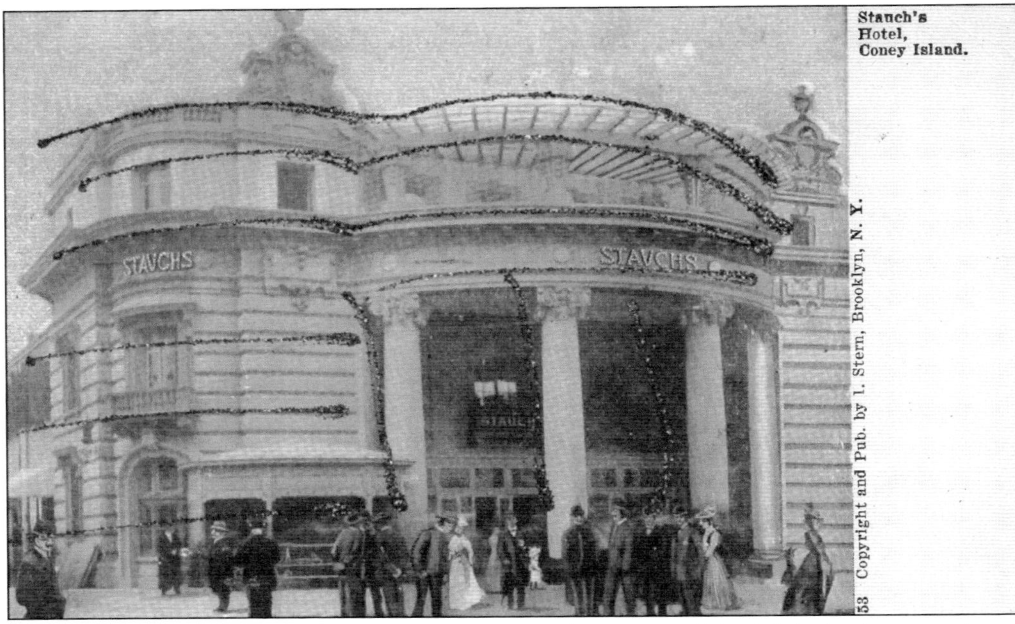

Owner Louis Stauch built Stauch's Restaurant and Dance Hall in 1904. At the time, it was considered the largest dance hall in the world. It extended from the Bowery to the beach along Stillwell Avenue. The Bowery burned several times, but each time, Stauch rebuilt.

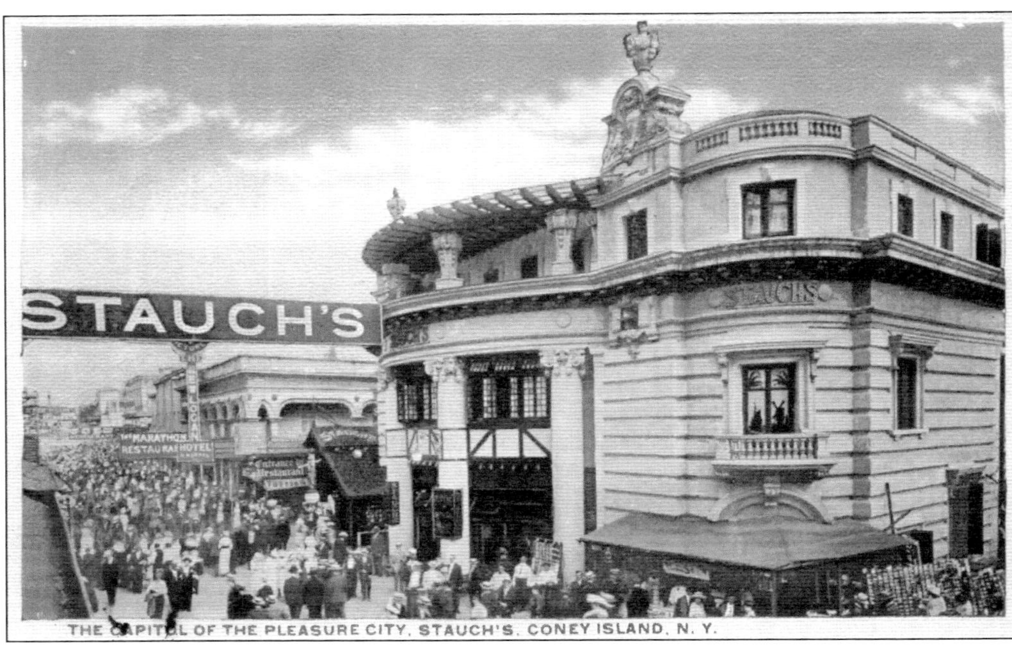

In the early 1920s, Louis Stauch claimed that he had not taken a single day away from work in 26 years. His dance hall could accommodate 1,000 couples, and the restaurant seated 5,000 people.

In 1923, Louis Stauch built a terra cotta and brick bathhouse along the Boardwalk. This postcard advertised it as the place "where the crowds go"—both the beauties and the beasts. The bathhouse building was demolished in 1992.

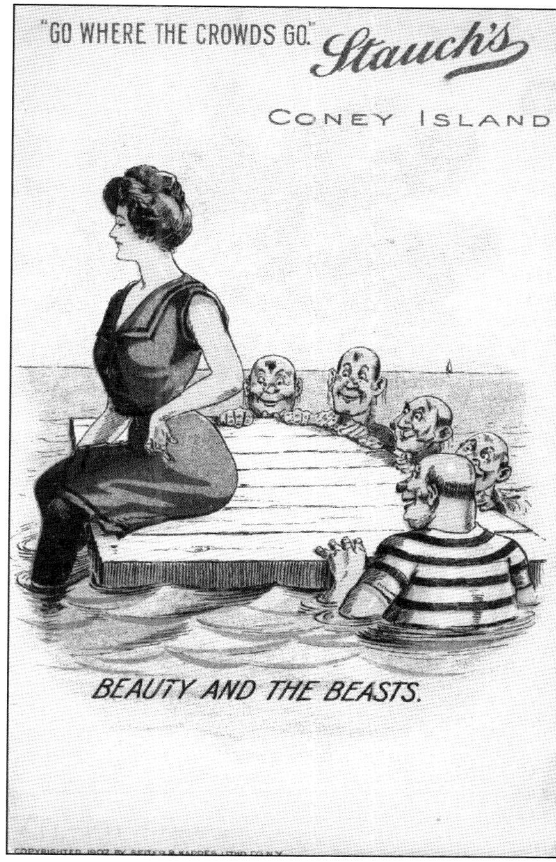

When Prohibition went into effect in the early 1920s, Louis Stauch finally sold his beloved restaurant. He died in 1929. The Bobsled roller coaster replaced Stauch's Dance Hall in 1941 after businessman Joe Bonsignore purchased the ride at the 1939 New York World's Fair and brought it to Coney Island. It was demolished in 1974.

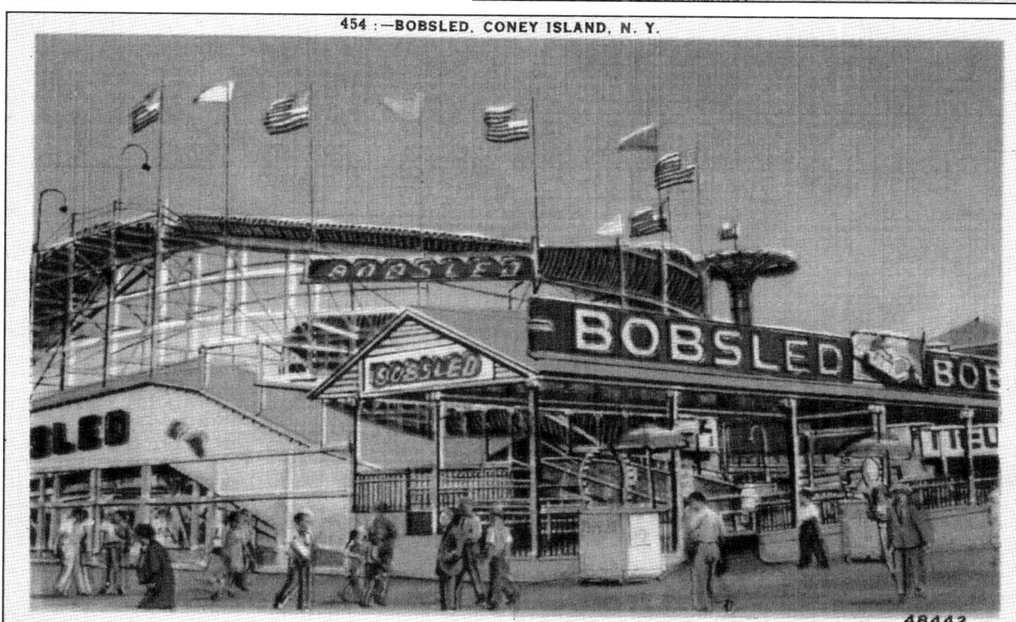

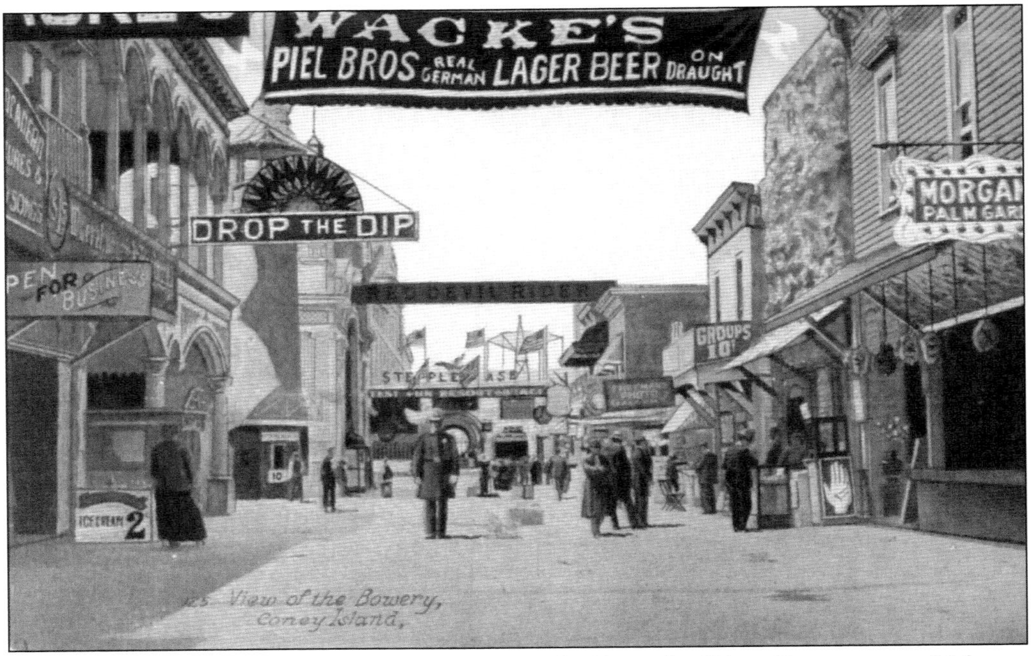

This view of the Bowery shows the entrance to the Drop the Dip roller coaster, which was moved to Luna Park in 1924 when the streets were widened on Coney Island. The Red Devil Rider, a coaster built in 1907, was located at the Bowery and West 15th Street.

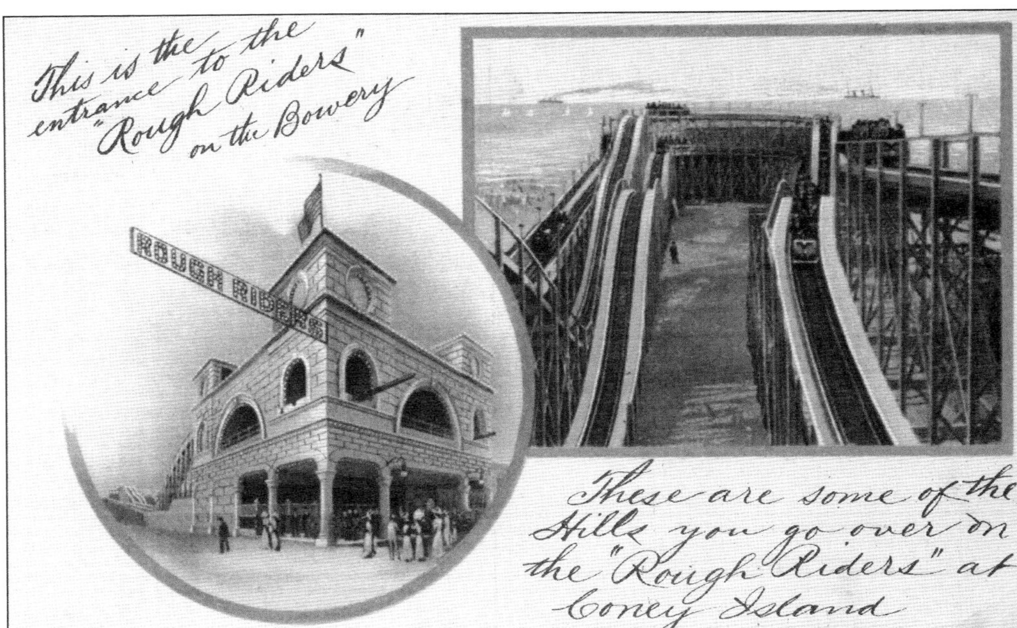

Rough Riders opened in 1907 at the corner of the Bowery Street and Jones Walk. After the ride caused a couple of deadly accidents, it was demolished in 1915.

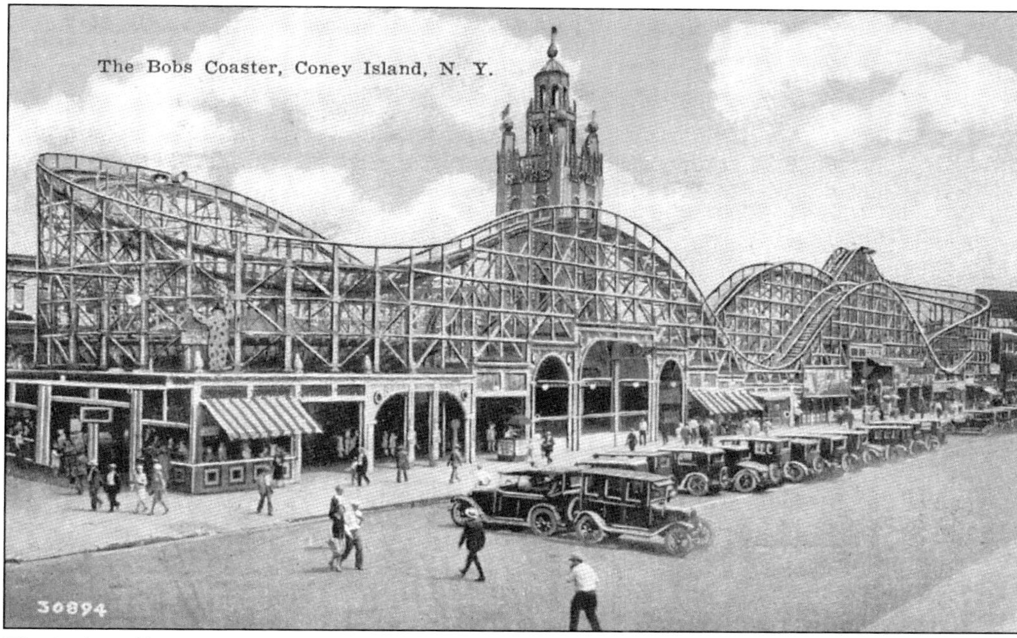

The Bobs roller coaster, built by the L.A. Thompson Company in 1926, was located at Stillwell Avenue and the Bowery on a difficult, narrow lot that was only 70 feet at its widest and tapered to only 50 feet. It was a hybrid coaster with a wooden track and a steel structure, and it featured a large tower in the middle. It opened on Memorial Day in 1926.

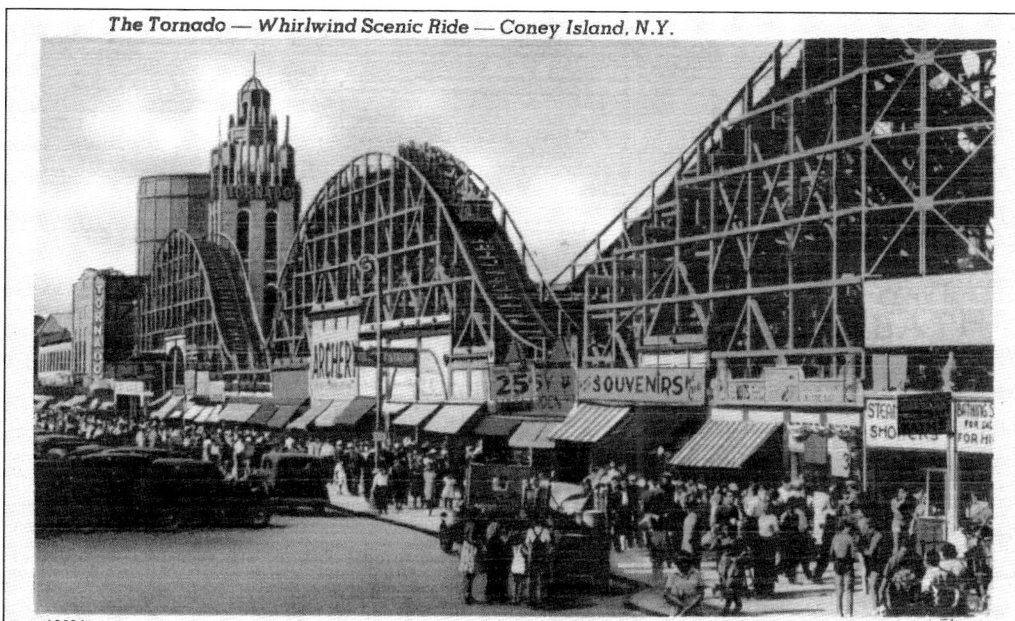

The Bobs roller coaster, later renamed the Tornado, was demolished in 1978 after it was heavily damaged by arson.

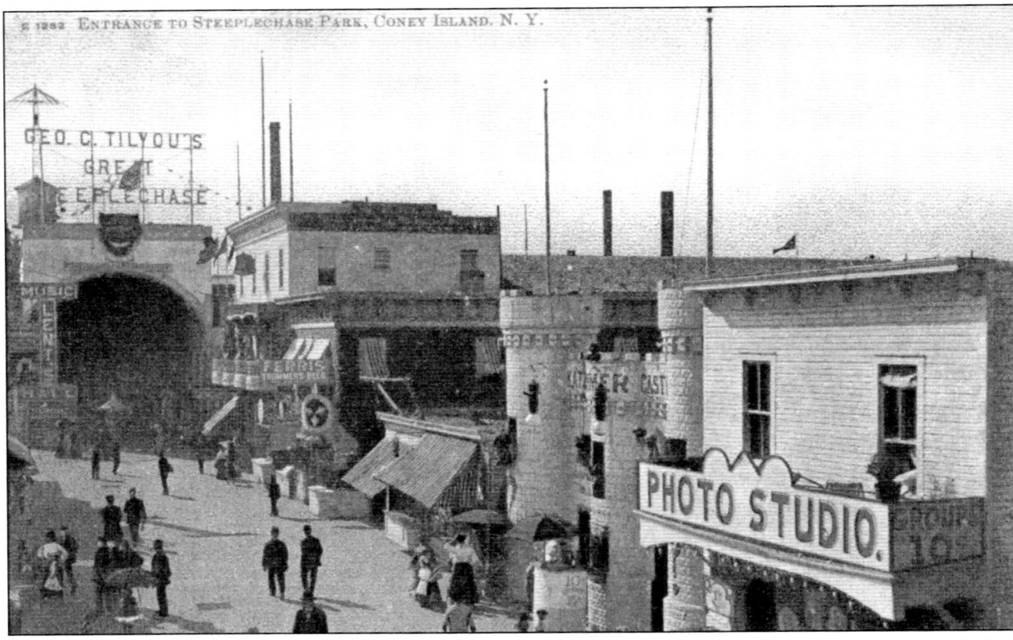

The Steeplechase Park entrance on the Bowery was surrounded by various concessions, including one of the ever-popular photography studios. For 10¢, groups could pose on different stage sets, and the photographer would use the images to create real-photo postcards—personalized souvenirs that could be mailed home.

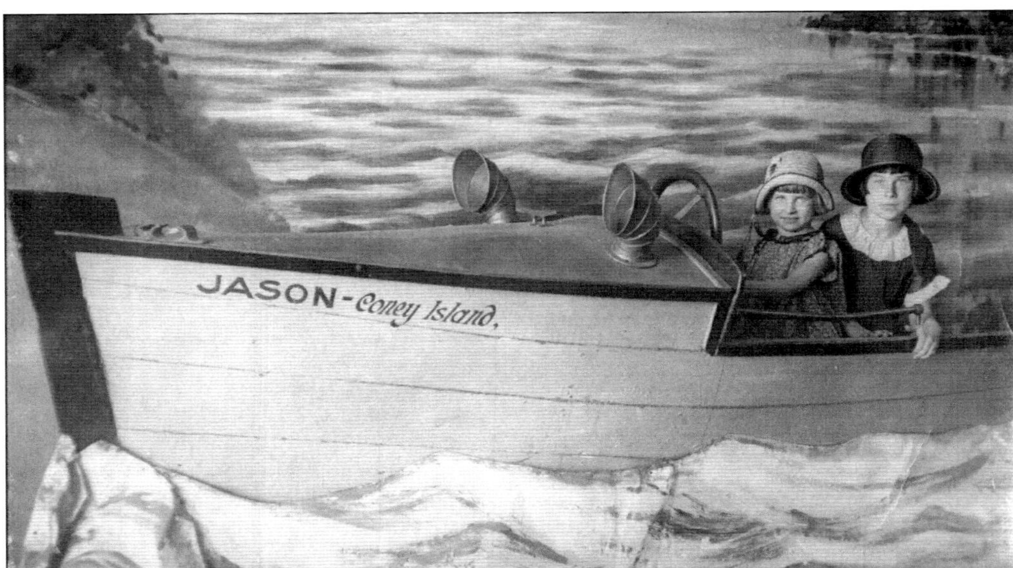

Real-photo postcards contain photographs developed by a professional photographer on thick paper with postal markings. This enable senders to write on the cards, which could then be stamped and mailed. Each card is unique, even if the backdrop is repeated. Real-photo postcards were very popular in the first two decades of the 20th century, a time known as the Golden Era of postcards.

Although most families owned cameras by 1910, photographs were still a novelty, and the thrill of posing for your own postcard to send to friends and family was irresistible. The backdrops varied, but the most popular in Coney Island featured boats, trains, and automobiles.

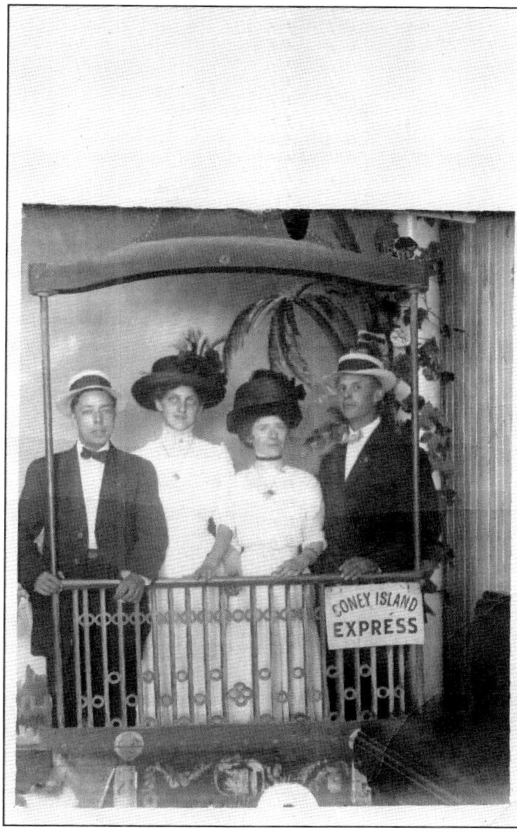

Real-photo postcards could be viewed as a form of social media that existed 100 years before the term itself. The popularity of real-photo postcards waned around the time of World War I. Other factors that contributed to the cards' demise included the doubling of postal rates for mailing postcards and increased usage of the telephone to communicate with family and friends.

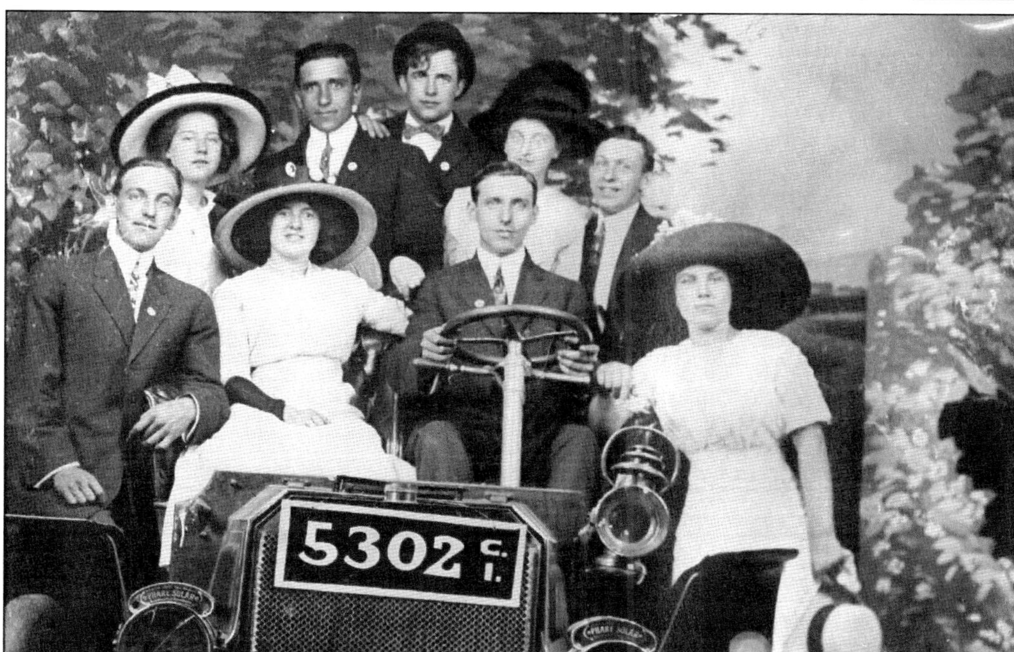

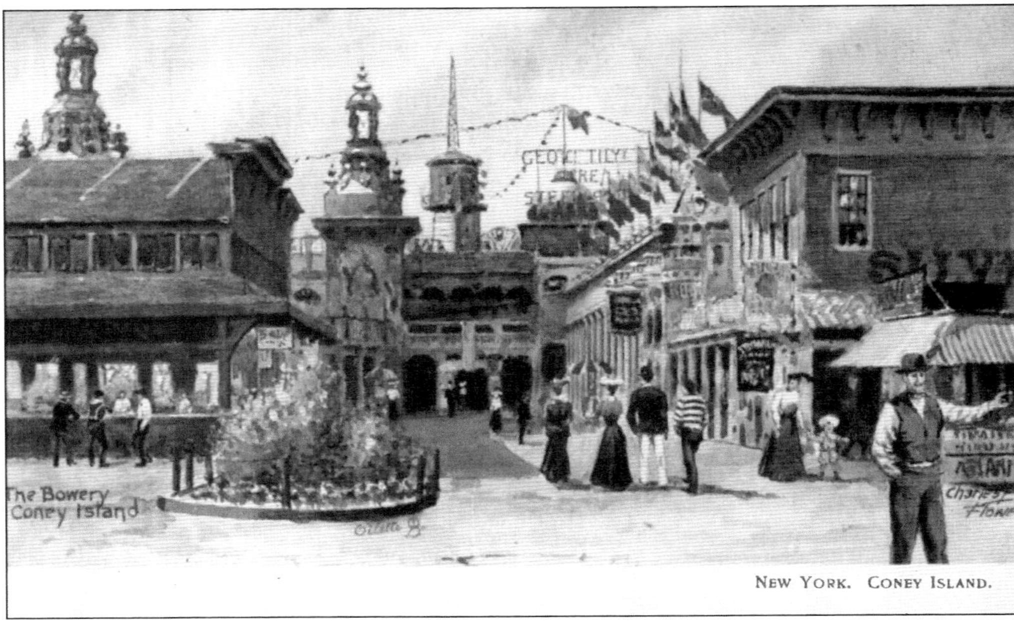

This painting by Charles E. Flowers was featured as part of the Coney Island postcard series printed by Raphael Tuck & Sons in 1905. The painter would have been facing west, and a Steeplechase Park sign rises above the buildings in the center background.

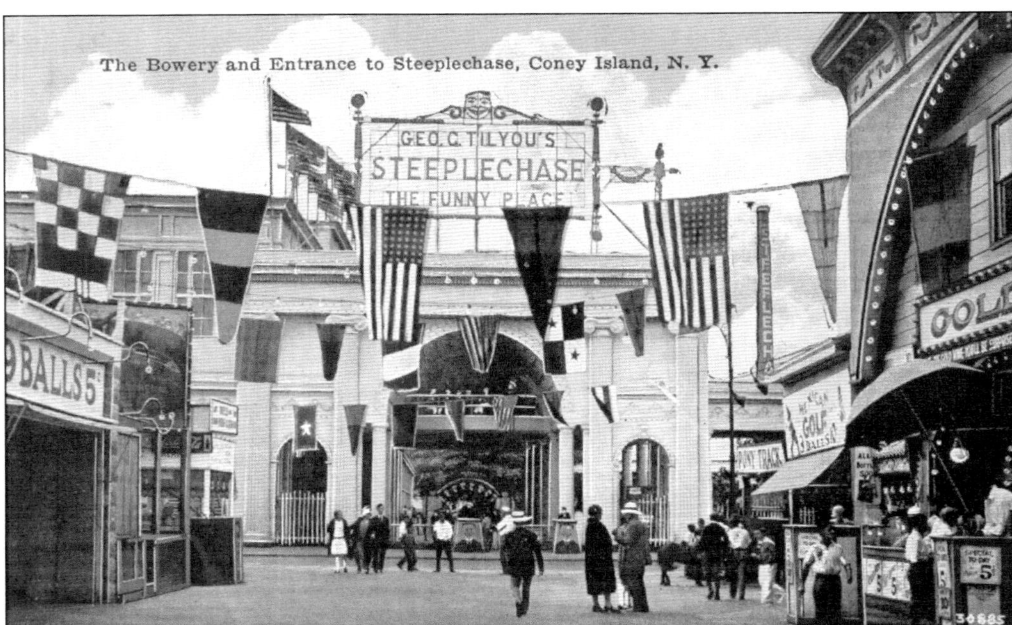

A later view of the same Bowery entrance to Steeplechase Park shows flags hanging across the street and various concessions flanking either side of the walkway.

Seven

The Beach and Boardwalk

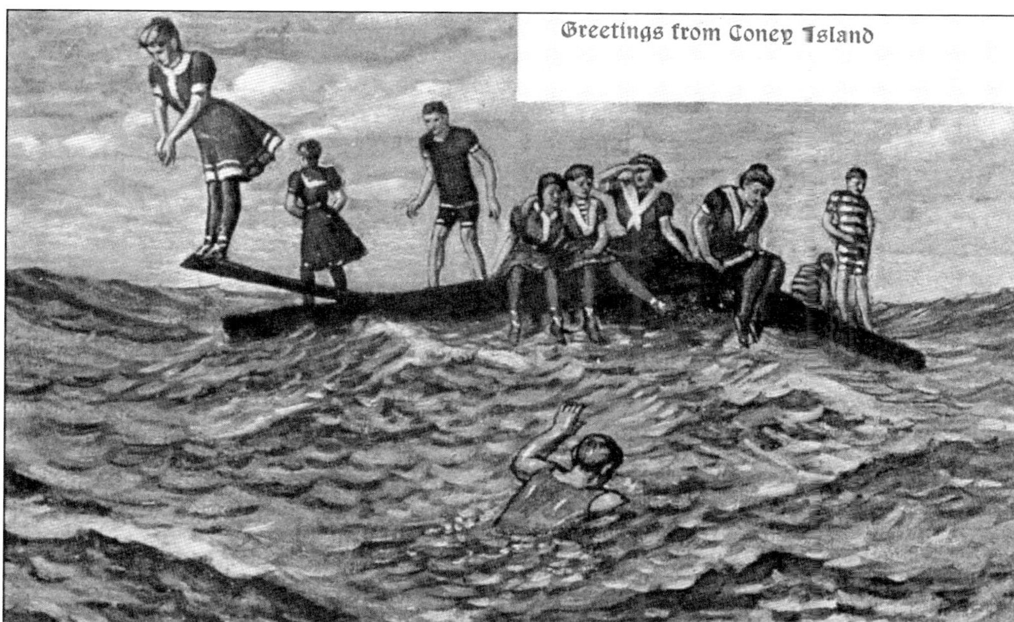

This undivided-back postcard, entitled "Greetings from Coney Island," was published by Arthur A. Martin of New York. It shows the bathing attire that people wore at a time when mixed bathing had only recently become socially acceptable.

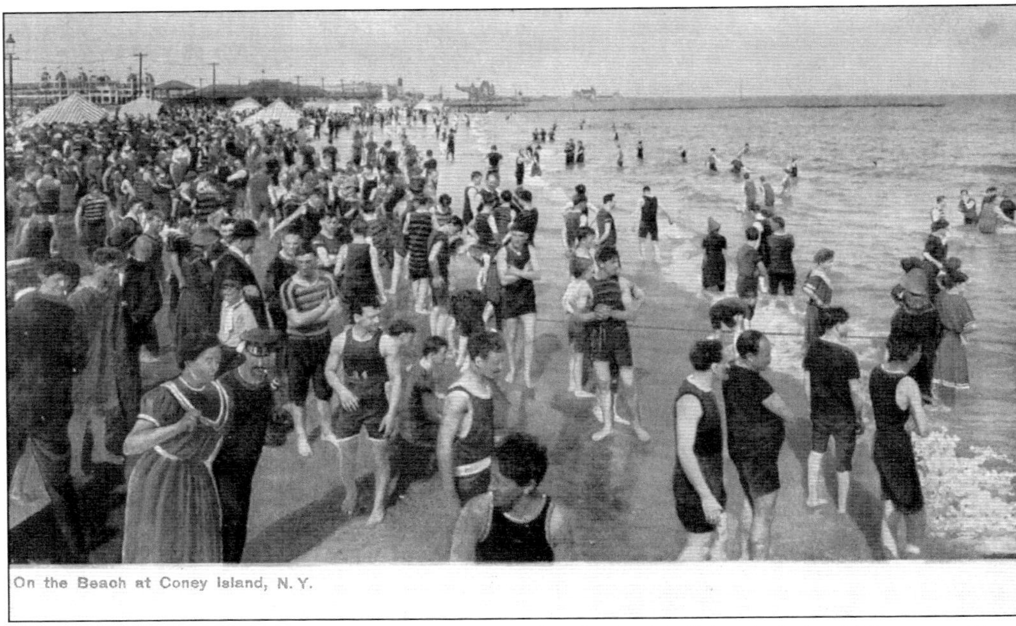

The Lenape Indians that once inhabited Coney Island called it "Narrioch," which means "land without shadows." The position of the beach and lack of significant obstructions means the entire beach is in sunlight virtually all day.

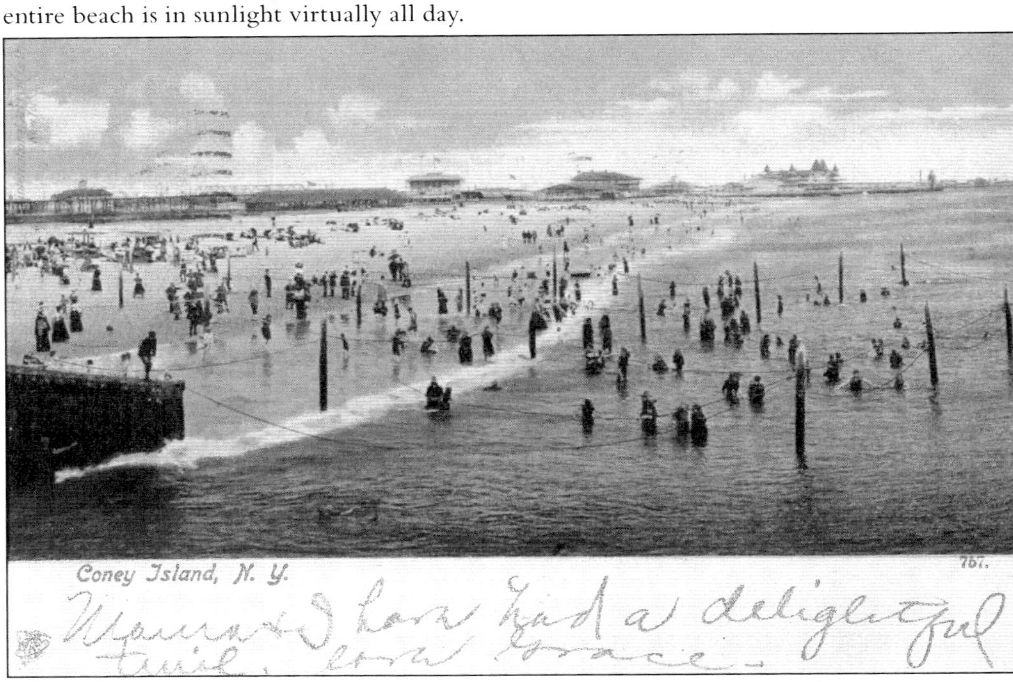

Swimming areas were designated with ropes in 1906 to keep swimmers safe. In 1903, Bernarr Macfadden, known as the "Father of Physical Culture," founded the Coney Island Polar Bear Club, which is still active today. As the oldest winter bathing organization in the United States, the group celebrates an annual tradition of taking an ice-cold dip in the Atlantic Ocean on New Year's Day.

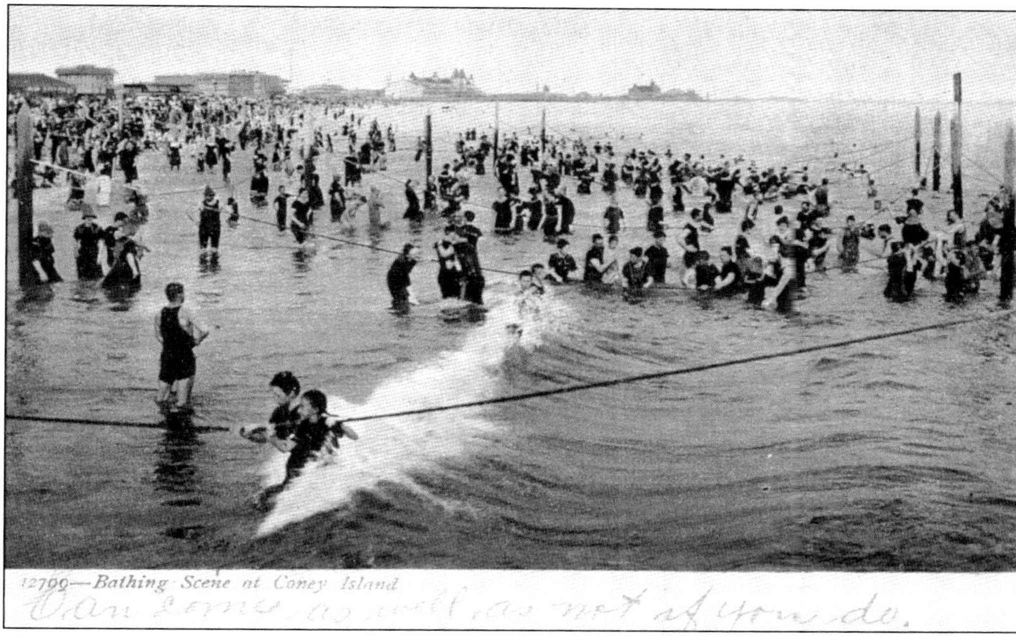

The swimming costumes worn by women before 1900 consisted of a pair of pantaloons, a corset, a blouse, and a jacket—often made of wool. When these clothes got wet, they could weigh as much as 10 to 15 pounds. In the first decade of the 20th century, women's swimming outfits gradually evolved to dark-colored dresses worn with stockings. Police captain Byron R. Sackett assigned a squad of policewomen to deal solely with the issue of improper beach attire. In 1918, when women dared to remove their stockings on the beach, they were publicly humiliated and escorted out of the area.

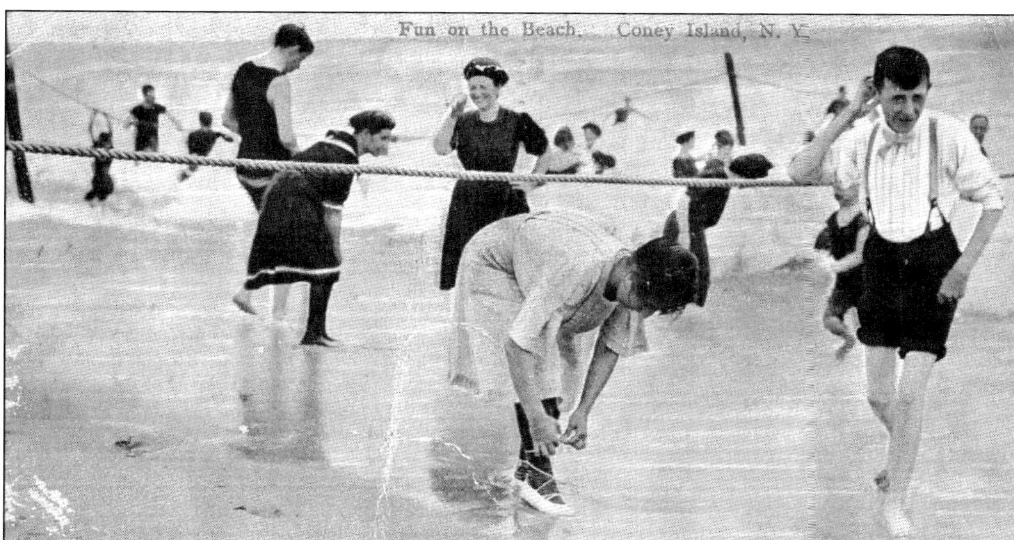

Beach bathing attire changed drastically over the course of the 20th century. In 1907, men could not expose their chests, and women wore dresses and stockings with shoes. In Coney Island in the early 1930s, men were arrested and given jail time for appearing on the beach without shirts, but by the end of the decade, men were stripping down to short pants.

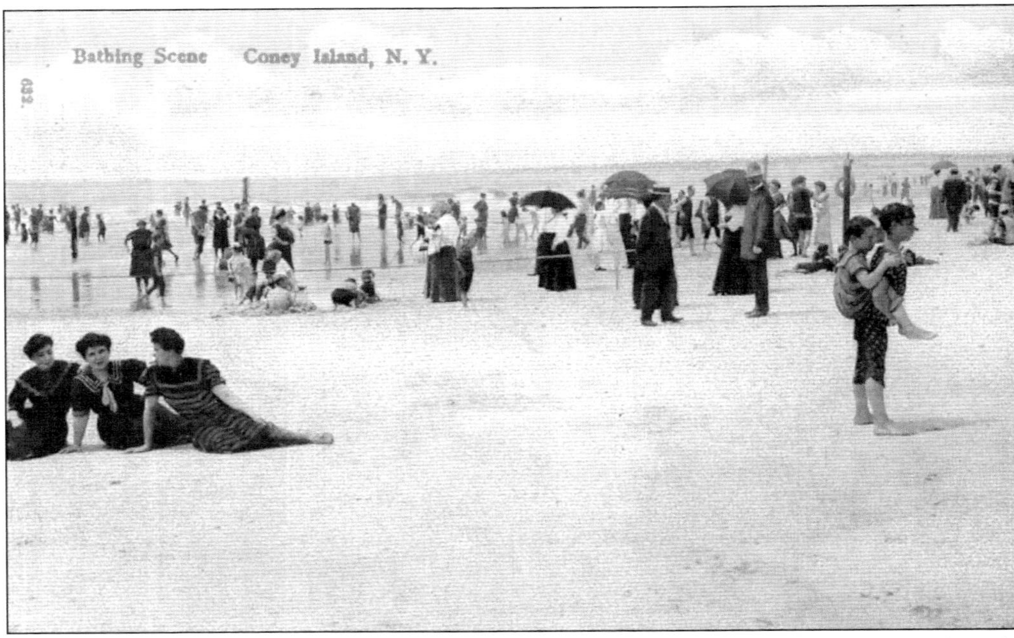

During the first half of the 20th century, Coney Island had it all: the beach and pier, the rides and amusements, and the sun and surf. The beaches were packed to capacity during Coney Island's heyday.

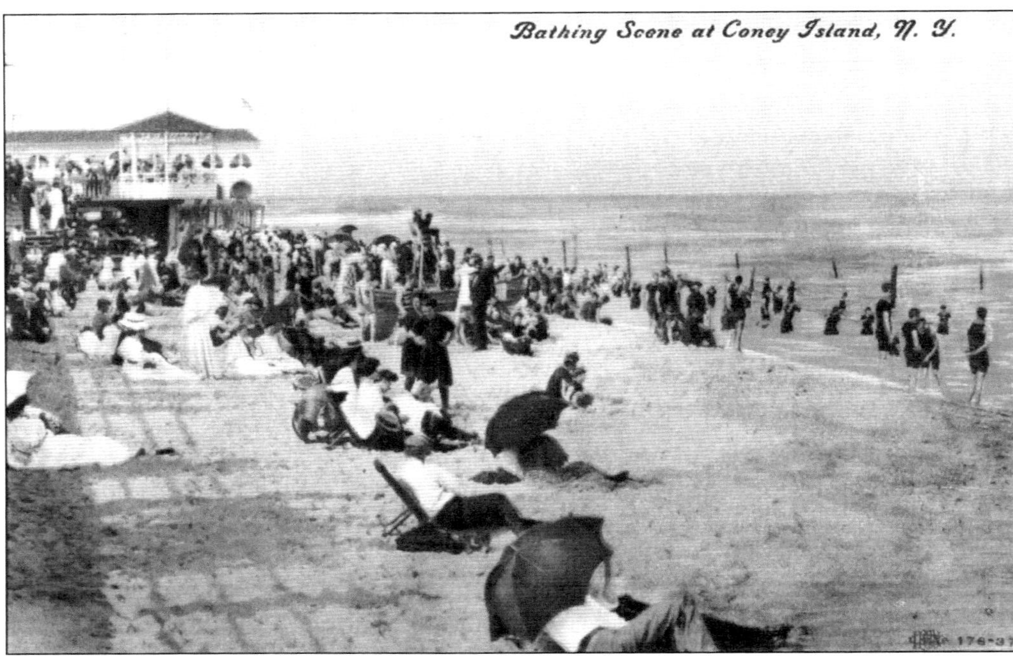

On the back on this postcard, someone named Percy wrote, "An eighteen year old girl was drowned at this Beach, day before yesterday. One of the roomers saw it. The Life Savers recovered the body in a few minutes, and everything was done to revive her, but all to no purpose. Mrs. Edwards says the girl's Mother was perfectly frantic with grief."

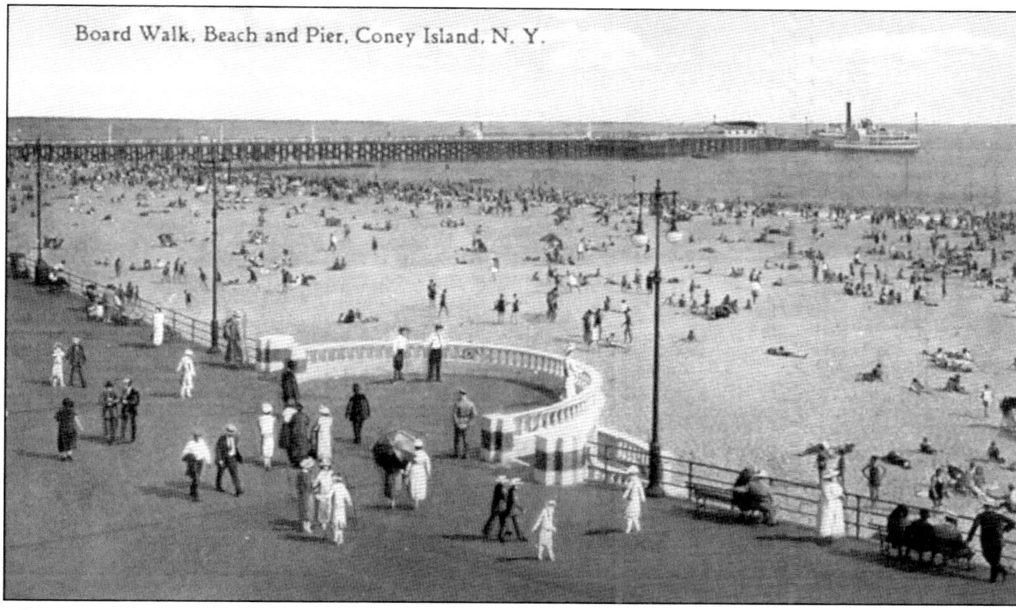

The Riegelmann Boardwalk, which the city built in 1923 along the southern shore of Coney Island, was named for Brooklyn borough president Edward J. Riegelmann, who worked hard to make sure that all Coney Island visitors had public access to the beach. Most refer to it simply as the Coney Island Boardwalk. The Boardwalk stretches for 2.51 miles from West Thirty-seventh Street, at the border of Coney Island and Sea Gate, east through Brighton Beach to the beginning of Manhattan Beach.

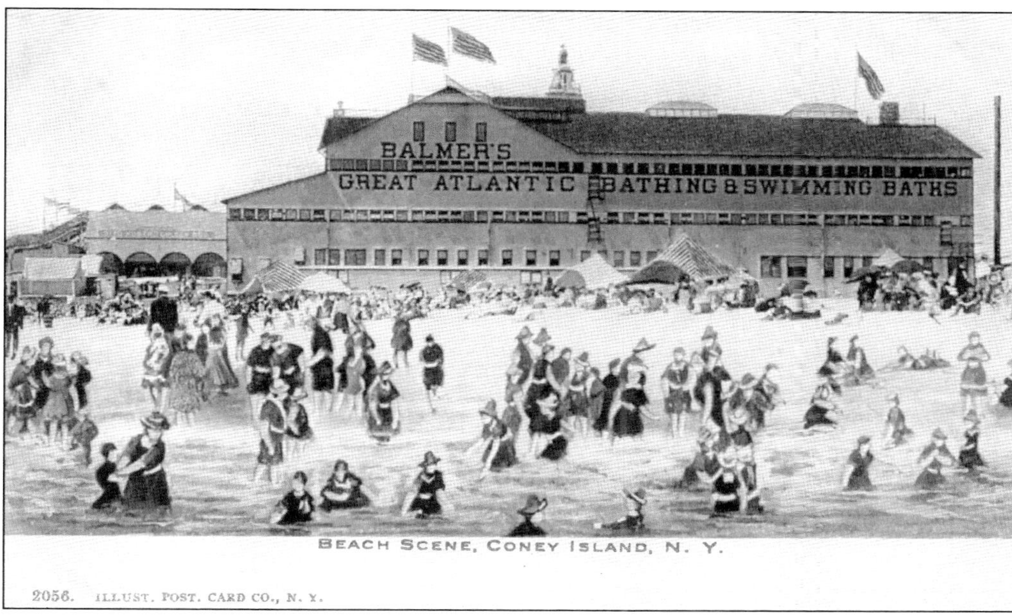

Balmer's Great Atlantic Swimming Baths were destroyed in the Dreamland fire of 1911. Over 40 bathhouses existed on Coney Island. Before the city built the Boardwalk in 1923, the beach was private, and the only way to gain access was to pay admission at a bathhouse. Some of the fancier bathhouses had restaurants and saltwater swimming pools.

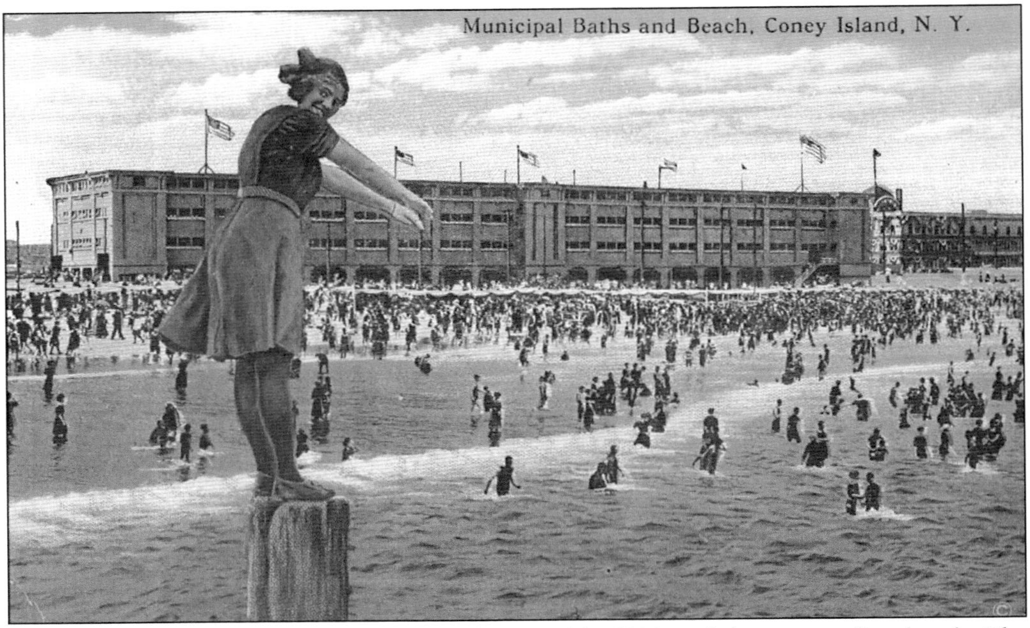

This card shows the municipal baths, which opened in 1911, and the surrounding beach. The public bathhouse had lockers and showers and was the only bathhouse that did not charge an admission fee. The beach is now open to all without restriction.

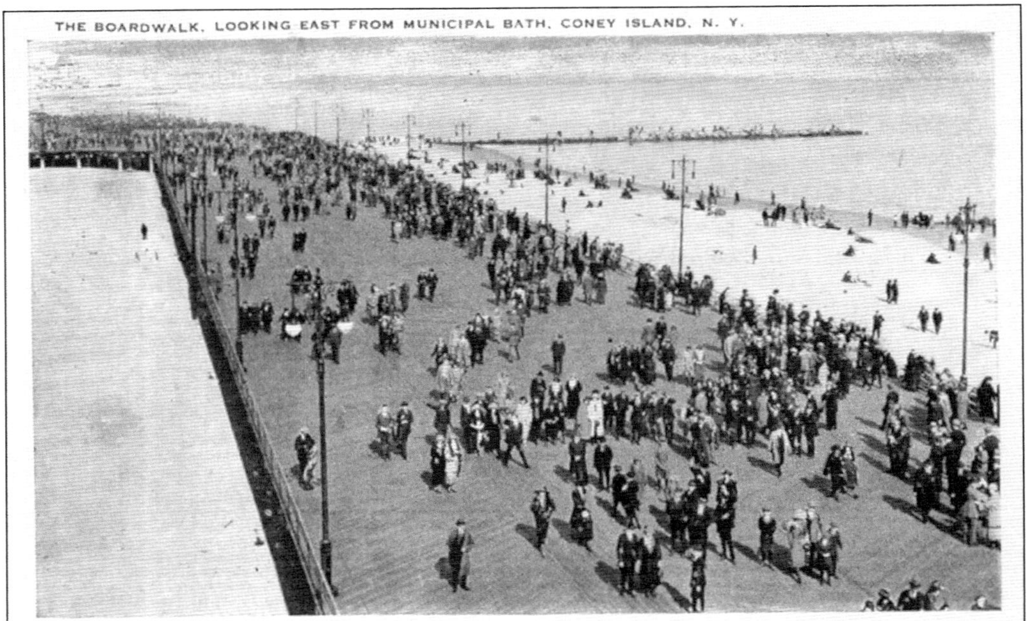

This card shows an aerial view looking east from the municipal baths as crowds stroll along the Boardwalk.

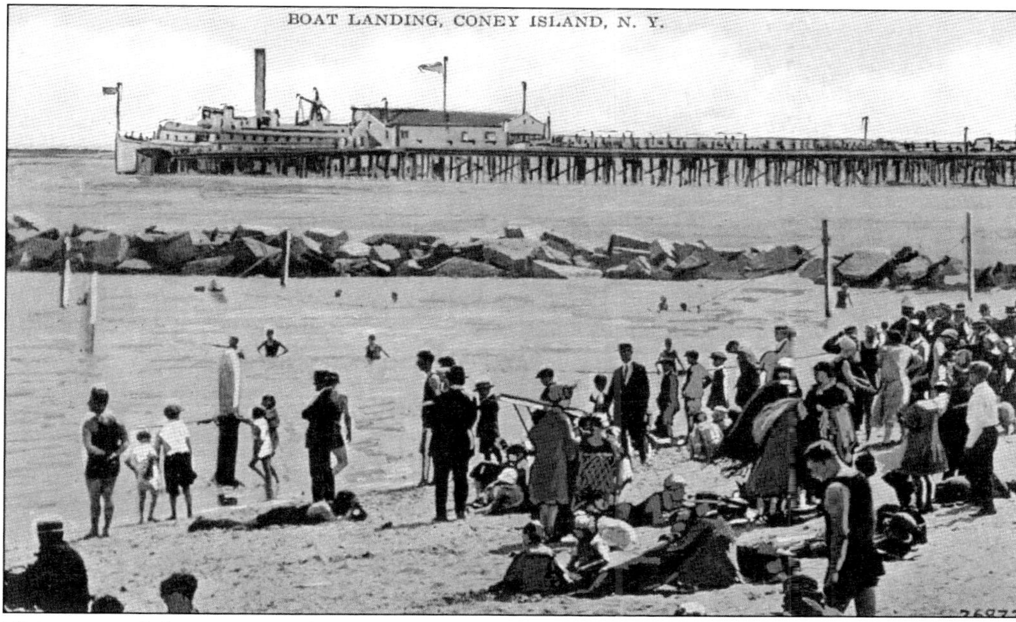

This postcard shows a typical summer day at Coney Island with a crowd on the beach and in the designated swimming area of the ocean. The steamboat docked at the pier in the background likely brought more visitors to enjoy the day at the beach.

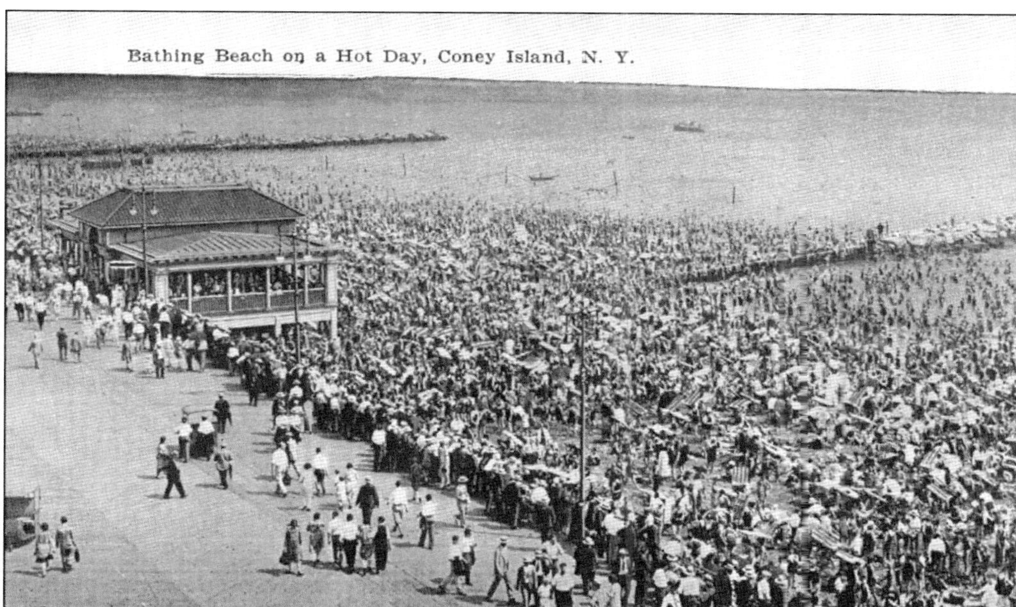

This postcard, sent in 1931, claims that "the beautiful beach at Coney Island is now long enough and wide enough to accommodate almost the entire population of New York at one time." Numerous bathing houses with unlimited facilities were located along the beachfront. After an exhilarating dip in the ocean, the sun-heated sand could be a welcome haven for swimmers.

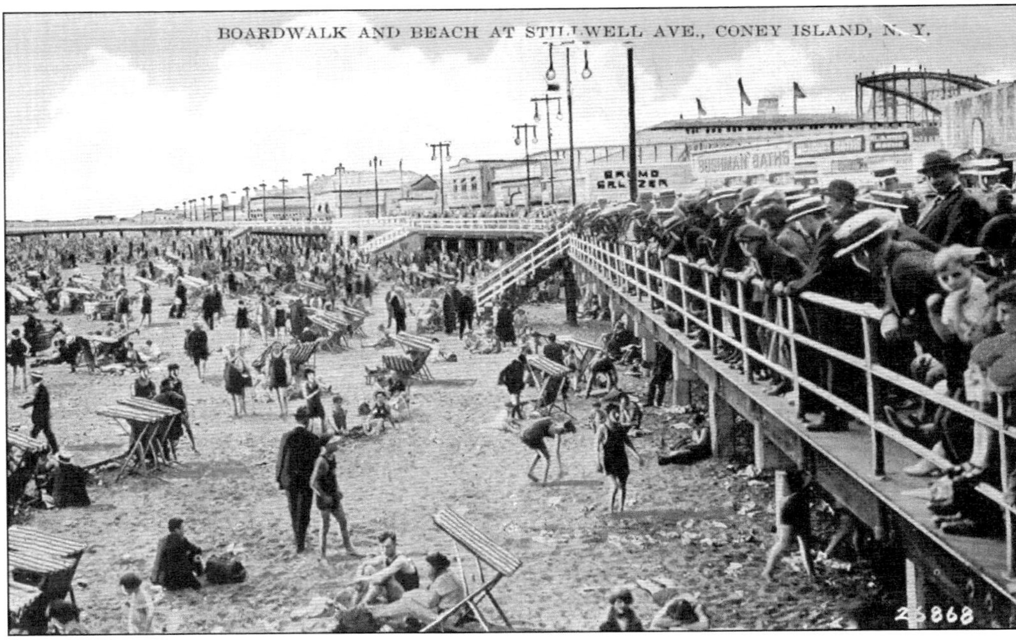

In this postcard, the Boardwalk along the beach at Stillwell Avenue is packed with folks ready for fun. The elevated Boardwalk was built with stylish lighting, railings, benches, and stairs.

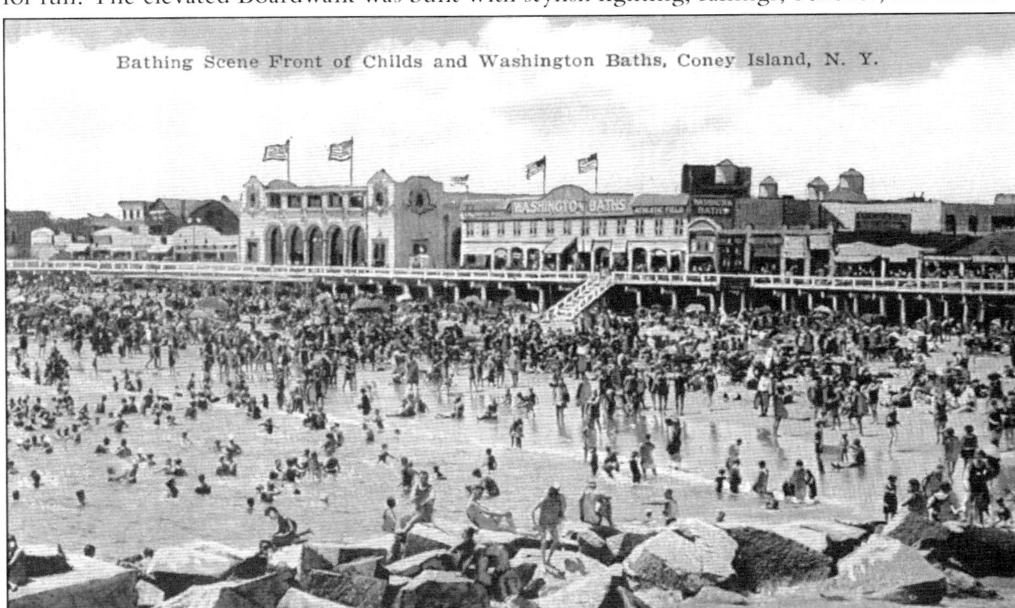

This postcard features the scene in front of Childs Restaurant and the Washington Baths. During the winter of 1923–1924, Surf Avenue and the Bowery were widened to create better access for firefighters. The loss of 25 feet of property on each side of Surf Avenue—and a similar amount on the Bowery—required the demolition of many businesses. Stauch's Restaurant and Dance Hall and Nathan's Famous rebuilt on the same sites, while Childs found a new home on the Boardwalk.

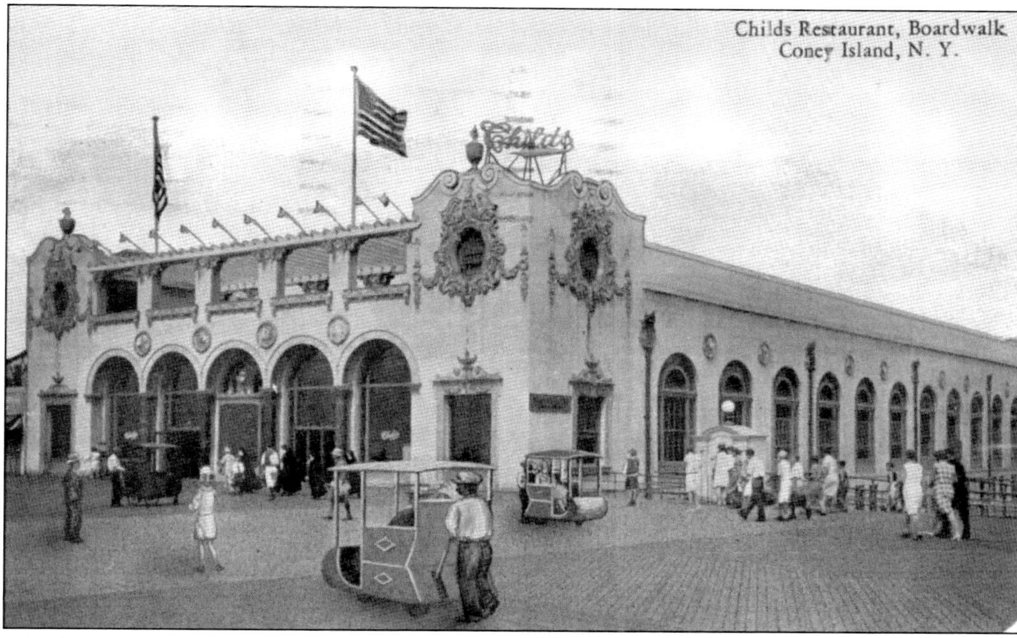

The firm of Dennison and Hirons built Childs Restaurant, located at Twenty-first Street and the Boardwalk, in 1923. This beautiful terra cotta building is adorned with sea creatures in the molding and roundels. The restaurant closed in 1947, but the building is still intact and could potentially be preserved.

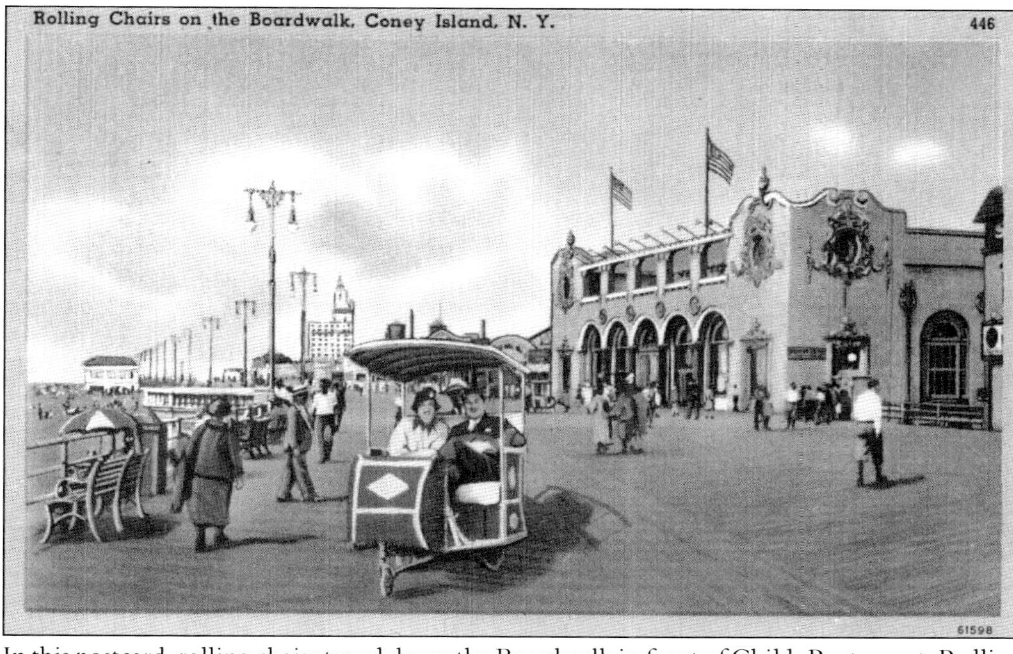

In this postcard, rolling chairs travel down the Boardwalk in front of Childs Restaurant. Rolling chairs first appeared on the Boardwalk in 1923. The Ocean Rolling Chair Company operated these two-passenger covered chairs on wheels until the mid-1960s.

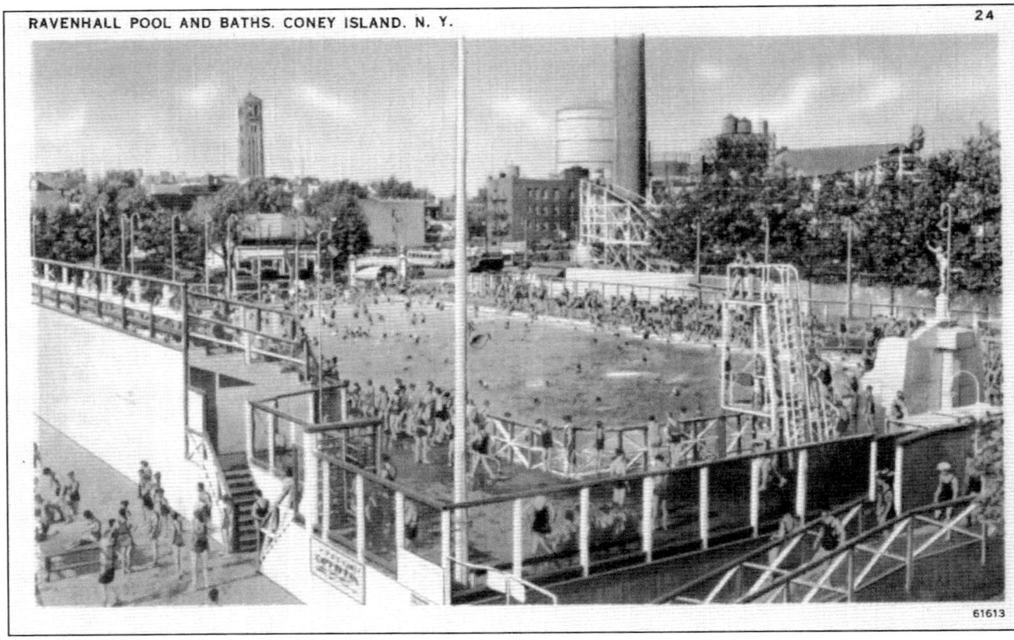

Ravenhall Pool and Baths opened in 1867 as a hotel and expanded into a large resort until it was destroyed by fire in 1963. It occupied the entire block at West Nineteenth Street between Surf Avenue and the Boardwalk, where the Abe Stark Ice Rink is now located. The saltwater Ravenhall pool was the largest in Coney Island and had four diving boards that were named Jack, Queen, King, and Ace, based on their height.

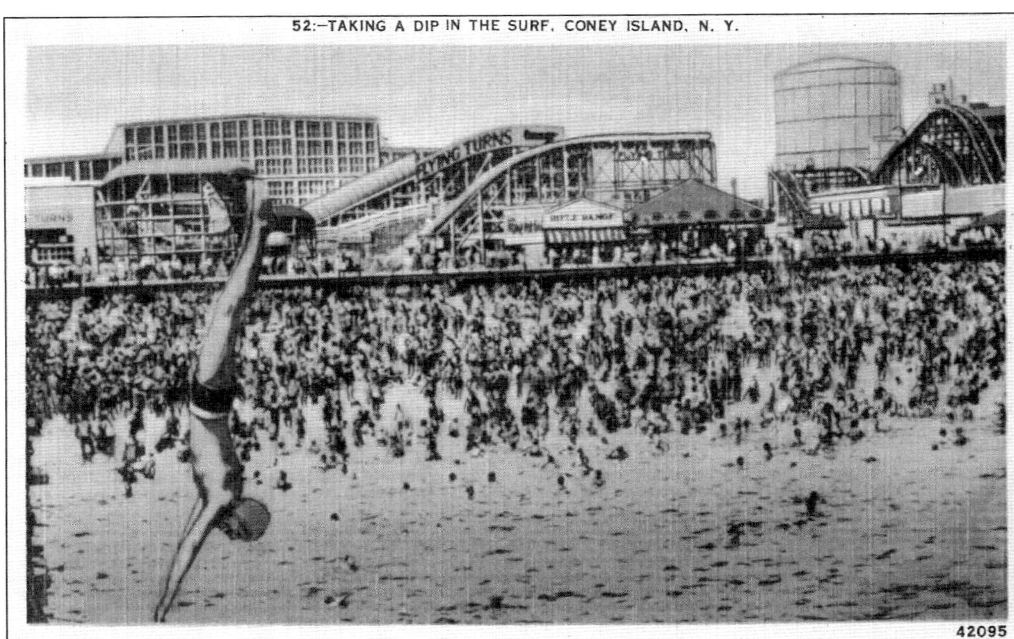

The beach stayed crowded for most of the summer. The Flying Turns coaster, which came to the pier in 1934, is visible in the background; five years later, it was destroyed by fire.

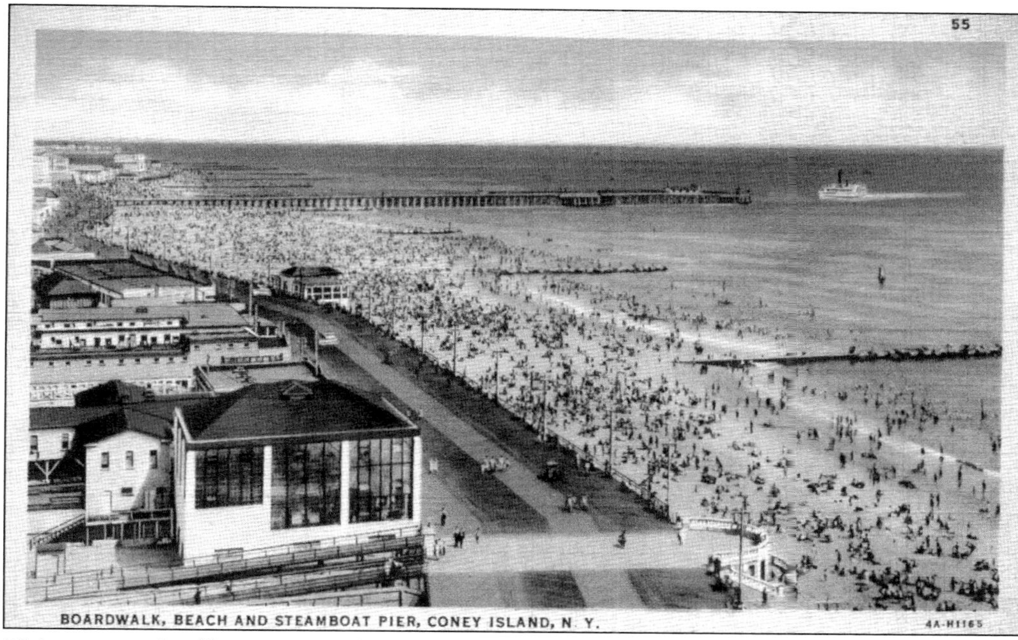

This postcard offers an aerial view of the boardwalk, beach, and steamboat pier at Coney Island.

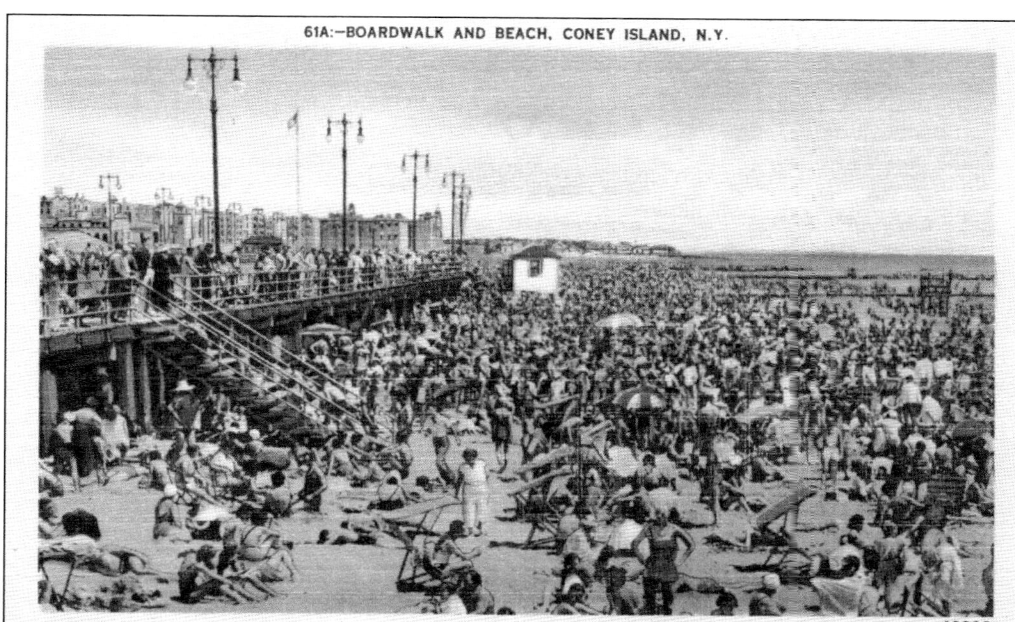

This "linen" postcard shows the size of the crowds that flocked to the beach at Coney Island to escape the summer heat.

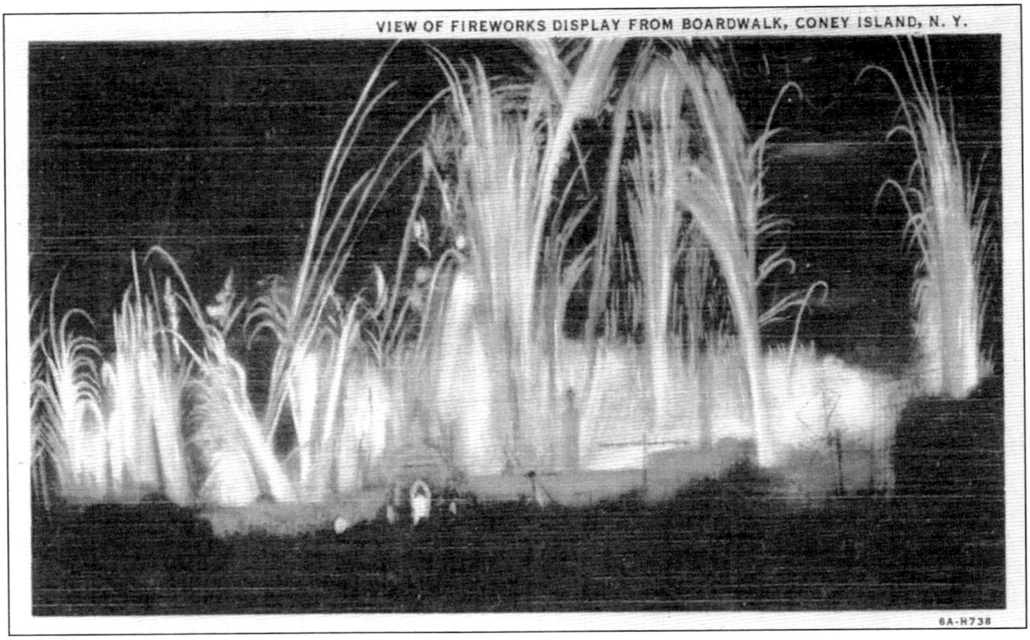

Fireworks have long been a part of the beach and boardwalk experience, and today's visitors can still see plenty of fireworks at Coney Island. There are regular fireworks displays every Friday night during the summer, on the Fourth of July, and after Brooklyn Cyclones home games.

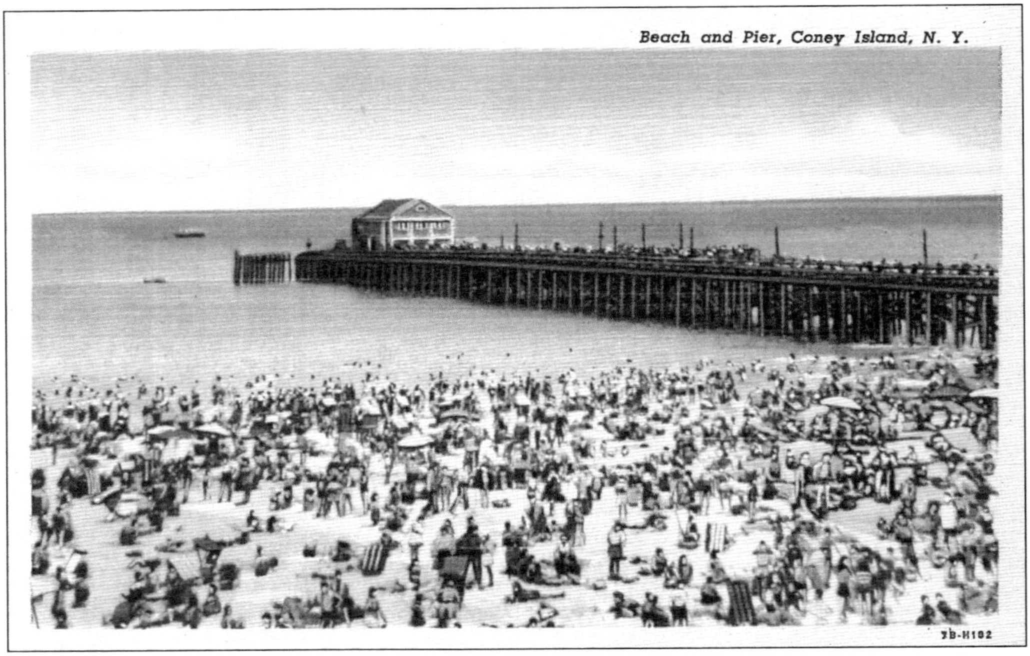

As if preserving the past is not hard enough, Coney Island sustained much damage during Superstorm Sandy on October 29, 2012. Fortunately, Coney Island's Steeplechase Pier reopened about a year after it was seriously damaged.

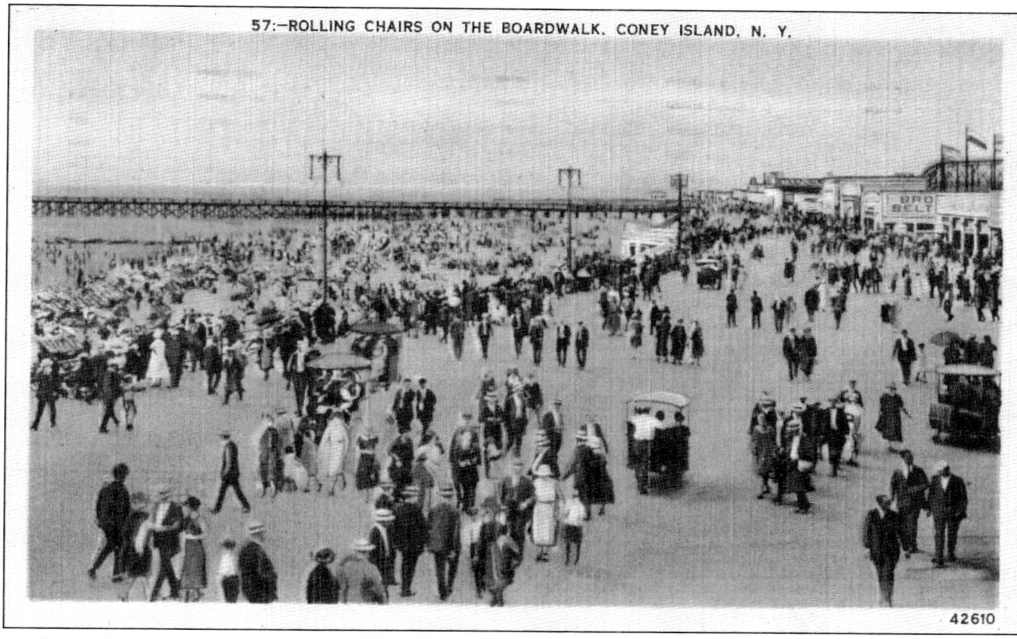

Rolling chairs, a fixture on the Boardwalk in the early 1900s, were used to increase the ease of transportation along the shoreline.

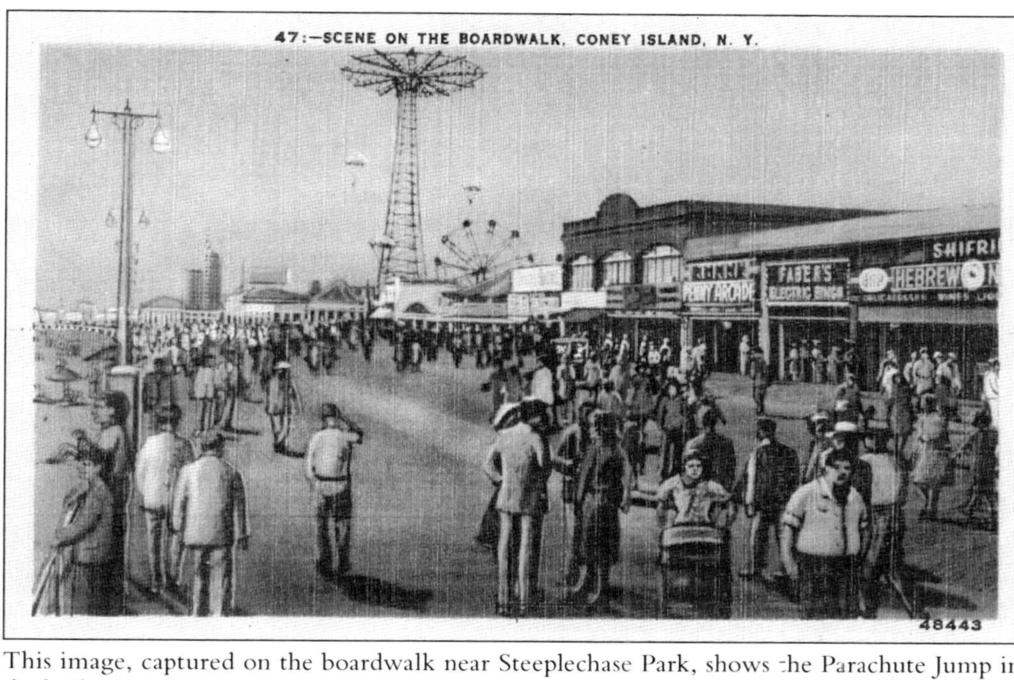

This image, captured on the boardwalk near Steeplechase Park, shows the Parachute Jump in the background.

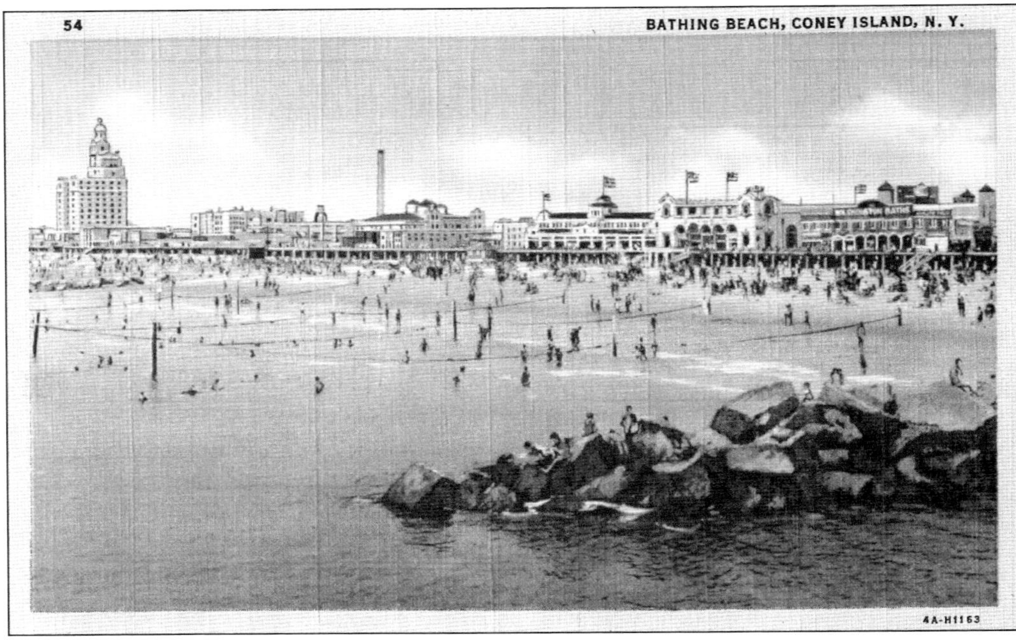

This card shows the Coney Island shoreline from the Half Moon Hotel to Washington Baths. The buildings on the Coney shoreline were low enough that they did not block the view for those brave enough to open their eyes while enjoying the Wonder Wheel, the Parachute Jump, or one of Coney Island's many roller coasters.

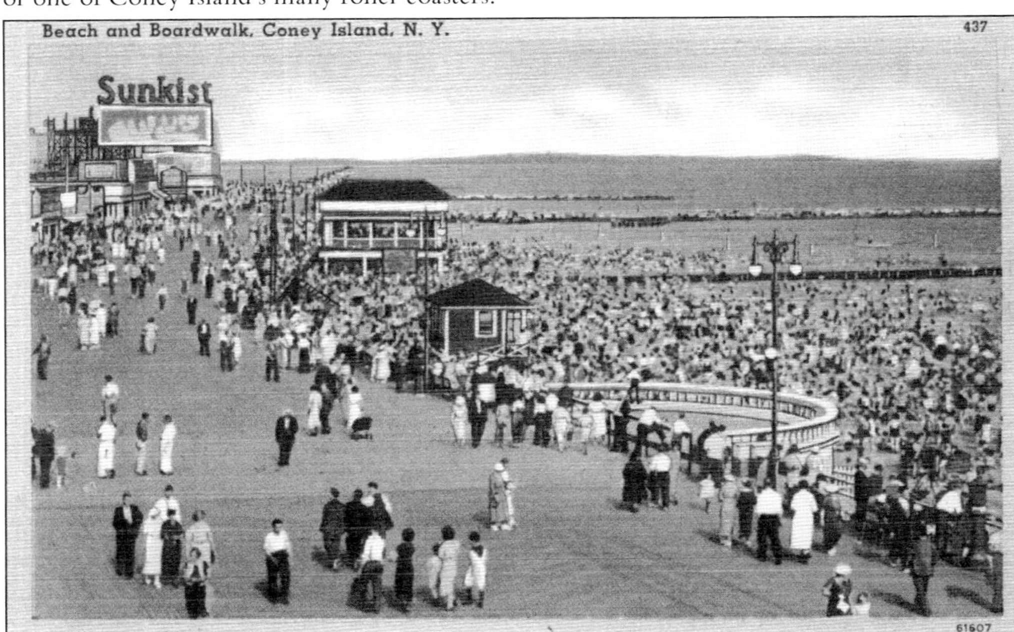

Joseph Heller, author of *Catch-22*, grew up in Coney Island in the 1920s and 1930s. In his 1999 autobiography, *Now and Then: From Coney Island to Here*, Heller says, "Coney Island still presents a Boardwalk that seemed then, and probably still does, the longest, widest, and most splendid boardwalk in the whole world."

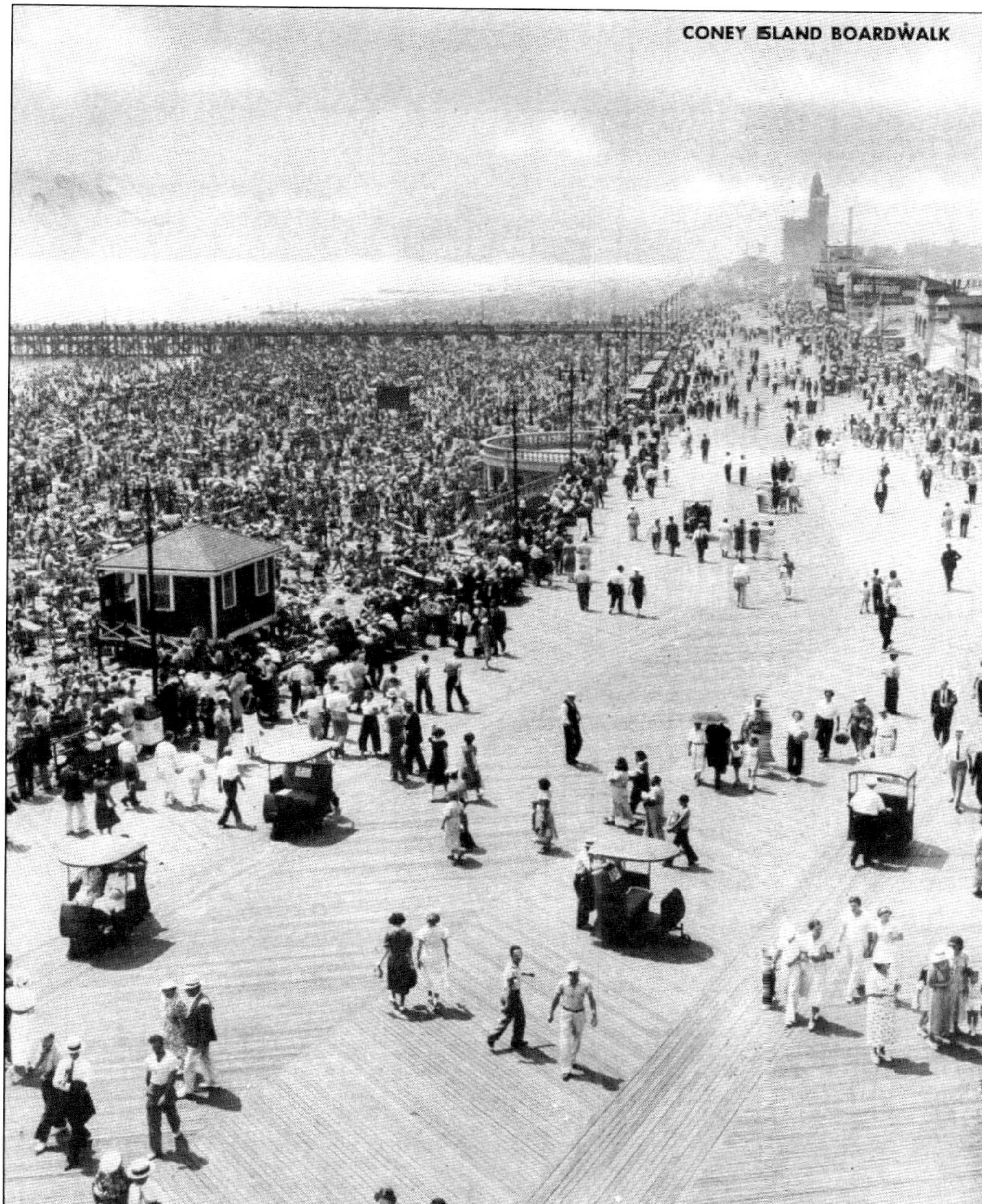

This jumbo postcard, which is about three times the size of a traditional one, shows the Coney Island Boardwalk, which is 80 feet wide and 2.5 miles long, with rolling chairs traveling down the boards and the Half Moon Hotel in the background. The Steeplechase Pier is also in the background, and the beach teems with thousands of visitors.

Halt Moon Hotel on the Boardwalk, Coney Island, N.Y.

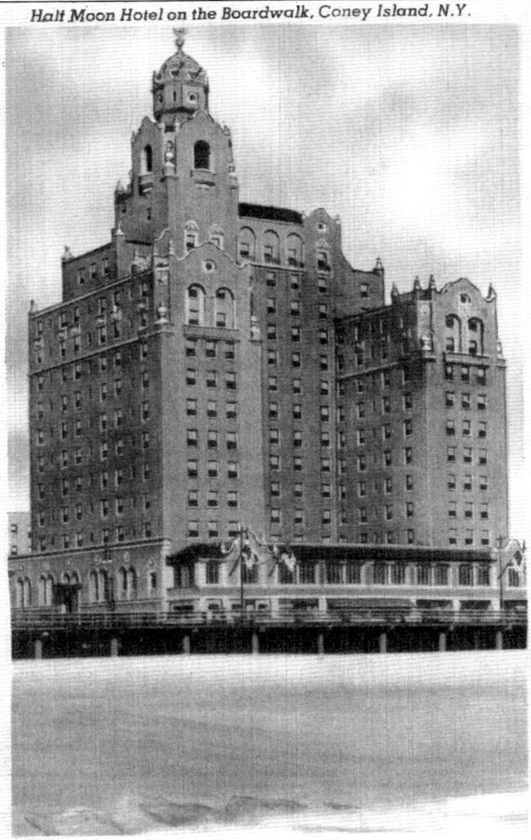

The 14-story Half Moon Hotel opened on May 5, 1927, on the Boardwalk at West Twenty-ninth Street. Its builders placed it on the outer fringe of the amusement area with the idea that the Boardwalk between the hotel and Stillwell Avenue would fill in with other luxury establishments. However, the Great Depression befell the country in the 1930s, and this expected development never happened.

The Half Moon Hotel gained notoriety in November 1941 when gangster-turned-informant Abe "Kid Twist" Reles jumped, fell, or was pushed to his death from a sixth-floor window. He was being held in protective custody until he could testify against fellow mobster Albert Anastasia. After his death, Reles became known as "the canary that could sing, but couldn't fly."

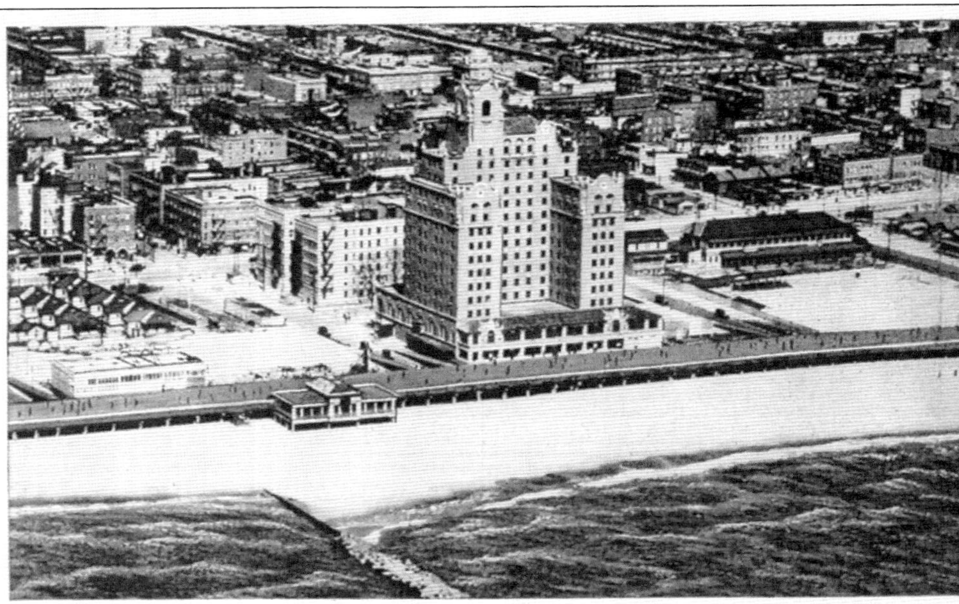

AEROPLANE VIEW, HALF MOON HOTEL, CONEY ISLAND, N. Y.

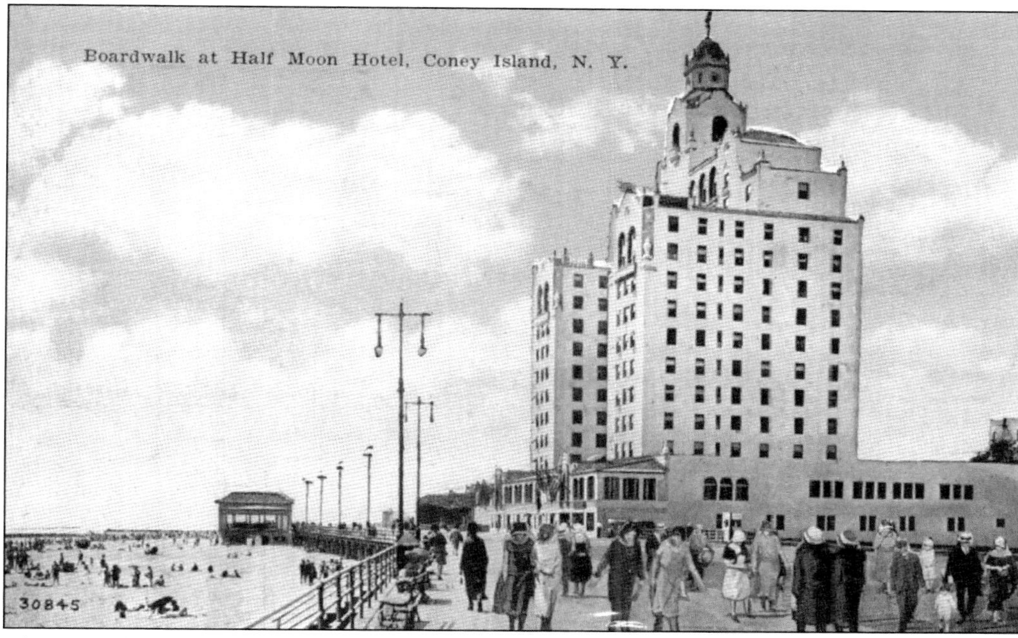

The Riegelmann (Coney Island) Boardwalk extended west past the Half Moon Hotel in the 1920s. The Half Moon Hotel was converted to a Navy convalescent hospital during World War II, and then it became a nursing home. It was demolished in 1996.

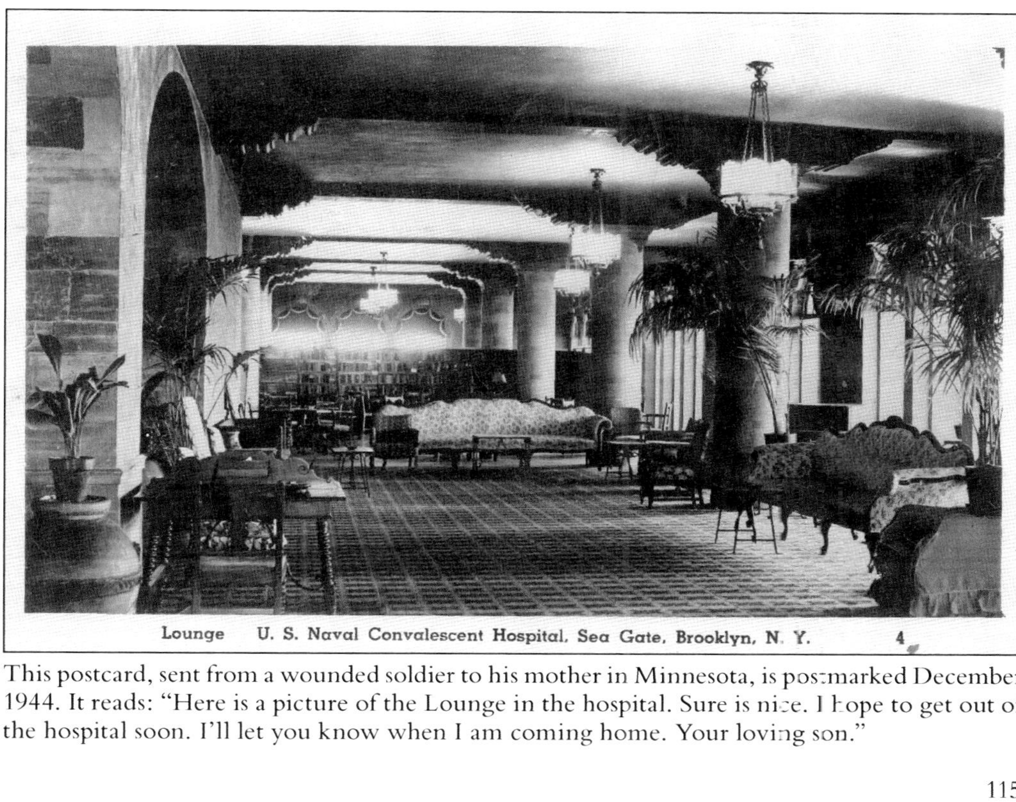

This postcard, sent from a wounded soldier to his mother in Minnesota, is postmarked December 1944. It reads: "Here is a picture of the Lounge in the hospital. Sure is nice. I hope to get out of the hospital soon. I'll let you know when I am coming home. Your loving son."

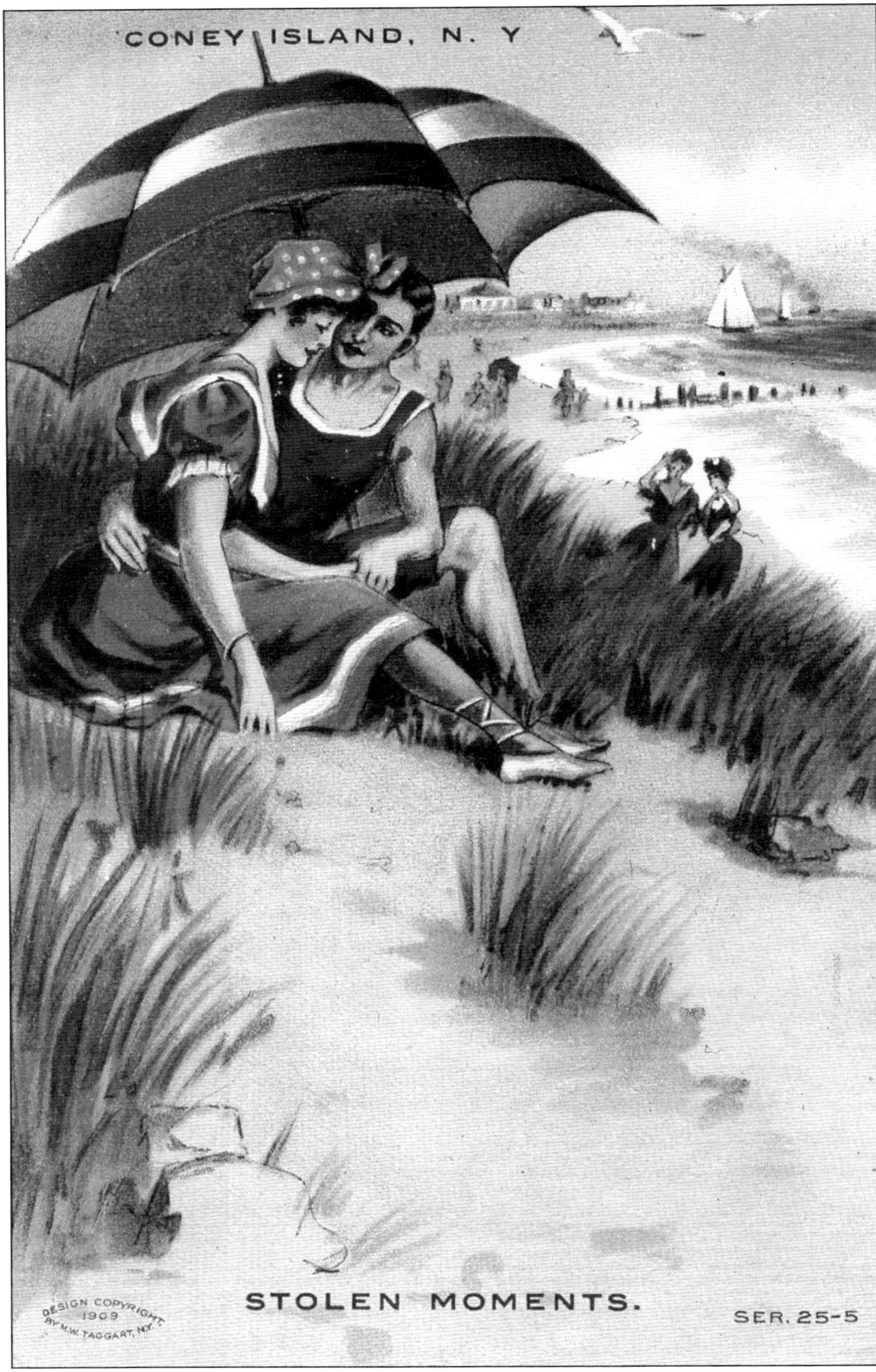

The couple is enjoying a few "stolen moments" on the beach in Coney Island.

Eight

Brighton Beach

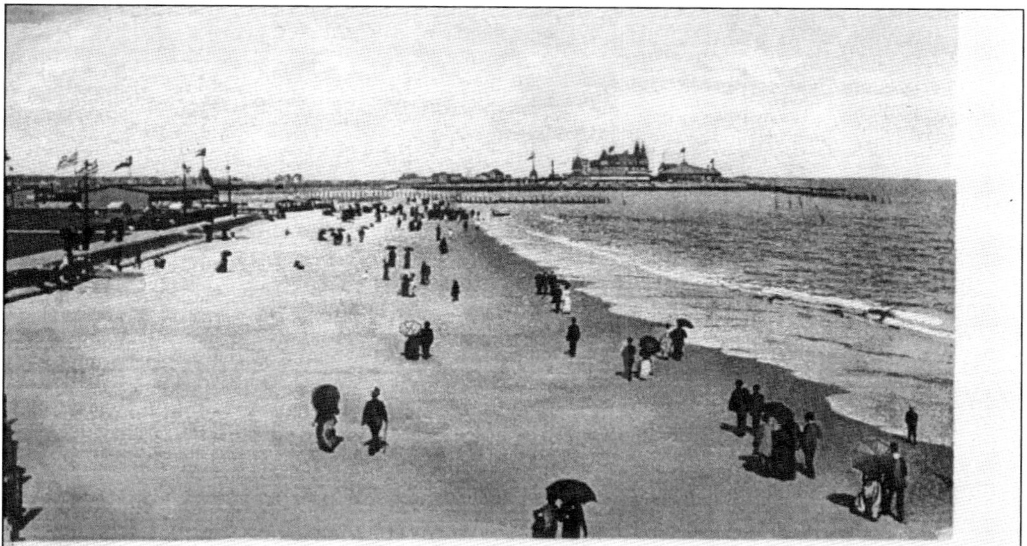

This private mailing card shows Brighton Beach, a community located due east of the Coney Island amusement area. Known for its large population of Russian-speaking immigrants, it was developed in the late 1860s by William A. Engeman to cater to the wealthy horse-racing crowd.

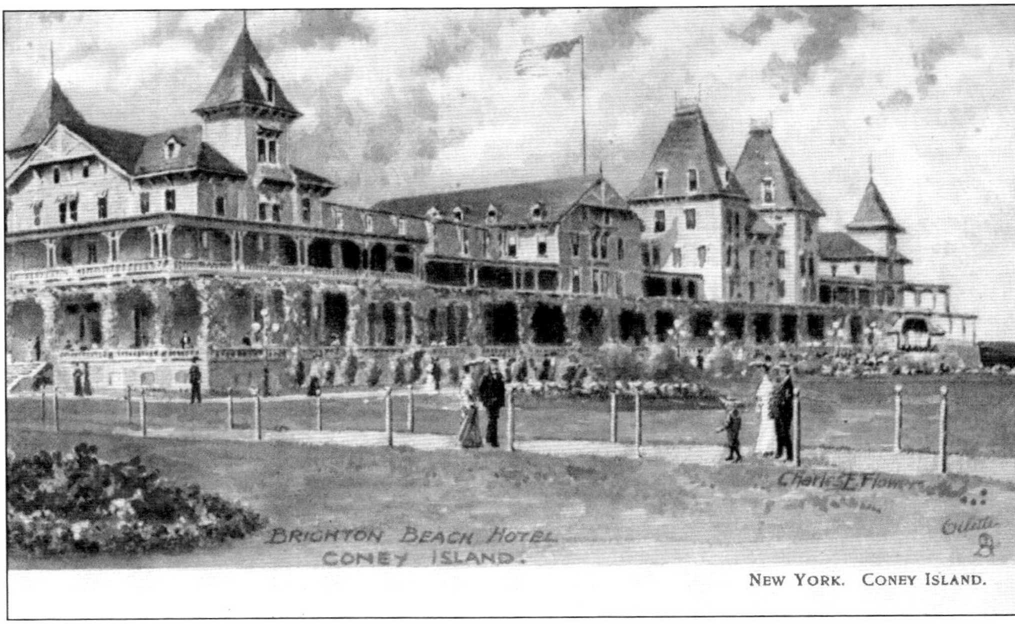

The centerpiece of the resort area was the Brighton Beach Hotel, which opened in the summer of 1878. This postcard is another from Raphael Tuck & Sons that features a painting by Charles E. Flowers. This series was printed in England and issued in 1905.

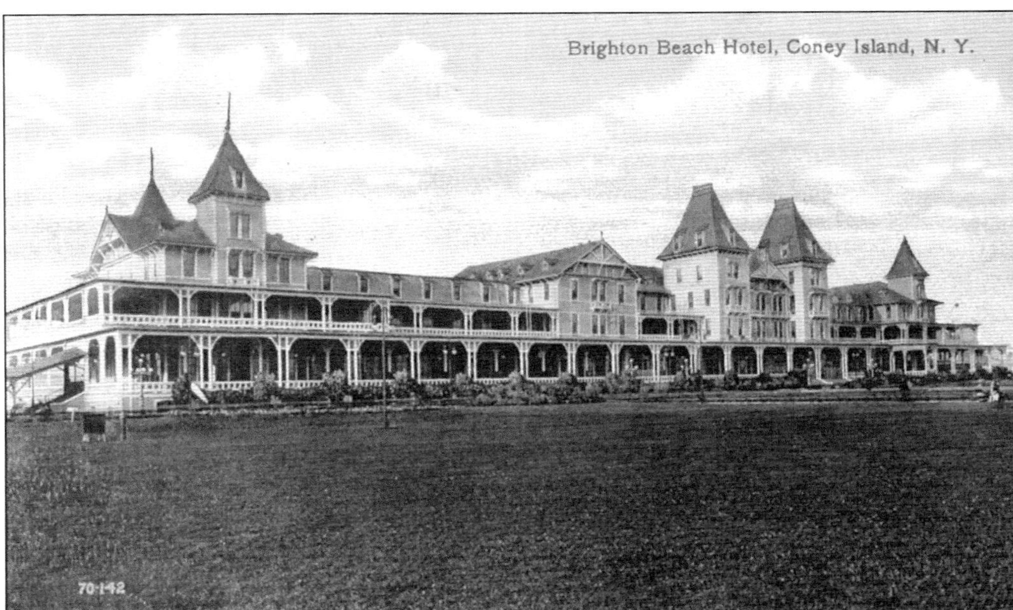

After serious beach erosion, the city decided to move the Brighton Beach Hotel 600 feet away from the sea by raising it up and setting the building on 112 railroad flatcars pulled by six steam locomotives, which took nine days in April 1888. This became the largest building relocation of the 19th century. The Brighton Beach Hotel closed in 1924.

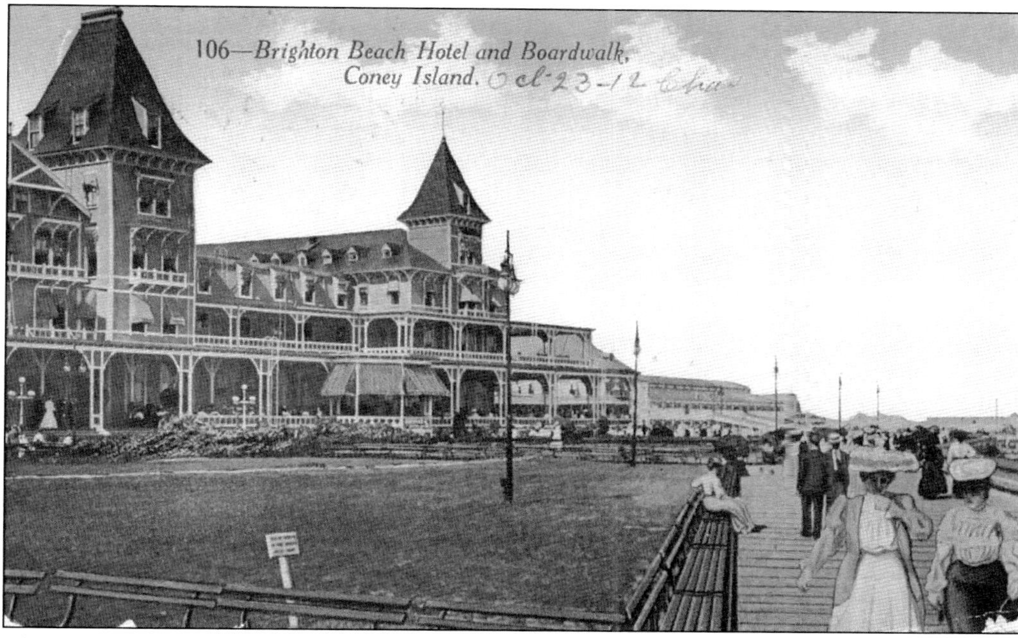

The Brighton Beach Hotel was known for its fine cuisine and live entertainment. There was music every night of the week during the summer season, and fireworks, too. In 1883, William "Buffalo Bill" Cody and his cowboys rode into town along with a band of Sioux Indians.

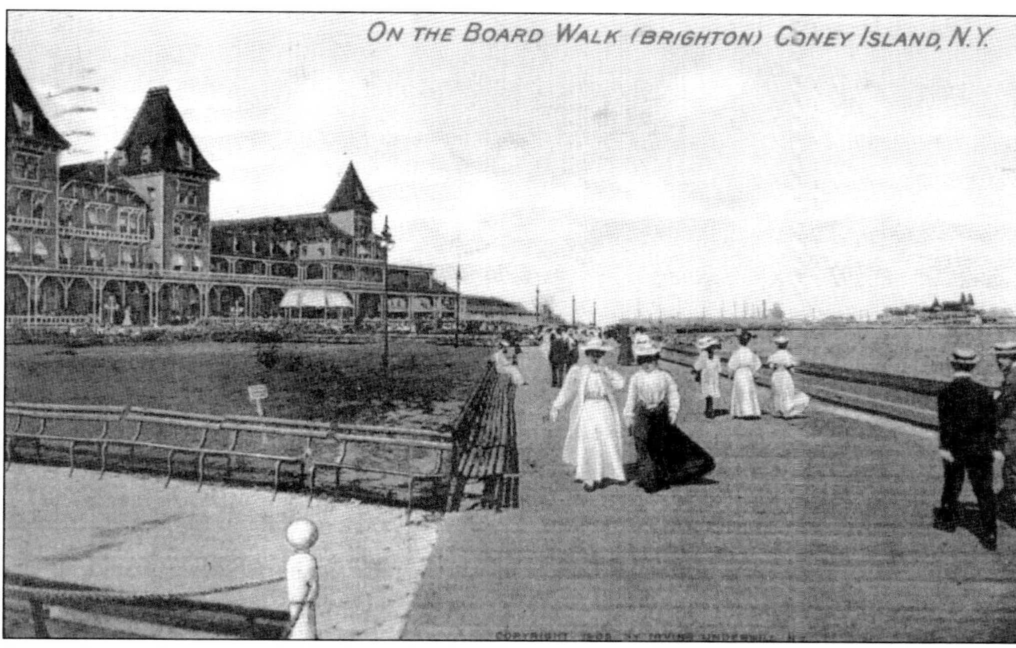

A wooden walkway was built along the shoreline as part of the Brighton Beach Hotel. In the 1920s, the walkway became part of the Riegelmann (Coney Island) Boardwalk, which extends 2.5 miles from West Thirty-Seventh Street in Sea Gate, on the western end, to Fourteenth Street in Brighton Beach.

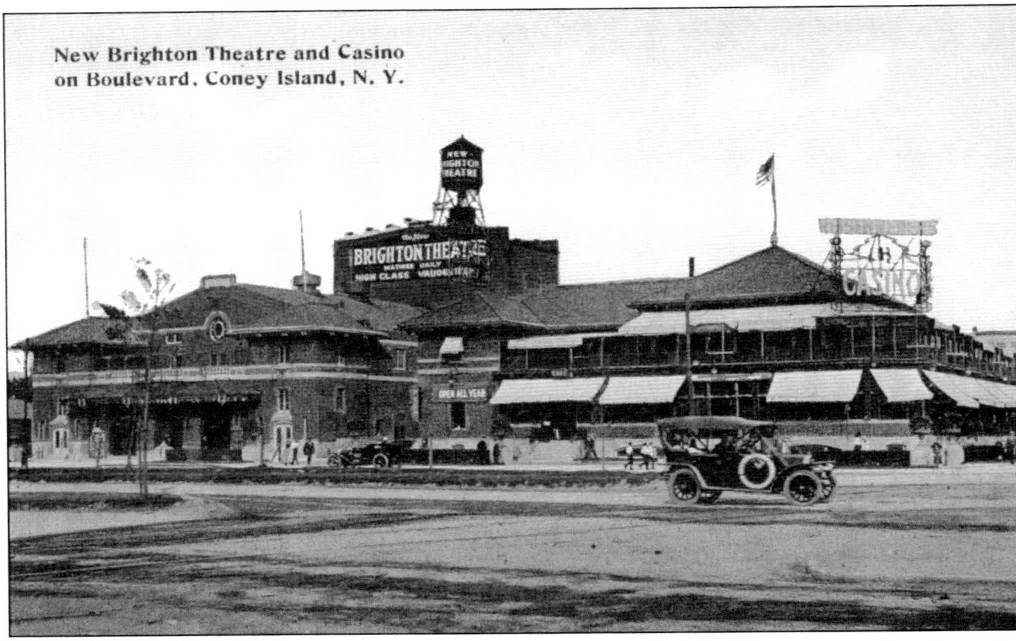

Reisenweber's Casino was an elegant ballroom, restaurant, and nightclub that catered to the racing crowd from the adjacent Brighton Beach Race Course in the early 1900s. The casino closed during Prohibition and then reopened as Publix Baths. After it closed in the 1950s, a bingo parlor and event hall opened in its former location. It was replaced by apartments in the 1980s.

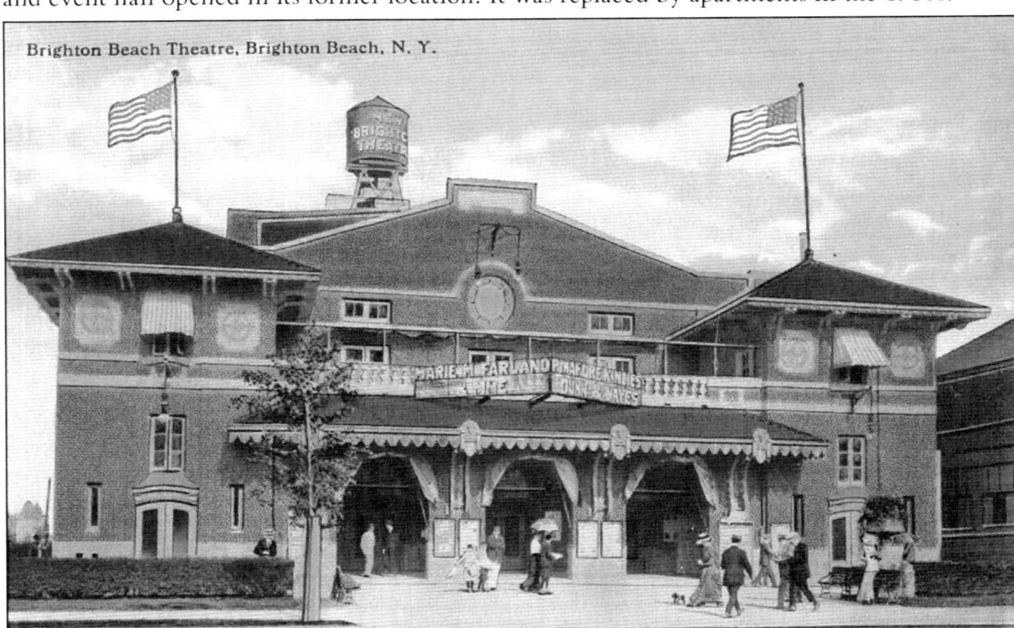

Two theaters opened in Brighton Beach to provide various types of entertainment. The New Brighton Theatre was located at the ocean end of the New Iron Pier. The Brighton Beach Theatre, which opened in 1909 at Ocean Parkway and Brighton Beach Avenue, exhibited "High Class Vaudeville" during the summer, according to this divided-back postcard.

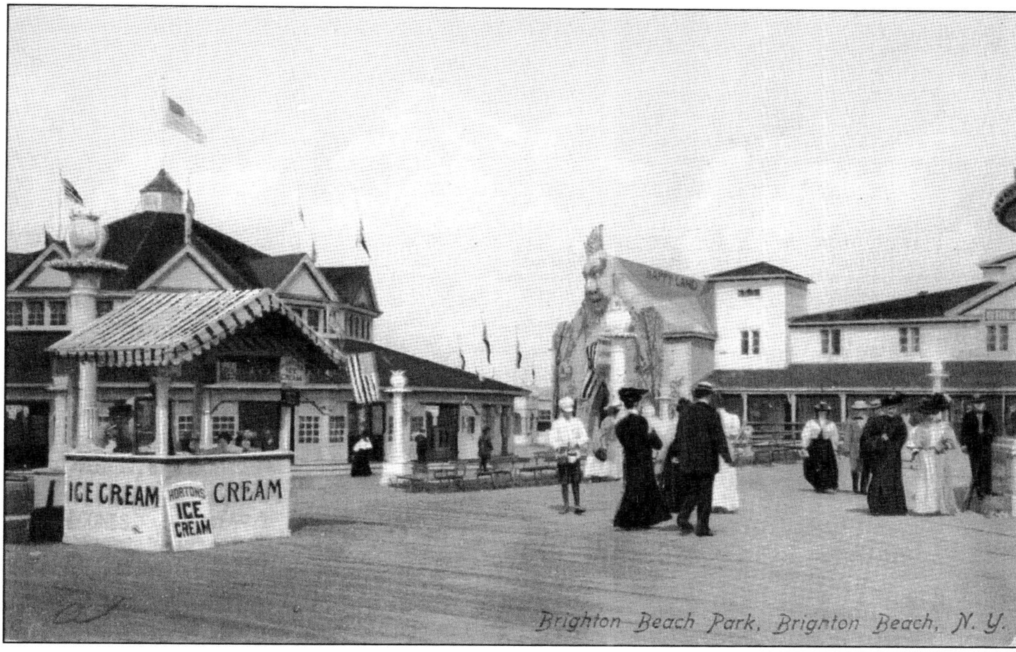

In 1905, Brighton Beach Park opened with a mile-long open midway called the Brighton Pike. The park had its own scenic railway, carousel, pavilion, fun house, animal shows, Wild West shows, and a large roller coaster. Brighton Beach Park closed in 1919 after a fire destroyed many of the attractions along the Brighton Pike.

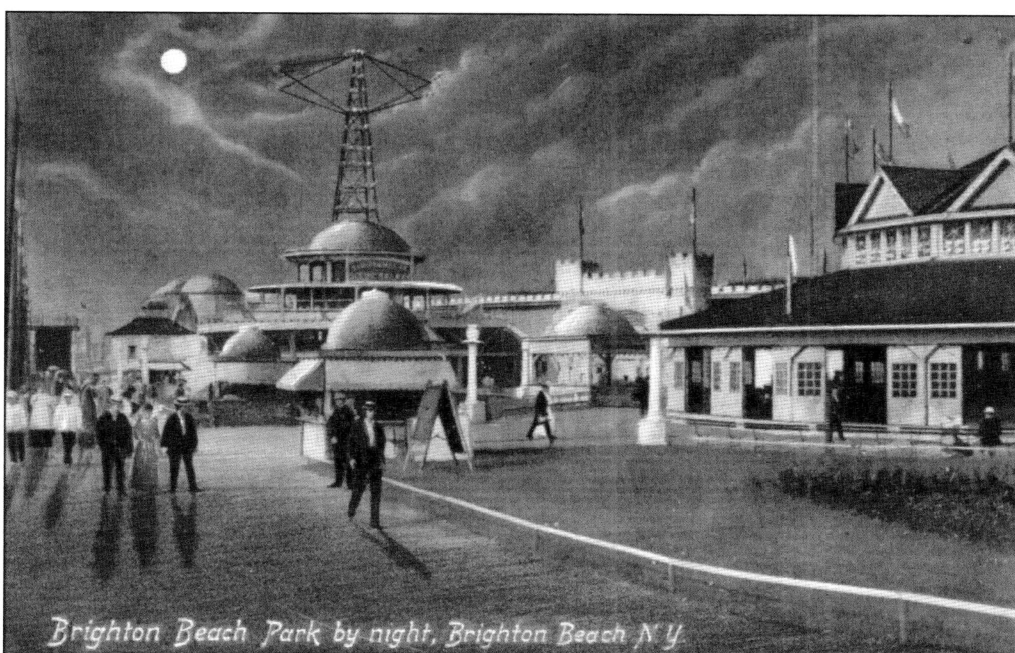

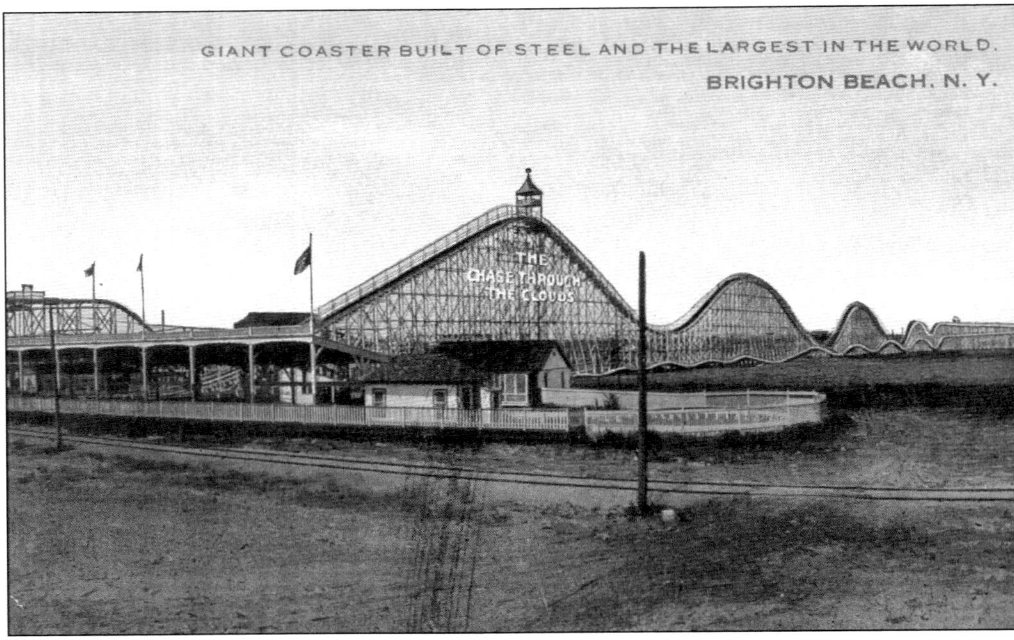

When it opened in 1910, The Chase Through the Clouds was the largest steel roller coaster in the world. A 1919 fire destroyed the Brighton Pike amusement area, and The Chase Through the Clouds stood unused for four years. In 1923, it was moved to Luna Park, where it enjoyed a new life as the Mile Sky Chaser. The coaster's creator, Arthur Jarvis, was responsible for its second chance at Luna Park. It had a good run as the Mile Sky Chaser but was destroyed in the 1944 Luna Park fire.

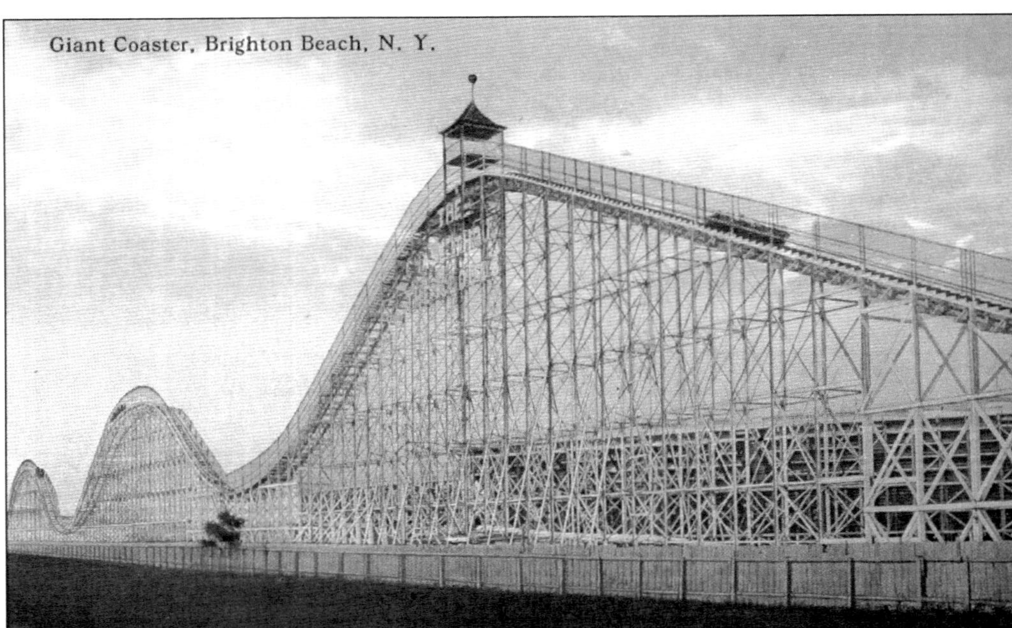

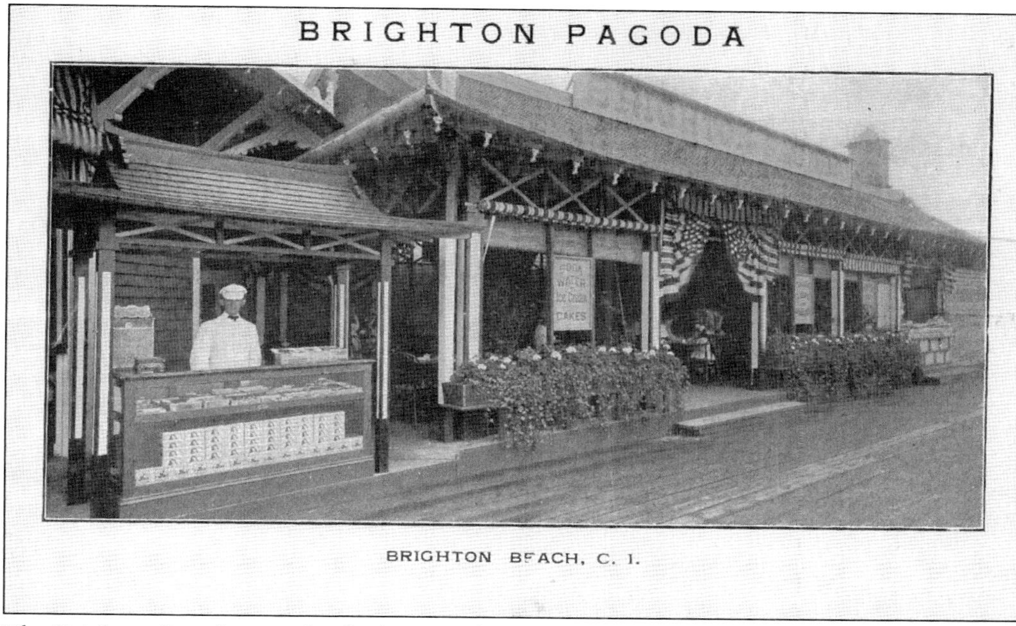

The Brighton Pagoda served refreshments along Brighton Beach's midway, Brighton Pike.

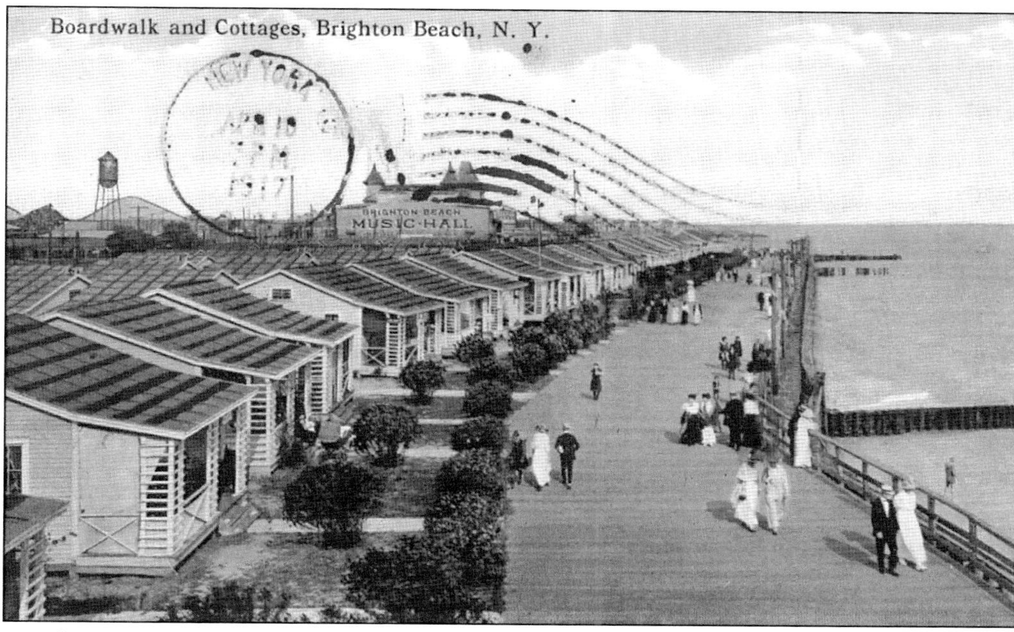

Families could rent cottages for the summer along the Brighton Beach boardwalk. The Brighton Beach Music Hall and the Chase Through the Clouds coaster are visible in the background.

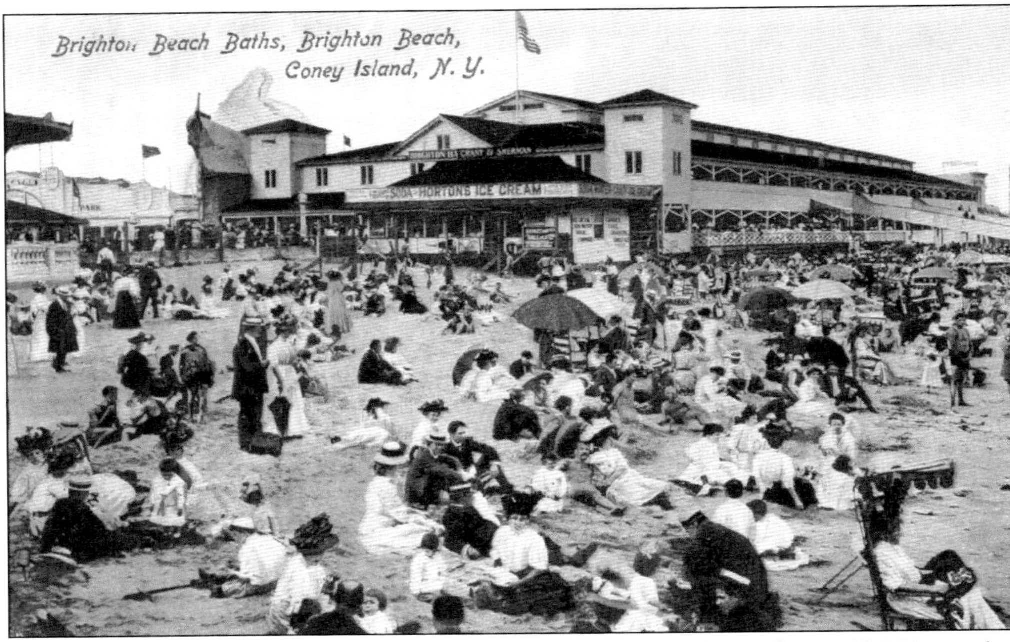

Brighton Beach Baths, opened in 1907, was a private club that boasted over 12,000 members at its peak (between the 1950s and the 1970s). The club offered three swimming pools, various recreational sports, and even a nude beach. It closed in 1994; the Oceana Condominium and Club now occupies the site.

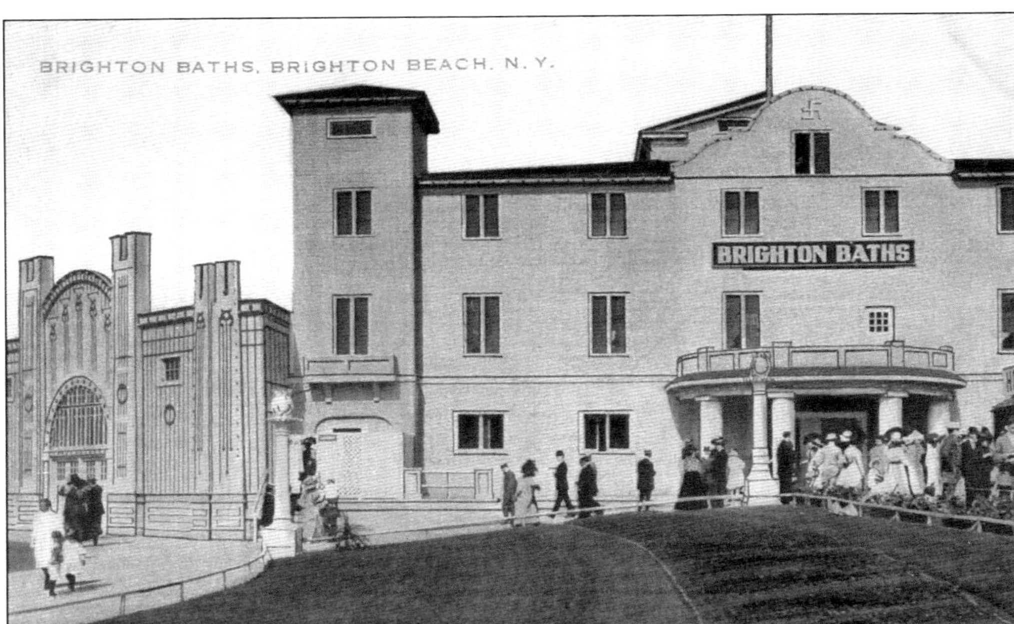

The Brighton Beach Baths and Horton's Ice Cream (barely visible at the far right side of the image) made for a perfect combination on a hot summer day, as shown on this postcard mailed in 1913.

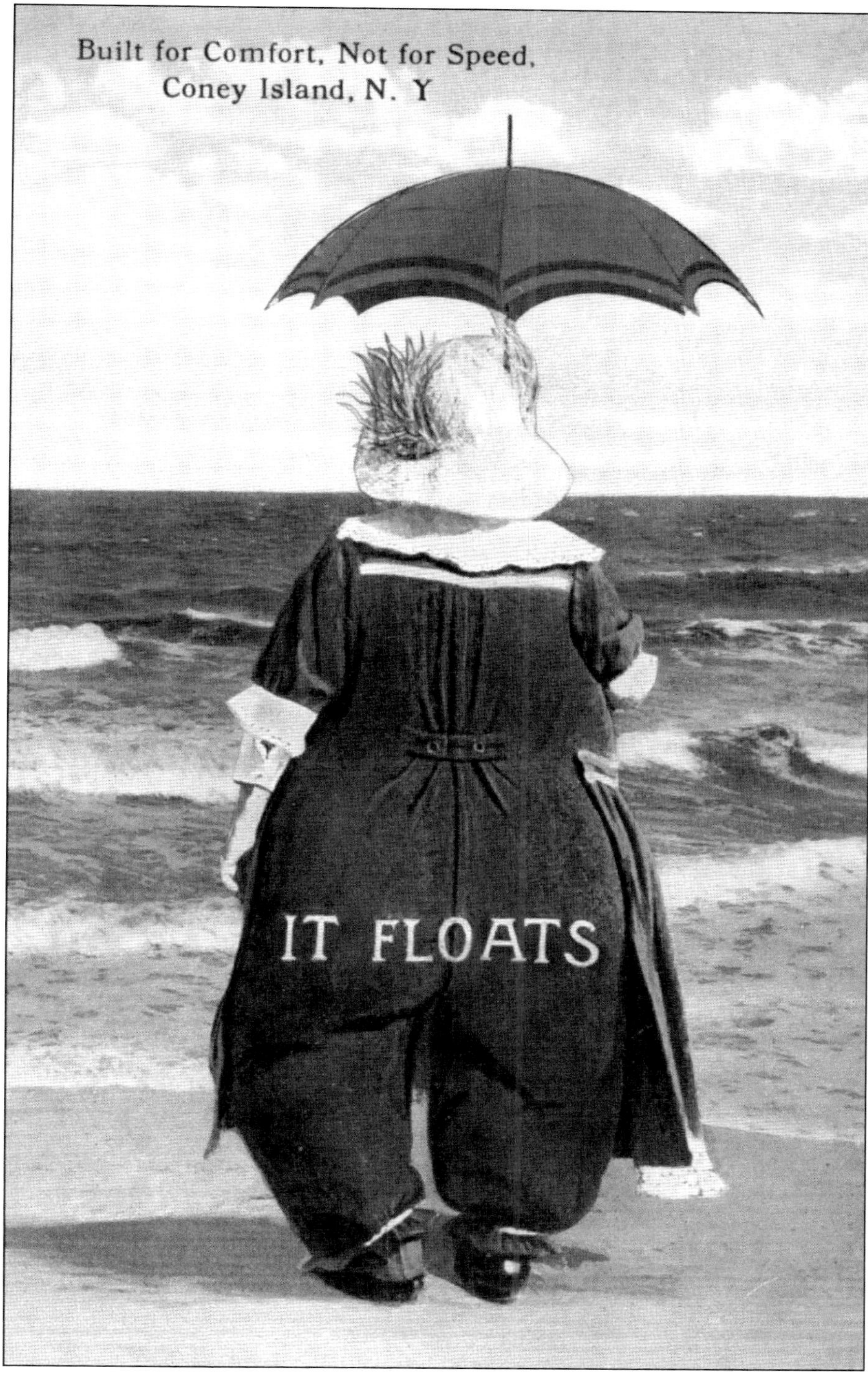

This postcard, with the tagline "Built for Comfort, Not for Speed," touts Coney Island as "the Playground of Greater New York," going on to state that "during the summer months it is visited by approximately forty million bathers." The end.

INDEX

BIBLIOGRAPHY

Clark, Gary W. *Real Photo Postcards KwikGuide: A Guide to Identifying and Dating Real Photo Postcards of the 20th Century*. PhotoTree.com, 2013.
Daly, Michael. *Topsy: The Startling Story of the Crooked-Tailed Elephant, P.T. Barnum, and the American Wizard, Thomas Edison*. New York, NY: Atlantic Monthly Press, 2013.
Denson, Charles. *Coney Island: Lost and Found*. Berkeley, CA: Ten Speed Press, 2002.
Heller, Joseph. *Now and Then: From Coney Island to Here*. New York, NY: Random House, 1998.
Immerso, Michael. *Coney Island: the People's Playground*. New Brunswick, NJ: Rutgers University Press, 2002.
Kasson, John F. *Amusing the Millions: Coney Island at the Turn of the Century*. New York, NY: Hill and Wang, 1978.
Pilat, Oliver and Jo Ranson. *Sodom by the Sea: An Affectionate History of Coney Island*. Garden City, NY: Doubleday, Doran & Company, Inc., 1941.
Register, Woody. *The Kid of Coney Island: Fred Thompson and the Rise of American Amusements*. New York, NY: Oxford University Press, Inc., 2001.